Fiona Bruce is one of the country's top female journalists and presenters. On BBC1 she presents the *Ten O'Clock News* and *Antiques Roadshow*, and presented *Crimewatch* for eight years. She is involved in the charities Victim Support and Refuge.

Jacqui Hames is one of Britain's most famous real-life detectives, having co-presented *Crimewatch* for sixteen years and served with the Metropolitan Police for over twenty-five years. Jacqui makes regular contributions to programmes such as *GMTV* on bullying, drug- and date-rape, illegal minicabs and other crime issues.

www.**rbooks**.co.uk

Savvy!

THE MODERN GIRL'S GUIDE
TO DOING IT ALL
WITHOUT RISKING IT ALL

FIONA BRUCE & JACQUI HAMES

BANTAM PRESS

LONDON · TORONTO · SYDNEY · AUCKLAND · JOHANNESBURG

TRANSWORLD PUBLISHERS
61–63 Uxbridge Road, London W5 5SA
A Random House Group Company
www.rbooks.co.uk

First published in Great Britain
in 2008 by Bantam Press
an imprint of Transworld Publishers

A CIP catalogue record for this book is available from the British Library.

ISBN 9780593059890

Extract from *They Call Me Naughty Lola* edited by David Rose is reproduced by kind
permission of Profile Books.
'Out of the Tunnel' by Rachel North is published by kind permission of The Friday
Project Ltd.

Addresses for Random House Group Ltd companies outside the UK
can be found at: www.randomhouse.co.uk
The Random House Group Ltd Reg. No. 954009

The Random House Group Limited supports The Forest Stewardship
Council (FSC), the leading international forest-certification organization.
All our titles that are printed on Greenpeace-approved FSC-certified
paper carry the FSC logo. Our paper procurement policy
can be found at www.rbooks.co.uk/environment

Typeset in 11/15pt Baskerville by Falcon Oast Graphic Art Ltd.

Printed in the UK by CPI William Clowes Beccles NR34 7TL

2 4 6 8 10 9 7 5 3 1

To Sam and Mia

For Annie and Oliver – have wonderful,
free, exciting lives – but safely!

Contents

Introduction

THERE ARE ENDLESS BOOKS OUT THERE TELLING US HOW TO BE better dressed, better shoppers, better cooks, more glamorous, better in bed, more in control of our destinies. We've read most of them, and Fiona's wardrobe is still full of clothes she'll never wear and Jacqui's cooking still tastes like wet cardboard. HELP!

These books are great fun, but they aren't what we really need. What we're crying out for is a smart handbook for surviving the modern world (and we're not talking about how to avoid bad-hair days, where to find a 'life-saving' online deli, how to build a leaf hut or an organic compostable loo). We mean surviving in a real and practical sense – making sure you are safe and secure in your home, when you're travelling, in your finances and in your relationships. The stuff that we have to deal with every day that really matters.

Surveys suggest that most of us believe crime is rising (even though it is mostly falling), and up to half of us feel unsafe most or all of the time. We're most afraid of being attacked but we're significantly worried about being burgled too.

If you're a homeowner, a tenant, or are about to buy or rent somewhere new to live, if you live alone, if you're a student, if you're working, if you drive a car, ride a bike, if you bank or shop online, if you're travelling, if you like going out to clubs or restaurants, if you're going out on a hot date, if you use a credit card – this book is for you. These are just a few of the countless situations in which you can become a victim of crime or plain old sharp practice. Whoever you are, whatever stage of life you've reached, we will minimize the risks of everyday living for you. And it's so simple – it's easy to stay safe as long as you're armed with the right information.

My work as a reporter and presenter for the BBC, and in particular for *Crimewatch* and *Real Story*, has brought me into daily contact with people and scenarios that have constantly made me think, 'If only they'd had the right advice, if only someone had told them, it could all have been avoided.' Take the woman who was burgled while she slept because she didn't have the right locks on her front door; the girl who lost her earrings but couldn't get the money back from the insurance company because she'd taken out the wrong policy; the person who had her computer nicked from the back seat of the car when she stopped at some traffic lights because she hadn't locked all the doors. And those are just the things that have happened to me. FIONA

As well as co-presenting *Crimewatch* with Fiona, I served as a detective with the Metropolitan Police for over twenty-five years. Every day I helped people who never dreamed they'd find themselves victims of crime. Sometimes it wasn't a question of an obvious, straightforward crime being committed – who hasn't fallen foul of dodgy operators who take you for a ride just because you lack knowledge and experience? The world is changing so rapidly in terms of how we live, where we live and who we live with that increasingly we're on our own when it comes to navigating our way safely through the everyday and, very occasionally, the not-so-everyday dangers of modern life. Why is it that so often we only engage with these matters when we hear Fiona read them out on the news or see them in a *Crimewatch* reconstruction? It's because we don't have time – we believe we don't have time to find out what we need to know, we don't have time to take in the details, and particularly we don't have time to imagine ourselves as victims. It'll never happen to us, we think. What I have learned over the years is that an hour or two thinking about and planning how to protect yourself and your property now can keep you safe for the rest of your life. JACQUI

In this book we'll do all the research for you. We'll help you avoid the kind of common low-level crime that most of us have got used to but which can seriously affect the quality of our lives. And we'll show you how to reduce your chances of becoming a target for more serious or violent crimes. We'll also give you tips to help you steer clear of those infuriating and often expensive times when you can fall foul of thieves or crooks in a variety of guises, just because you don't know how to deal with them.

We're not going to preach to you. We've been there and done it ourselves, made stupid mistakes or just not bothered to think things through. Learn from where we went wrong – Fiona once came home from an office party so wasted she forgot to close her front door and left it wide open all night for any passers-by to pop in. In fact, she's done it twice!

Mostly, we'll tell you about the everyday kind of crime that happens to us all but we either don't think about or don't know how to avoid – when we're at home, in the car, on the bus or using the computer. We'll also deal with the more serious aspects of personal safety – protecting yourself from burglars or intruders in your home and keeping safe when you're out and about. But we will keep it in perspective – you are far less likely to be bothered by a stranger lurking in an unlit alley than you might think. Above all, we promise we're not aiming to turn you into timid teetotallers who don't venture out after dark. We'll show you how to live dangerously – but play safely.

1

Home is Where the Heart is

OK, LET'S START HERE – THIS IS THE BIGGIE BECAUSE THIS IS
what you spend most of your money on, where you spend
most of your time and, unfortunately, the place one in four of us
is likely to experience crime. Your home is a place of refuge, the
one place you should be able to feel comfy, warm, safe and confident. When you come home and open the door, you should
instantly feel better, no matter what kind of day you've had. It's
the place where you can put your feet up, put your music on,
wear your most unfashionable slob-out clothes, not care what
your hair looks like, wear those cosy old slippers that you love
but wouldn't be seen dead in, pour yourself a glass of wine, eat
Marmite on toast, keep out unwelcome visitors – and not have to
make polite conversation with anyone. Bliss.

If your home doesn't feel like that, let us help.

BEFORE YOU MOVE IN

So, you've found your dream house, flat, bedsit, caravan, house-
boat . . . or at least one you can afford. Good for you, that's
the first hurdle out of the way. But before you hand over your

hard-earned cash ask yourself: do you really want to live here? Along with all the other things you have to consider before buying or renting, you need to consider how safe both your prospective home and neighbourhood are. Here are some things to think about before you sign on the dotted line.

The Neighbourhood

⚿ **Take a look at the area by day but also by night,** as it may feel very different when the sun's gone down. No matter how lovely the house or flat, would you feel safe living there? If you are travelling to and from work, how would you make that journey? How far would you have to walk from the tube or bus to get to your front door? Would you feel comfortable making that journey in the dark in the winter months? If you've got a car, think about where you'd park it, how easy it is to park and how far you'd have to walk to your front door. Does that inviting local pub become irresistible to every drug addict and yob in the area at night? Or does that chippy next to the station attract every passing drunk on their way home?

When I left university, a million years ago, I lived in a tiny old three-bedroom railway worker's cottage in the centre of London with four other people (yes, it was VERY crowded). The house was on a lovely road but there were so many cars and so few parking spaces that I had to park several streets away and walk through a dark and pretty intimidating estate to get to it. Most nights it was OK but sometimes there were gangs hanging around who'd call out things I'm too well brought up to repeat, or occasionally men would come up to me making some unwelcome suggestions of how we might develop a not-so-lasting relationship. I loved living in that house, and I had a lot of fun there, but I certainly would have thought twice about moving in if I'd realized what I'd have to go through most nights just to get to the front door. Location, location, location – always consider it before you buy. FIONA

O⌐ **When renting it's worth asking the letting agent about any disputes.** The tenancy agreement will only give you information like when the boiler was last serviced. The landlord is not legally bound to inform you and may not be forthcoming about disputes. If the agent isn't too helpful, check out some of the others in the area (take numbers from To Let boards in the same street). Take the time to ask around the neighbours and local shops – it'll pay off.

O⌐ **What are the neighbours like?** The paperwork that must be completed when you sell a property includes a questionnaire sent out by solicitors in which the seller must include details of their relationship with their neighbours. If disputes amount to no more than cross words over the garden fence then the seller may take the chance and not mention it. However, if a formal complaint has been made to the local authorities, about noise, for example, then the sellers are legally obliged to declare it.

Ensure this questionnaire is completed before you sign, and look out for any strangely worded answers which may be trying to cover up disputes. 'We have lovely neighbours and very much enjoy hearing their children play' could be code for 'Their children have just been slapped with their own personal ASBOs and are terrorizing the neighbourhood.' The last thing you need is difficult neighbours and boundary disputes.

O⌐ **How secure is the place?** Have the doors and windows got good locks and bolts?

⌖ **Write or email the local police** and ask some searching questions – which you are perfectly entitled to do under the Freedom of Information Act 2000 – such as:

1 How many domestic burglaries were there in the area last year?

2 Has this property ever been burgled? If so, how did they gain entry?

3 How many times were police called to disturbances in the street or to neighbouring houses in the last few months?

4 Have any Anti-Social Behaviour Orders been given to the people living in the neighbouring properties?

5 Where are the crime hotspots in your area? Most police forces have their own websites now. The quality and quantity of local information varies, but they are worth checking.

6 There are quite a few property search sites on the web. We looked at www.findaproperty.com, which also gives you the local crime stats and www.primelocation.com, which has buying/selling/renting guides. For a totally independent view use www.homecheck.com, which allows you to input a postcode and gives you environmental info, amenities, planning applications and also crime figures. If you feel like wading through statistics try the British Crime Survey Local Authority Statistics (be prepared to age during the process: it will take that long), but if you want anything more specific you need to contact the local police with your request.

Renting and/or Finding a Flatmate

If you're renting, you'll have different things to think about than if you are living in a home you actually own. And you may be living in solitary splendour or you may be sharing with flatmates. Here are some of the issues we think you should consider:

─────────────── YOUR FLATMATES ───────────────

We're not just talking about whether they wash more than once a month, whether they cut their toenails in the sitting room (and leave the clippings on the coffee table) or whether they pick their nose while watching telly. These things are undeniably important to the quality of your life but we reckon you can work that lot out for yourself. What about how you safely find a flatmate in the first place?

Obviously, in an ideal scenario you'd share with some friends, but if you're moving to a new area, or all your smug married friends are happily ensconced with their other halves, you may need to share with relative strangers. If you do, there are a few things to consider. Decide whether you mind sharing with a man or whether you only want to share with another woman. If it's a female flatmate you're after, make sure you stipulate that up front. If you advertise in the local paper, newsagent or on a website, don't put your name and address, just put the area where you live and a contact number. When you arrange to see a prospective flatmate, don't see them in the house or flat alone. Make sure another flatmate or a friend is with you. Whoever you finally choose should be able to provide some form of reference. If they're employed, get the number of their office and check they are who they claim to be. If they've rented before, get a reference from their previous landlord – a very handy way of finding out if they have any bad habits, such as not paying their bills or playing loud music in their room at 3 a.m.

If you're the one who's looking for somewhere to rent, take someone with you when you go to look at a place or to meet prospective flatmates. And make sure you meet all your prospective flatmates. It's no good thinking how friendly everyone is and only realizing once you've moved in that you never got round to meeting the one who can't cook but survives on baked beans – with predictable results. Or the one who can't stop helping herself to your things and never returns them.

When it comes to security, you may have a very different approach to the others in your flat. While you would never dream of going out without double-locking the front door, your flatmate might think nothing of inviting back that nice bloke she fancies at the bus stop and giving him a key so that he can let himself in to make a quick cuppa if the number 39 is going to be a long time coming. Agree some ground rules. Go through what you think the security issues might be and decide on a common approach. Think about the kind of door and window locks you have, who has a front-door key, whether you have an intercom, who you do and do not let into the flat or building. The rest of this chapter should help you identify the issues you need to be considering and what to do about them.

YOUR LANDLORD

You have different rights depending on what kind of tenancy agreement you have. But landlords have an obligation to carry out repairs, allow tenants to live peacefully in the accommodation provided and to meet certain safety requirements. Talk these obligations through with your landlord before signing on the dotted line.

You may find that the person giving you the trouble is not your flatmate, an intruder or a burglar: it's your landlord. Harassing tenants is a serious criminal offence, so know your rights. Harassment can take many forms, for example, coming into your flat without your permission, or interfering with your possessions or power or water supplies. If asking your landlord to stop in writing gets you nowhere, you can get legal advice from a solicitor, go to your local Citizens Advice Bureau or contact the council, which has the power to prosecute landlords. If you're a student, you can always get advice and back-up from your college or university.

Illegal eviction is also a criminal offence and your rights differ depending on what kind of tenancy you have. If you have an *assured shorthold tenancy* you must be given two months' notice to leave and the landlord has to say why you are being told to go if it falls within the fixed term of your tenancy. If you have an *assured tenancy* you must be given two months' or fourteen days' notice of eviction. The former comes with the most common type of agreement, which gives you a legal right to live in your rented property for an agreed period, at the end of which the property reverts to the landlord. The latter is what you would generally get from Housing Associations or Trusts.

If you live with your landlord you are what's called an *excluded occupier*. This can be a much less formal agreement and you can simply be told to go and the notice should be equal to the timescale in which you pay rent, i.e. a month's notice if you pay a month at a time.

BURGLARY

Making your place burglar-proof should be at the top of your checklist. In many areas the burglary rate is going down, so take heart, but remember: it could still happen to you. From someone nicking your bike from outside the front door to coming back from holiday to find your house empty except for that toasted sandwich-maker Aunt Mabel gave you which you never wanted anyway, your house or flat is the one thing you really need to think about protecting. The good news is, it's easy. Whether you're buying or renting a first home, or whether you've been in your home for some years, it's quite likely that your considerations – and your weak spots – will be similar. As we've already mentioned, if you're about to move to a new area there are steps that you can take to investigate what both crime and safety measures are like there. Once you're settled in you can make sure that your home is safe with you and your property inside it. We'll give you some simple routine steps to build into your everyday life to make sure it stays that way.

Who are You up Against?

Most burglaries are committed by small groups of people who are usually known to the local police. Some officers I've worked with have taken to sending Christmas and birthday cards to these known criminals to unsettle them and let them know the police are on to them. It seems to work! JACQUI

Jacqui's met more than a few burglars in her time – they vary from career crims making their living from raiding other people's houses to drug addicts needing to nick something which they can easily flog for a quick fix. They are almost always young men. No surprise there. And they are usually opportunists looking for a fast and easy way to get in. Maybe a window's been left open, maybe there's no alarm, or maybe it's obvious you've gone on holiday. Opportunistic burglars wander through the streets looking for the easiest home to enter and exit, with the lowest risk of getting caught, for the most reward. It's as simple as that, and if you and your neighbour have identical homes, but yours is the one with the window open or easier access round the back – then you know which one he's going to go for.

About six years ago my husband arrived home to discover the back door of our house had been kicked in. Thankfully, the children and I were out and our very old Golden Retriever was discovered hiding under the kitchen table with his paws over his eyes and ears! There was mud everywhere and the place had been ransacked – drawers and cupboards emptied on to the floor, cigarettes stubbed out on the carpets, make-up tipped out on to the floor, cut electrical wires waving about loosely. One awful mess. In the main, smallish items had been taken, including my jewellery box and credit cards from our desk. As my husband was head of CID in Surrey at the time, a police officer and scene-of-crimes officer arrived fairly quickly – all right, within thirty seconds – and luckily we were able to give them a fairly extensive list of missing items, which was in turn circulated quickly.

Later that evening, about 25 miles away, a local lad was stopped, searched and found to have some of our stuff on him, including a credit card, and he was duly arrested. It turned out that he and a mate had travelled down to our sleepy and generally crime-free village for a day trip and had wandered about until they saw our place, which gave easy access (not any more, it doesn't) to the back, which also wasn't overlooked. Their motive was to get money for drugs. On their way back on the motorway they'd thrown out of their car window any items like jewellery which they didn't think were worth anything.

Probably the thing I miss most is the locket my mother gave me on my fortieth birthday. In it I had put pictures of each of my children. It still breaks my heart to think of it being thrown from the window of a car on the M25 and ending up under the wheels of a lorry or in a ditch somewhere. Since then we've learned our lesson and fitted better locks and an alarm. If only we'd thought about proper security sooner the burglars would have moved on to the next house and I'd still have the family jewellery that meant so much to me. JACQUI

Jacqui's experience is fairly typical – except, unfortunately, for the response from the local police. But what it does show is how important it is to circulate an accurate and detailed description of what's been stolen. We'll give you details of the best way to do this later on (see p. 32).

Teams of two or three burglars sometimes work together, and it's not unknown for a team to send in someone to recce an area and mark out potential properties to break into using chalk-marks on fences, gates or driveways – worth keeping an eye out for. Most burglaries are committed during the day, when you're out. Instances of householders coming downstairs in the night and confronting a burglar are very rare; generally, burglars don't want to meet you any more than you want to meet them. Jacqui's burglars came mid-morning on a weekday, when adults are likely to be at work, children at school. Roughly 20 per cent of burglars don't have to force entry; they just get in through an open door or window. And an alarm is proven to be a real deterrent. So if you make sure you lock up and you get an alarm, you've already significantly reduced your chances of being burgled. How hard is that?

My elderly parents were broken into a couple of years ago. The thieves got in through the back door and stole the usual small things, like jewellery, but also the hi-fi, TV, etc. The policeman who came pointed out a chalkmark on their front-garden gate and said they'd received several reports of break-ins in the area with similar marks. A few weeks later when they had replaced all the electrical stuff they were burgled again. This time the police asked if they had left the new packaging outside for the dustman. They had to admit they had, and he said it was highly likely the original burglars had kept an eye out for it. CAROL, SURREY

Protect Your Property

Whether you live in a mansion, a two-bedroom semi or a room in a shared flat, you want to make it impregnable, or as near as dammit. You can speak to your local crime-prevention officer (just call the local police station) and he or she will come round and advise you on how to make your home more secure. There is no end of things you can do to make it burglar-proof, but we're suggesting what we think is realistic and practical. You want your home to be your fortress, but not to feel like Fort Knox.

Insurers have calculated what it will cost, on average, to make your home reasonably secure. According to 2006 prices, to have a decent alarm, door and window locks and good internal and external lighting will cost about £600–700 for an average three-bedroom semi-detached house. If that's outside your price range, read on and work out what you can afford. As you'll see, having something is much better than having nothing.

And if your house or flat is a new-build, check whether it's been approved by the Secured By Design initiative. SBD is the name of a group of national projects involving the design of new and refurbished homes and a number of other crime-prevention measures. The initiative is run by the police and private industry together with the Association of Chief Police Officers. They aim both to prevent crime in the future and lower the fear of crime – so not only does it reduce the chances of someone breaking into your home but you also feel safer in it. It's not compulsory for every new build, but check out the SBD website (www.securedbydesign.com) to see if your house or builder is listed. It also has the details of companies and products that meet the police safety and security standards, but the property will generally have approved door and window locks if approved by SBD.

BOUNDARIES

There might be fences, hedges, walls, metal railings or no boundary at all. Some of the newer open-plan estates have very little demarcation between one house and the next, which can make securing your own property a bit trickier. About as many burglars break in at the front of the house as at the back, so you need to check your property all round. As a rule of thumb you want the front of your house to be easily visible so that burglars don't have somewhere to hide while they're trying to force the front-door lock. If you have a high hedge or fence around the front, you might think about scaling it back. The possibility of someone passing by on the street and seeing him is a real deterrent to an opportunist thief.

What about getting round the back? How easy is it? If a burglar can just scale a fence or if your side door has a rickety old lock, you need to make any means of access at the sides of your house more secure.

And then there's the back garden. Once a burglar is there, he's home free, with all the time in the world to work out how to get into the house and little chance of anyone disturbing him. Ideally, you want a high perimeter around the back which is difficult or impossible to climb over.

What's best to make the boundary secure? You've got a few options.

- **Walls** are the strongest, but if they're too low they can provide a useful leg-up for a burglar and a good thing to hide behind.

- **Wooden fences** can be climbed, too, if they're strong enough. Or if they're a bit flimsy, a hole can easily be kicked through them.

- **Metal railings** can be the priciest option but they are very secure, particularly if they've got nasty spikes on the top. It's very time-consuming and noisy for a burglar to saw through them.

- **Hedges** are the prettiest option and if you choose the right ones the thorns will put off all but the most determined crims. It can take up to several years for a decent hedge to grow high enough and thick enough to be useful, but you can buy some pre-grown at garden centres.

   Our tips for the prickliest hedges are holly, *pyracantha* (white flowers in June, orange or red berries in winter, fierce thorns) or blackthorn (spiny with white flowers. And you can make sloe gin from the fruit – what more could you possibly want?).

○⌐ **Trellis** This is genius because it's simple and cheap but is a real deterrent. Think about putting a trellis on the top of your fence or wall to make the boundary too high for a burglar to climb over. He will know that if he tries, the trellis will probably break and that will make a lot of noise, attracting unwelcome attention. And he may well fall and injure himself, which you may regard as a bit of a bonus, since that means his robbing days will be over for a bit. And if you grow some pretty climbing plants over the trellis, you'll have a secure perimeter that looks and smells nice. You might need planning permission if you make the fence or wall more than 2 metres at the back and more than 1 metre at the front, so check with the council planning office.

○⌐ **Gravel** Not just for parks and public gardens, gravel can be really useful around your property too. Try sneaking in over a gravel path and see how quiet you can be. It's impossible. And the sound of footsteps over gravel in the still of the night can be as good an alarm as a foghorn going off. Remember – the vast majority of burglars just want to get in and out quickly and undetected.

○⌐ **Barbed wire** Hang on, you're thinking, this is my home, not Colditz. Yes, but a line of barbed wire along the top of a wall or fence is not something most burglars will tackle willingly. And if you grow climbing plants along it, you won't ever see it – but someone sizing up the place to assess how easy it is to get in will detect it pretty quickly. Remember to check with your neighbours if you're thinking of putting barbed wire along a shared boundary. We heard of one council that banned the use of barbed wire on a private garden for health and safety reasons. Apparently, they were concerned that a 'poor little' burglar might injure himself trying to climb over. We haven't found restrictions on its use by the Health and Safety Executive other than to say it should not be used in a 'dangerous way'. So as long as it's kept to a minimum, has no detrimental effect on innocents and your neighbours are happy – why not?

Gate Your boundary is only as secure as your gate. If it's easy to get in through your gate, all your other protective measures are a waste of time. Treat your gate as you would your front door: make sure it's strong and the locks are up to the job. More on locks as we go through your options.

I bought a new lock for my front door eighteen months ago and was a bit overwhelmed by the choice and different level of cost. In the end I went for one which looked pretty robust and weighty and wasn't too pricy. Last month I took the rubbish into the front garden and stupidly managed to lock myself out. Luckily, a kindly neighbour let me use his phone to call a locksmith, who arrived a short while later. It took him about thirty seconds to open my 'robust and weighty' lock and charged me £77 for the privilege of watching this neat trick. Having seen how easy it was for him to get in, I wish now I'd spent a bit more money and got a really good lock, as I no longer feel as secure. Still my neighbour and I are so friendly now, he's holding a spare key for me. AMANDA, LONDON

THE FRONT DOOR

This is what you want to think about first, because this is often how a burglar gets in. Make it as strong and tough as you can, and that includes the frame. There's no point having a heavy, secure front door with a flimsy frame – one push and it'll still give way. You want to make sure that whatever you're buying is fit for the purpose, so as a general rule look out for the British Standard Institute or BSI mark. This is the UK's national standards organization, which ensures a level of quality in a whole range of areas. Some insurance companies require BSI products to be fitted before they will insure and in some instances will offer a discount. If a product is recommended to you it's always worthwhile checking if it has a BSI number before buying (www.bsigroup.com).

The British Standard for doors is PAS24. At the risk of stating the obvious: always lock the front door when you go out, even if it's only for five minutes. You want at least two locks – make one of them a five-lever mortice lock (British Standard 3621) and place it about a third of the way up the door. A mortice lock fits into a hole cut into the door and has keyholes on both sides, creating a dead lock. It is the most secure type of lock, as the door frame has to be broken in order to get past it. Think about installing hinge bolts too – they slide into the frame of the door when it's shut, making it much more difficult for the door to be forced or kicked in.

Even if you lock the door when you go out, what about when you've come in, put your bag down, reached for that cup of tea/glass of wine/vodka shot and you're about to put your feet up? If you've just closed the door behind you and left it at that, you might as well leave your door wide open with a welcome mat outside. You need to lock the door from the inside. It's best to use a bolt lock, the kind you just pull across, or a lock with a snib that you can just push down (again, British Standard 3621). The latter is a Yale-type lock that can be just pulled to, or deadlocked if the key is turned again. The small button which is pushed down to deadlock it is the snib. This has the advantage that it locks the door against unwanted intruders trying to force their way in but you can still open the door from the outside using a key – handy if there's more than one of you living in the property. Also, it's not too fiddly or time consuming if you need to get out of the house in a hurry as with the case of fire.

NEVER lock your door from the inside using your keys – scrabbling around to find your front-door key so you can get out when there's a small inferno raging in your house isn't a good idea.

I have been burgled twice. Each time I was in and had just pulled the front door to, without locking it. The first time, I was downstairs having Sunday lunch. The aroma from my slightly burnt roast chicken was wafting from the open window; I was sitting down at the table in the kitchen in the basement with my husband and baby son, clearly visible from the street. A burglar took the opportunity, and let himself in the front door, snatched my handbag, my husband's wallet and our coats, and scarpered. The front door was just five steps from the kitchen. The first I knew of it was when I went to answer the phone and wondered why on earth the front door was open.

You might think that I'd learned my lesson, particularly given how many police officers I come across and how much free advice I get. But no, not me. A year later, I had been out with the girls, had a few drinks, poured myself out of the taxi at the end of the night, slammed the front door behind me, didn't lock it and fell into bed with my make-up still on. I tottered downstairs the following morning, and the front door was wide open. Yup, bag gone, coat gone. Fortunately, the car keys weren't by the door or they'd have been nicked as well. Thank god the guy breaking in was more interested in my personal possessions than in my person. FIONA

Incidentally: each time Fiona's bag was stolen, she went looking for it in the streets around the house the following morning and found it both times. It's worth doing because if the burglar is a kid or an addict looking only for money, chances are they'll take the cash and ditch the bag and its other contents as quickly as possible.

─────── CHAINS, PEEPHOLES AND INTERCOMS ───────

You might think this is becoming a very long list for the front door but, honestly, it is all worth it. Have a peephole installed in the front door so that you can see who is outside. Don't open the door unless you know who it is. DON'T WORRY about appearing to be rude or unsympathetic; we've heard of scams where women and children have been employed to try to talk their way into your home. If you're still unsure and want to speak to the person or see some identification, this is where the door chain comes in. It can feel a bit embarrassing appearing quite so cautious, but that's a small price to pay. Not all burglars break into homes – some will try to con their way in.

We've lost count of the number of cases featured on *Crimewatch* where this method has been used to rob people. Often distraction burglars (as they're known by the police) may pretend to be on official business from the local council or utility company. Or they may tell you about some urgent repair that needs doing immediately. Anyone from a reputable company will have ID on them and will be used to having to show it when requested. They will also be happy to allow you to ring and check with the office before you allow them in. So make sure you do that and satisfy yourself that they are genuine or, even better, ask them to make a fixed appointment rather than turning up on spec.

Incidentally, if someone comes to your door trying to sell insurance, offering to do building work or tarmac your front drive, NEVER take them up on the offer. The service they provide will almost certainly be rubbish. If it sounds like an incredible bargain, it will be just that – incredible. One exception – people from charities who come round every few months selling dusters and dishcloths. You never actually want them but it seems churlish not to buy a few. Go on, don't be so mean (but don't let them in the house!).

One Sunday afternoon the doorbell rang, and I had no peephole or chain so couldn't see who it was before I opened the door. When I did, I saw a man in his twenties, looking a bit dishevelled and distressed. He asked if I could help him and went into this long and heartbreaking story about how he'd broken up with his wife, only had access to his son at the weekends and had to get to Kent to see him that day. He said it was an especially important trip because it was his son's birthday and his son would be devastated if he didn't make it. Trouble was his car had broken down and he didn't have the money to get it fixed, so he was going to take the train but didn't have the money to buy a ticket. The whole story took about ten minutes and the upshot was, did I have a few quid I could lend him so that he could get to see his little boy? He swore he'd pay me back as soon as he got back, he only needed a tenner – please, he was desperate. Now, I was a bit sceptical

(I'm not a complete idiot), but he seemed so upset and he'd put so much into the telling of the story that I reckoned if it was true, he deserved a bit of help and if it wasn't true, he deserved some cash for all his effort. So I handed over a tenner and off he went. About a year later, the doorbell rang and it was the same bloke. This time he told me that he was supplying fish for the restaurant over the road and the staff were supposed to be there to meet him and put the fish in the fridge and pay him. But there was no one there, his fish was in danger of going off, could I just lend him a tenner to go and get some ice which he could put in his van to keep the fish fresh? As soon as the restaurant staff turned up, he would be paid and he'd be able to give me the money back. I couldn't believe the man had the front to come back to my house for a second time and concoct another tall tale in the hope of parting me from my money. Maybe he thought I was such a mug the first time, it was worth another go. Anyway, after asking him how his son was – 'What son?' he said – I sent him packing.
FIONA

To be sure who's outside your front door, your best option is to have an intercom. It's the priciest option, but at least it means you can speak to the person before you decide to open the door. If you live in a flat, it's essential – and saves you traipsing down the stairs only to discover that a) they've got the wrong address, b) they wanted the person in the flat above and pressed the wrong bell or c) it's the local Jehovah's Witnesses. (Sorry, no offence, but who *does* sign up to join when they come to the door? Have you ever met *anyone* who has?)

When you're in a flat or shared house, you have to rely on your flat/housemates to be as security-conscious as you are. Have a quick chat to them about it and try to agree some common ground rules. For example, agree that everyone should always lock the street door and never let anyone in that they don't recognize – even if they do say they are a friend of Karen on the top floor.

WINDOWS

Windows are the other obvious way for a burglar to get in. Get some window locks – if they're clearly visible some chancers will be deterred because it means they'd have to break the glass and risk attracting attention. So fix key-operated locks to all your downstairs windows and any ones that are easily accessible on floors above (if you've got a flat roof or a handy drainpipe, for example). There are various British Standards numbers to look out for, depending upon the types of window you have – if you want to be sure that you have the right type, you can talk to your local crime-prevention officer or contact NACOSS, the national security inspectorate. You could also think about putting bars or grilles on vulnerable windows. It depends on how you feel about them. You can buy extendable grilles, which can be easily opened when you are in the house and locked shut when you go out.

Another option is laminated glass, which is very hard for a burglar to break through. It won't put them off trying, as it doesn't look any different to normal glass, but when it is broken, a special interlayer keeps intruders out. Laminated glass is used to replace bars in prisons and it can be constructed to withstand bullets or bomb blasts – so we reckon it's probably strong enough to protect your home. But think about the fire risk – breaking a laminated window to get out in a hurry isn't an option.

You definitely want one of these. Some people cheat and just put an unconnected box on the front of the house, but it's really worth investing in an alarm, because it's proven to be a serious deterrent. There are a number of different systems you can choose from, so you're best off getting some specialist advice (see websites and addresses at the end of the chapter). Only speak to installers that offer you a written quotation without obligation. Turn away any company that tries to shock you into purchasing with stories of burglaries in your locality. If you feel a particular company has tried 'hard-sell' tactics you should consider contacting your local police or trading standards office.

You can opt for an alarm that makes a loud noise or a siren, which should scare off the intruder and alert anyone passing by (and seriously irritate your neighbours). With one of these, the police won't come unless someone calls them, but remember: if it goes off too often in error, you could find yourself blacklisted. You can guarantee that the one day there is a genuine burglary will be the day no one comes!

We recommend that you get a remote signalling alarm. It will send a signal to an alarm-receiving centre, who will call you or a key-holder you've chosen in advance and, if they get no reply, will then call the police.

I've used this system for years and I've found it really useful that the alarm company calls me on my mobile first. If I don't answer they call my husband, my children's nanny and then my brother. If none of us picks up the phone, they call the police. Once I came home to find the alarm going off, and the police in the front garden and trying to get into the back garden. I thought two things at the

When you go to bed at night, it's useful and reassuring to be able to part-set your alarm. That means to set the alarm for only a predetermined section of the house – the ground floor, for example – so that you can move around at night upstairs, in your bedroom, go to the bathroom, etc., without setting it off. Jacqui sets an area that her dog can move about in at night. But if someone tries to break into any other part of the house the alarm will sound loud and clear.

One extra bit of kit that you might find useful is a personal-attack device. You can get it installed as part of your alarm system and you push a button to set it off at any time, even if the alarm itself is switched off. It can be portable or fixed to the wall. It's to be used if you suddenly find yourself face to face with a threatening or unwanted visitor at your door or inside your house. And we're not talking about the Jehovah's Witnesses again (we know – we will burn in hell). Best places to put it – within easy reach by the front door and by your bed. Very reassuring. If you buy a device that has a police response built in, the police will come straight away.

We all hate coming back to our front door in the evening and fumbling around for the key. It makes us feel vulnerable and it's always a nightmare to find it when it's right at the bottom of your bag. And if you are coming home in the evening, what you don't want are dark places in your front garden or by your front door where someone could lurk unseen. Get some PIR (passive infrared) security lights. Not only will your fumbling-for-the-door-key days be over, but burglars don't like them. If you put them by the front door, any intruder will be beautifully floodlit as soon as they enter your property and more inclined to scarper as a result. You could also think about putting security lights by your back gate and around your front or back garden. The idea is to make the burglar feel visible and therefore vulnerable. They're not expensive and you can get ones that work on a simple switch, or on a timer, or ones that are triggered by movement sensors.

As well as external lights, it is a good idea to put some of your internal lights on timers. They can come on and off at particular times of day and night to give the impression that you're in even when you're away on holiday. Incidentally, you can do this with radios too. It all creates the illusion of occupancy. You can now even buy a gadget that switches lights on remotely via your mobile phone. Called a Remote Phone Switcher, this gadget costs around £50 and is designed for the remote switching on and off of any item of electrical equipment plugged into it. You can access it from any telephone anywhere in the world and it is operated by a coded telephone call. All these things can be bought at your local hardware centre.

GARDENS, SHEDS AND GARAGES

Not the most popular choice for a prospective thief you might think. But no – they are like catnip to your cat burglar, containing all sorts of tools and bikes that can easily be taken away and flogged. Use a padlock on your shed and make your garden difficult to access with secure boundaries and prickly planting – and stick lights in too, as above, as a further deterrent.

As for your garage, make sure that your alarm system encompasses that too. Fiona's had her garage burgled, even though the house was left untouched. The thief was caught – a rather sad individual who nicked her bike to feed his drug habit. An alarm would almost certainly have frightened him off.

As a detective at Kingston Police Station CID I dealt with a prisoner one day who'd been arrested for stealing meat from a freezer in someone's garage. Not the crime of the century, you may think, but the value was over £100 (and this was twenty years ago). After extensive interviews he admitted carrying out more than thirty other burglaries over a couple of months in which he had stolen the contents of people's freezers and then sold them on. He even came out with me in a car and pointed out the houses concerned. Nearly half of these incidents hadn't been reported and I was amazed to discover a lot of those people hadn't even realized stuff was missing – or had realized but didn't think it worth reporting. It's worth considering how much it costs to stock your freezer if you keep it in your shed or garage, and think about how you can secure the door or lid. JACQUI

LOVE THY NEIGHBOUR

It might not be immediately apparent, but your neighbours can be your best protection against being burgled. Make friends with them. They can be your eyes and ears when you're not around. If you know them well enough, they can have a key to check up on things when you're away. They may be the ones who notice a suspicious man hanging round and alert the police. Find out if your area has a Neighbourhood Watch group. Information sheets or emails with details of crimes, arrests, appeals for witnesses, etc., are regularly sent to scheme members so you can keep up to date with what's going on in your area. If joining and going to meetings is too much for you (despite our best intentions, we have to admit it probably would be for us), go along at least once and have a chat to them, be aware what they're up to and what they think the security risks are in your area. Some groups run email-alert schemes to let you know if burglars or scammers are operating in your area.

KEYS

What type of front-door key do you have? And how many people have a copy of it? Fiona reckons, at the last count, five people have a copy of her front-door key. That's probably too many.

The best type of key to have is one that cannot be duplicated at your local key-cutters. It's a pain in the bum if you lose one, but if you can afford it, buy a security key which can only be copied at a special store against the security of your signature.

Ideally, if you've lost a key, or have just moved into a property, change the locks. Then you have total control over who has access to a key and, therefore, your property. If you do lose a key, remember: most insurance companies will cover you for getting new keys and locks, but do check your policy.

Things to consider:

- ⊙ᴇ **Try to avoid having your keys and your address in your bag at the same time.** If someone nicks your bag, they've got it made.

- ⊙ᴇ **Where do you keep your keys when you come in?** Hopefully not right by the front door. That old wives' tale about burglars fishing through your letterbox to nab a set of keys is true. Make sure your letterbox is at least half a metre from any locks so no one can reach in and open the door.

- ⊙ᴇ **Don't leave your keys with a builder, workman or estate agent unless you trust them absolutely.** They might not burgle your property themselves, but they might have a nice little sideline in flogging off duplicate keys to the highest bidder.

- ⊙ᴇ **Don't leave your keys outside under a flower pot, garden gnome, dustbin.** We've all done it but it's a seriously bad idea. The hiding place you think is so brilliant is bound to occur to a burglar. And it's possible he may have even seen you putting it there. And NEVER do what Fiona did . . .

When I was in my early twenties, I was going away for a holiday. I'd agreed that a friend of mine could use the flat while I was away but hadn't managed to find the time to see her and hand over a key before I left. So what did I do? I sent her the key through the post with an accompanying letter with my address and my departure and arrival dates. Well, I can hear you saying, I would never be as stupid as all that. OK, but I'm not all that stupid either and I still did it. Luckily, I got away with it and nothing was touched while I was on hols. But my friend has never had much regard for my IQ ever since. **FIONA**

If you get your milk or newspapers delivered to your home, make sure they come early enough for you to be able to take them inside before you leave the house. And make sure you cancel them when you're on holiday. Obvious advice, but you'd be amazed how often people forget. If you leave any kind of delivery outside your house you might as well put a banner across the front door saying, 'Look! I'm out! Wanna come in?' If something is going to be delivered and you know you won't be there to collect it, make sure it can be left with a neighbour and give the delivery company the details. (We told you those neighbours would come in handy.)

Protect Yourself and Your Belongings
Right, so you've done everything you can to stop someone getting into your house or flat. But if your burglar is *utterly* determined and much brighter than the average, there is still a slim possibility that he will manage to get in. So how can you make sure that he is able to walk off with a minimum amount of your stuff?

Far and away the most popular items for a thief are your purse and money, followed by computer equipment, jewellery, electrical goods and, finally, CDs and DVDs. So, take a note of which of these items you have in your home, write down the serial numbers of those items that have them and photograph them. Put this information somewhere safe, or else send it off to the insurance company to keep. That way there are no arguments afterwards.

Ideally, register your most valued possessions at www.immobilise.com. This is the website for the National Property Register and Recovery Service. It's the world's largest and *free* register of possessions with over 25 million entries and is supported by the police. Details of *all* your valuables including mobile phones, laptop and desktop computors, mp3 players, bicycles, jewellery, watches, antiques, keys and even your luggage when travelling, can be registered prior to any crime being committed. Anything you register on the website as having been nicked instantly appears on the police's national stolen equipment database, which is checked over half a million times a month by law enforcement officers to identify registered owners and whether the item of property is stolen. This will increase your chance of getting your prized possession back. Also, having access to those details will help you with the inevitable form filling required by the insurance company and police.

Another thing to consider is marking your property. The simplest and cheapest way of invisible marking is by using a UV pen, which can't be seen by the naked eye but shows up under fluorescent light. These can be bought online or at some DIY and hardware shops. You could also try a product called Smartwater. This is a liquid or sticker you can use to invisibly mark your property which contains a unique forensic code. If the police find a burglar in possession of suspect items, anything marked with Smartwater can easily be traced back to you and returned – and the burglar convicted: result. It's easily available from their website www.smartwater.com and costs about £44 for items in the average home and about £23 for a vehicle.

––––––––––––––––––––– JEWELLERY –––––––––––––––––––––

We bet you've got a jewellery box stashed on your dressing table somewhere. Any burglar worth his salt knows it's there too. So –

have two, one out on display for the stuff you like to wear but that isn't particularly valuable, the other, containing the collection from Tiffany's, Theo Fennell, etc. (should you be so lucky), hidden away. Obviously, a safe is the ideal answer, but if you can't afford one there are also some clever little gadgets on the market, such as boxes disguised as tomato-soup cans or books. If you're a Blue Peter disciple you could even make something yourself out of an empty food packet, just for while you're away on holiday. This is a particularly useful option if you live in a communal property, such as student accommodation, with flatmates you don't know very well.

―――――――――― ELECTRONIC DATA ――――――――――

If someone were to break into my house, I wouldn't care about losing things like passports or credit cards or electrical goods. They are a pain to replace but they are replaceable. My most precious thing is the hard drive of my computer, which has all my family photos on. I would be gutted if someone took it – I would feel like I was losing part of my history and that of my family. They're not worth anything to anyone else but they mean everything to me. Years' worth of holiday snaps, the first pictures of the children when I brought them back from hospital after they were born, that picture of my husband that I fell in love with and stuck on my fridge when we were dating. **FIONA**

One simple way to avoid losing those precious files on the computer is to back them all up on an external hard drive. It just plugs into your PC or laptop and you can copy everything on to it and then hide it away from the computer in another part of the house, in your safe (or cereal-box equivalent) or even at a friend's.

If you have a CD- or DVD-writer you have the ability to back up your files on to a disk. You should do this at regular intervals, depending on your amount of usage – say once a week, or just once a month if you're a light user. Again, remember to keep the disk in a safe place away from the computer.

<hr>

BE STREETWISE

Remember: your most precious things may not be the most obvious or costly.

As a general rule, if you would be grief-stricken if it was stolen or damaged, protect it! One of the easiest ways is to keep whatever it is out of sight, particularly from the street. If the contents of your house are clearly visible from the street, you might just as well have a yard sale – at least you'd make a few quid as everything walked out the door. Don't advertise what you own and, as far as you can, keep it hidden and keep it to yourself.

If you like to work at your computer by the window and it can be seen from outside, chances are a burglar's clocked it and is wondering how to get in and relieve you of it. So either move it or invest in – dare we say it – some form of *net curtains*. Aaagh, the horror! But listen up, net curtains have moved on. In these days of home makeovers, we are talking voile, linen, organdie, darling. Or what about nice wooden slatted blinds? Much more tasteful. Do you mind if you and your possessions are completely visible to anyone passing by outside? You should – and we're not just talking about people looking in when you get undressed in the bedroom. (If you are into that, you need to be reading a different book . . .)

The voile, etc., is particularly important if your bedroom is on the ground floor or in the basement. It should never be apparent to anyone on the street that you sleep in a room which, without the right precautions, can be so easily accessible. We can't stress this enough. It amazes us when we walk past people's houses and have a nosy in the windows that it is often immediately obvious that there is a bedroom at ground level or below – and sometimes it's easy to see that it belongs to a woman too. This book is not written to frighten the living daylights out of you, but that kind of information to the wrong sort of man is seriously dangerous. Think about it and make sure you keep the location of your bedroom private.

What to Do If You Have been Burgled

If you get home and the burglar alarm is going or the front door is wide open, what should you do?

As a young PC I would be sent to report a burglary and, when I got there, my first action was always to search the premises. Would you believe, on several occasions the burglar was still inside hiding – sometimes in the loft, a wardrobe or the garden shed – in the hope of slipping away later, having been surprised by the homeowner's arrival and terrified of being caught.

While working at Clapham Police Station in south London I answered a call about suspects seen leaving a house carrying property. My mate and I arrived, found the front door forced open and went in to investigate. From the odd noises we were hearing it was apparent someone was still there, so we searched each room. The only room we couldn't get into was locked, but the door had a loose lower panel. I pushed it open and crawled through. Inside, it was dark but I saw three sets of feet up against a wall and inhaled the unmistakable smell of fear. I let my mate in and we arrested all three for burglary.

Down the road another cop had found the suspect seen earlier with property and recovered a large amount of hi-fi and electrical equipment and music paraphernalia, including a large number of gold discs, belonging to Bob Geldof and The Boomtown Rats. Yes, he and Paula were very grateful.

I have to say, in my experience, most people caught in the act of stealing are absolutely terrified (even more than you are) and just want to get as far away as quickly as possible. But you can never be absolutely sure how they may react, so probably best not to take the risk of approaching them. JACQUI

If you think someone is still there, the first thing is to ring 999 from your mobile or a neighbour's phone. Unless you're mob-handed or feeling particularly brave (or your name is Jacqui), don't go inside and have a go at tackling the person alone.

I came back from broadcasting late one night to find a police officer outside my home. A windowpane had been shattered and shards of glass were strewn inside, but a neighbour had raised the alarm and the culprit had fled empty-handed. Foolishly, I went to bed without barricading the window effectively, and woke at 2 a.m. to find a man opening the door to my room. I'm not sure who was more startled, but he had the presence of mind to lie. 'I'm a police officer,' he told me. 'There's been a break-in. Please get dressed and come downstairs.' And then he vanished. So now I'd been broken into by a burglar not once but twice within twenty-four hours. I slammed on the lights, leapt after him and got to the

If you're in and you think a burglar is inside your home with you, what should you do? This is, frankly, a pretty scary scenario (but not a likely one, so don't panic). Remember, as Jacqui says, the burglar is likely to be far more terrified than you are. If you have a panic alarm, this is the time to press it. If you can, get out of the house or flat. Call 999 and make sure you tell them an intruder is in the house, as the police will come a lot more quickly. Some advice suggests you should shout and make as much noise as possible to try to frighten the burglar off. But this is not the time to be brave or foolhardy, and there's no way of knowing in advance exactly what the right thing to do is other than make yourself as safe as possible. If that means locking yourself in the bathroom or hiding under the sofa while you call the police, you go for it.

DON'T TOUCH

If your place has been burgled, it's very tempting to start putting things back in their right place, to go through drawers to see what's been taken. Wait. Depending on the seriousness of the burglary, the police may want to evaluate the scene and dust for fingerprints. You don't want to go round hoovering up vital evidence.

GET A CRIME REFERENCE NUMBER

When you report a crime of any kind, the police will take the details and give you a crime reference number. If they don't offer one, ask for it, as you'll need to give it to your insurance company. When you come to report the burglary to your insurers, don't be tempted to make up a whole load of stuff you've never owned but wish you had. (We know, it's so tempting. Even if you didn't have a pair of Christian Louboutin shoes, you *deserved* to have them.) In the case of a burglary, the police will note down what's been stolen, and if the two accounts don't tally, you'll be found out and possibly even prosecuted.

———————————— MOVE ON ————————————

We don't mean literally, though in rare cases people find the experience of being burgled so traumatic that they feel they have to move house in order to put it behind them. Having your home invaded by an unwanted stranger can give rise to all sorts of emotions, ranging from irritation and a sense of violation to real grief. You are going to react differently to having your bike nicked from the garden shed than to coming home from holiday and finding your house has been ransacked. You may feel that your home is no longer a refuge; that it feels like just a building. Your feeling of safety and peace has been corrupted. Every time you go up the stairs, you may imagine the burglar going up them too. Whenever you go to take some jewellery out of your dressing table, you might imagine the burglar doing the same. It can be seriously stressful, and don't try to pretend those feelings aren't there or are in some way shameful. They are perfectly under-standable, and you should talk to your friends or a counsellor about them. There is also an organization called Victim Support, which does what its name suggests (see Further Information). The police will probably give you the number of your local branch and, if they don't, ask for it. Victim Support should be a source of comfort and practical advice, and if you end up having to give evidence in court, they will come with you and help you.

If you feel as if your home has been violated, there are things you can do to make it feel like your home once more.

- ○⚊ **Decorate** The sense of newness that a coat of fresh paint gives will help override the sense that a thief was there. It won't just look different, it will smell different too, and that all helps to create the feeling that you are making a fresh start and getting rid of the 'contamination' brought in by the burglar.

- ○⚊ **Remove** Sell, take to the second-hand shop, eBay or simply chuck out anything you feel has been tainted by the burglar. If you hate your bedside table because you associate it with the burglar rifling through it, get a new one. If you hate wearing your clothes or underwear because you know the thief went through your drawers looking for valuables, get new ones.

- ○⚊ **Throw a party** Always a good idea, and no better time than when you've put your home back together after a traumatic burglary. Invite all your friends, get in lots to drink, ban all conversation about the break-in and have a great night. You will create all sorts of new happy associations for your home which should help get rid of the bad memories.

How to Stop Yourself being Burgled Again

Believe it or not, something like 1 per cent of homes account for over 40 per cent of burglaries. In other words, once a thief has found an easy place to get into, word gets around and the unfortunate homeowner will find their house burgled over and over – particularly as the thief knows that everything they stole the first time has probably been replaced by shiny new things by the nice insurance company.

If this has happened to you, firstly, do the obvious stuff. Find out how the thieves got in and make sure that is no longer possible. That will make you sleep a whole lot easier. You might need to call an emergency glazier or locksmith – your insurance company might cover this for you, so give them a call. Even if the door wasn't forced or the keys weren't stolen, you might want to get new locks as a precaution. Check for your chequebook and any credit cards or financial information you might have left lying around. If your bank statements have been gone through, you'll need to take steps to protect yourself. (See Chapter 6 on financial protection.)

You might think the mansions on millionaire's row are the places most likely to be repeatedly burgled. After all, you're thinking, I haven't got much, no one in their right mind's going to break into my place, there's nothing worth taking. Well, those megabucks mansions have megabucks security too and are pretty off-putting to your common or garden thief. It's much easier to get into somewhere that looks a bit run-down, with no obvious signs of security. A thief can be in and out in a couple of minutes with a purse, or a DVD player, which is easy to flog. And that is the kind of place that gets burgled again and again. Make sure the security in your home is obvious and don't let the place get too run-down. If a house or block of flats looks unkempt, a burglar will reason that the inhabitants aren't making much effort with the security either. Be house-proud – it'll save you money in the long run.

BE HAPPY IN YOUR HOME

Being confident and secure in your home isn't just about preventing crime or keeping burglars out, it's about protecting yourself from the unexpected, the unwelcome and the potentially catastrophic. You might not want to do all of the things listed below – but at least try to do *some* of them.

Smoke Detectors

Get smoke detectors installed professionally or just put them up yourself. They are very cheap and you can get them from any DIY store. They will give you invaluable time to get out if a fire starts. They can be battery- or mains-operated. Some of the more expensive burglar alarms also include smoke detectors. They're wired in as part of the system and, once the detector goes off, the alarm company is alerted. They will then call to check if you are there, if you are safe, if there actually is a fire or whether the alarm's just been triggered by your burning the toast. If you are away and they get no response, they will call the fire service. If you rent, the landlord has to have smoke detectors fitted by law; it should be mentioned in the tenancy agreement health and safety regulations.

Your Own Emergency Exit

You can buy rope ladders or extendable ladders from DIY shops, which you fit to a top-floor window, and they are a brilliant safety device for getting out of the house if there's a fire. Our only tip would be: if you do get one, practise using it at least once. Give it a go during the day when you've got a spare moment. Otherwise, the first time you have to get down it, you may be blinded by smoke or terrified by flames behind you. If you are already familiar with using your rope ladder, you've got a head start. You never know, it could be fun. Talk to everyone who lives in the property about a plan of action should there be a fire. Where are your exit points? That way everyone will know what to do and how to get out quickly if a fire should break out.

Carbon-monoxide Detectors

Faulty heaters or boilers can kill you. If they aren't processing natural or petroleum gas properly, they can leak carbon monoxide into the room or building. The gas reduces the body's ability to carry oxygen, leaving your organs and cells starved. You will eventually fall unconscious and then die. Even if a faulty boiler isn't leaking enough carbon monoxide to kill you, it may slowly poison you. Symptoms include headaches, nausea, abdominal pain, sore throat and dry coughs, although, unlike a cold or flu, you won't get a raised temperature. You need carbon-monoxide detectors in your home. These can be battery-operated or mains-operated.

I made a documentary about the effects of carbon monoxide for the BBC a few years ago. Two stories in it particularly affected me. I remember a family mourning the death of their teenage son, who'd just gone off to university. He was setting out on his own independent path in life for the first time, and the hopes and dreams of his parents went with him. He couldn't get rooms in the university so he got himself a rented bedsit in some cheap student accommodation. The only source of heating for the room was a gas fire. When he turned it on in the winter, he didn't know that it was faulty and that carbon monoxide was seeping out. The fumes made him feel drowsy, but because he couldn't smell or see them, he presumably didn't notice anything was wrong. He died in his sleep from carbon monoxide poisoning.

I also interviewed a family who'd all been poisoned by carbon monoxide but lived to tell the tale. They had a faulty boiler in their home and hadn't had it checked or serviced for some time. The carbon monoxide fumes weren't strong enough to kill them, thankfully, but the family gradually began to fall ill and couldn't understand why. They kept going back to the doctor but he could find no reason why they were feeling so tired and under the weather. The mother felt worst, as she spent most time in the house. After months they managed to trace it back to the boiler and realized what was going on. But the mother was ill for years afterwards with aching joints and extreme tiredness. In neither case had a carbon-monoxide detector been installed. Few people knew that such detectors existed back then and how dangerous carbon monoxide can be. There's much greater public awareness now but still few people think of installing detectors. If I had my way, they would be mandatory in every home. FIONA

Carbon monoxide has no smell, and you can't see it, but if it's leaking into the room you may go to sleep and never wake up. Stick some carbon-monoxide detectors up (you can get them at hardware and DIY stores) and also make sure you or your landlord get the boiler and any heating appliances regularly serviced by a CORGI-registered engineer.

Torch

Always have one easily accessible, with the batteries charged up. If you have a power cut, it's a real pain trying to make your way to the fuse box in the dark. Instead of stubbing your toe, light your way through the darkness. It's a good idea to have a few candles and a box of matches handy too.

Living Alone

If you are a woman living alone in a property, try not to make it obvious to outsiders. If you have a label with your name on it by the intercom at the front door, just put your surname on it. Similarly, just use your surname and initials in the phone directory. When you answer the phone, just say 'hello'. (Lionel Richie, anyone?) Don't give out your name or your number, even if the caller claims to have dialled wrongly and asks you for it. And never say you are alone in the house to someone on the phone or at the door.

> A friend of mine lived alone, and when she left the house she would shout, 'Bye, Jim, see you later' or 'Down, Rover – you can have a steak later' (or something similar), just to make anyone listening think she had a large pet and an even larger flatmate. I don't know how effective this was, but she was never burgled.
> JACQUI

Silent or Abusive Calls

If you get abusive or silent phone calls, just put the handset down and walk away. Come back a few minutes later and hang up. Don't have a sneaky listen to see if the person is still there. Above all, don't say anything – your average perv or weirdo will be after a reaction. Don't give him one and most likely he'll give up. If, however, you do keep getting the calls, contact the police. They can put a tracing service on the phone and try to find out where the calls are coming from. British Telecom has its own unit (contactable on 150), which can investigate on your behalf. More details in Chapter 5.

INSURANCE

Discussing insurance can be monumentally dull, so we'll keep this brief, but we've learned from experience how much it matters. There are two types of home insurance, buildings and contents, and if you are a homeowner you need both. If you're renting or a leaseholder, you only need contents cover. If you are a student you may well find that your parents' home contents policy will cover you while you are living in student accommodation; if not, most companies will extend the policy to cover this for free, which is much cheaper than getting a separate policy.

Most people tend to take up the offer of insurance from the company making their mortgage offer or one of the big high-street lenders, just because it's easy and a familiar name. Our advice is: think first about what you need and then shop around. The trouble with the big, well-known lenders is that they usually offer a one-size-fits-all insurance, and that may not suit you. It may not be the cheapest either. Think about using a broker to negotiate the cheapest insurance for you. That may sound impossibly grand or only for the fabulously wealthy, but it's not. A broker should take into account all your needs and recommend the best and cheapest option. Always ask about their fees up front: some don't charge the customer direct but are paid commission from companies. They can also be helpful if you have to make a claim, as they may act on your behalf by completing forms and liaising directly with the company. When you understand the system and feel more confident, then there's no reason why you shouldn't take over the task yourself in future. Whether you pay monthly or annually, there is always a renewal date and it really is worth shopping around just beforehand for a better deal.

Alternatively, you can search for a deal on the web; there are several websites that will compare insurance options for you and select the cheapest. We like www.moneysupermarket.com, www.gocompare.com and www.confused.com, but you really need to search three or four comparison sites to ensure you're getting the best deal. This can be very time-consuming and most of them don't cover all the companies and are acting on behalf of just a handful. It's worth remembering that the comparison sites earn money from each company featured, and some pay them more than others. Some really big insurers don't use them at all. Make sure you compare all the product features carefully before you buy so you know exactly what you're getting for your money. www.uknetguide.com will help you navigate around all these sites, as will www.moneymakingexpert.com and www.money-magpie.com. Supermarkets can also offer great deals and are backed by major insurance companies.

Most of us will require little more than the basic off-the-shelf policies on offer, but if you have different requirements which don't fit the basic questions, then speak to a broker or insurer about a more bespoke policy. Some insurance companies will come out personally to assess your home and take photos if necessary.

Buildings Insurance

This is to insure the structure of the building, the bricks and mortar. If your home burned down or was damaged in some way, generally this policy would enable you to have it rebuilt or repaired to be just the same as it was before – *the same, not better*. You won't get that dressing room you always wanted or a swimming pool out of it.

Things to consider:

- Are there any insurance restrictions on the property? If there are, find out what they are and see if you can get them addressed or minimized. For example, if you have subsidence, you'll need to get that put right or your insurance premium may well be very high and you'll have difficulties when you come to sell the place.

- Is there a risk of flooding in your area? We've all seen the reports on the news about the havoc flooding can cause and how it can devastate your house and your belongings. An insurer may refuse to cover you for flooding if your house is considered to be at risk. If it's not too late, DON'T buy a house on a flood plain. No matter how much you love it.

When I first tried to buy my cottage there was a tree growing out of one corner. Luckily, the survey said that, once removed, it would not cause any structural problems, and just required infilling. However, my insurance company wouldn't give me cover until the tree was removed, I couldn't remove the tree until I owned the property, the mortgage company wouldn't give me a mortgage to buy it until I had insurance and I . . . well, you get the picture. Eventually, although the previous owner had died, I found one of their family members who agreed to give me permission to remove the tree on their behalf (after the council had given me permission to take down a tree in their area) and then I tracked

down the insurance company who had originally insured the property prior to the owner dying and they agreed to continue insuring it (once the tree was removed, of course). Despite the frustration (it was about then I discovered a love of large brandies and ice cream at night), it did all turn out OK, so don't give up.
JACQUI

Contents Insurance

This covers you for your belongings in your home. The furniture, the carpets, the curtains, the computer, the clothes, the TV – the lot. If you are burgled, if the house burns to a cinder or your belongings are damaged, a contents policy should buy replacements for what's been lost.

Keep your insurance company up to date with what you own. Computers and TVs are replaced every couple of years, on average, and as they go up in value you may find your policy doesn't cover them. Check with your insurer.

Does your insurance cover your belongings only when they are in the home? If you take your prescription glasses out to work with you and they are stolen or lost, will your insurer pay up? If you can, it's far better to get a policy that covers items in and out of the home. You never know what you may take out of the house for whatever purpose, and you want to know you're covered. It may also insure you for your belongings when you take them away on holiday. The advantage of that is you then don't have to buy two separate policies to cover your personal possessions when you're at home and away. So even if the contents insurance is a bit pricier as a result, it may well work out cheaper in the long run.

One night last year I trundled off to a pub in a nice part of London to meet some friends. The pub was quite quiet and we were reasonably well behaved, and about 10 p.m. we decided to make our way home. As we got ready to go it became apparent that I was no longer in possession of my handbag. The bar staff were mortified but confirmed that a number of bags had been stolen in recent weeks. I was devastated. Apart from the fact that the thief had taken my favourite Ted Baker handbag, my wallet, my cash and my cards, they'd also got away with a full bottle of perfume, about a hundred pounds' worth of make-up, my diary, my phone and my brand-spanking-new £200 iPod (sob!). When I added everything up it totalled over £500 and, to make matters worse, I had an unpaid water bill in my bag, together with a full set of keys, so I had to change all of the locks on my house. The next day a friend of mine pointed out that you can extend your home contents insurance to cover your possessions so I called immediately and was told that for a couple of pounds extra a month my bag and all of its contents would have been covered. If only I'd researched my insurance policy I would have been able to replace the sparkly video iPod that I so adored. SARAH, LONDON

Some policies specify that contents will be replaced new for old. So if your top-of-the-range plasma TV is nicked, your insurance will pay for you to have a brand-new one. If the policy does not stipulate new for old, you will only receive what the insurer decides the value of the item to be at the time it was taken. So, if you paid £2,000 for a new plasma three years ago but when it was taken the company rules it was only worth £300, that is all you will get. You are left with no plasma and you can't afford to buy a new one, even after the insurance company pays up. If you do opt for a new-for-old policy, check exactly what it covers. It may not cover everything.

> I took a look around my home and thought about what I would want to replace if it was burgled or burned down and how much it would cost me. I looked at the furniture, my paltry jewellery, the TV and music system and suddenly realized that replacing my clothes would be the highest expense for me. I have more than most people (with the possible exception of Paris Hilton . . .) because I need a variety of outfits for the different programmes I do on TV. I have lots of suits I wear for the news and I rarely chuck them out, in the usually vain hope that they might come back into fashion again. I checked my insurance policy and realized to my horror that it didn't replace new for old when it came to clothes. So if my entire wardrobe went up in a puff of smoke, the insurance would only pay out what they were worth second-hand and not what it would cost for me to buy a whole new set of outfits. That would have cost me thousands of pounds, so I quickly got myself a new policy that would pay up the full amount. Now, obviously, this predicament doesn't apply to most people and I still had a nagging worry that the insurers just wouldn't believe quite how many clothes I had ('What? Thirty suits, madam? Are you having a laugh?'), so I opened the wardrobe doors and photographed the contents, all just hanging in a line on the rails, so that at least they'd get a rough idea. FIONA

It's pretty common for an insurance policy to limit what they will pay out for any single item. It might, for example, be £1,000. That might sound like a lot of cash, but if you take a quick look around your home, you may well be surprised at the value of what you have. What about your computer? Or your TV? Maybe your engagement ring? Each of those could easily be worth over a grand and, if they are stolen, your insurer won't pay out the full amount if it's over their maximum limit. If you regularly take a valuable laptop or mobile phone out and about, check your policy for 'all-risks' coverage, otherwise you're not covered. Your insurer may offer you extra cover for particular items that are worth more than their stipulated maximum, but the insurer has to be made aware exactly what they are and what they are worth. If you're covered for a valuable painting, say, but forgot to mention the diamond ring you inherited from Granny that's worth a few grand, the insurer won't cough up if it goes missing.

Your own security precautions will affect your insurance. If you have a good alarm from a reputable company and if you have made your home as secure as possible with good locks, that should lower your premium considerably. But you need to check that all your good work isn't going to work against you. Some policies will offer you a 5 per cent discount but stipulate that if you are burgled when you are out and you didn't remember to set the alarm, you will not be covered. And if you forgot to lock the windows or left them open, they may not fork out either. In our view, this is absurdly restrictive and almost impossible to live up to. Be realistic about how safety-conscious you actually are. Can you be sure you will *never* forget to set the alarm? No, didn't think so. Don't waste your money on that kind of policy. If, however, because of where you live or the amount of coverage you need, the insurance company stipulates that you *must* have an alarm, then you are not bound by the same restrictions. You will still be covered even if you forgot to set it when you were going out. Make sure you choose an alarm that is NACOSS approved (NACOSS is the UK independent regulatory and certification body for the electronic security industry). When it comes to locks, the only BS standard specified by the insurance companies is BS3621 for doors. For windows, they just stipulate that you install key-operated devices.

If you are particularly negligent, the insurer may decide that you have rendered their cover null and void. Find out what the insurer considers negligent behaviour and make sure you are able to avoid it. Always read the small print on your insurance documents so you know what you need to do to be covered.

I went out to an office Christmas party a few years ago and had a few drinks – well, more than a few actually – and came home in pretty bad shape. I staggered upstairs to bed and fell into a virtual coma. When I dragged myself out of bed the next day, and went downstairs, the flat was freezing and the front door was wide open. I realized I must have been so wasted the night before that I'd gone to bed without shutting the front door. Amazingly, no one decided to wander in during the night and relieve me of some of my stuff. God knows what the insurance company would have made of it if I'd had to claim. I expect they'd have told me to get lost. And they might have had a point. FIONA

YOUR WORST FEAR . . .

We thought long and hard before including this, because it is so rare. But it's something we all fear, so it seems strange to leave it out. So here it is: you wake up in the night and there is a man in your house, possibly more interested in you than your property. But, remember, it happens in only 1 per cent of burglaries. It feels like it happens more often because it's the favourite scenario of crime writers and dramatists. The stories terrify the life out of us, but they're addictive. And if it happens for real, it's usually newsworthy enough (because it's so uncommon) to feature on the nightly bulletins. All of which reinforces our fear that finding an intruder in our home is a likely possibility. It's not. But we think the best way of easing your mind is to go through the worst-case scenario and get you to think about the best course of action – for you. Having a plan can help diminish the fear of the unknown and increase your confidence.

In the incredibly unlikely event that this should happen, you just need to do whatever makes you safest. This is not the time for brave heroics – get out of the house immediately if you can, try to get your neighbours' attention and call 999. If you manage to dial the number from a landline but aren't able to speak, the operator should be able to trace the call and the police should come to you to investigate – but that isn't guaranteed. If you're calling on a mobile, you will need to speak to the operator so that he or she knows the call hasn't been made as a result of the numbers on the keypad being pressed by mistake.

If you're feeling brave (or foolhardy) you could stay and try to defend yourself, though we would only recommend that as a last resort if you can't get out. A word of warning here – we've all seen stories in the papers of people who took action against an intruder in their home only to find themselves taken to court by the burglar for assault. The law states that you should not have anything by your bed, in your car, at work, etc., which you *intend* to use as an offensive weapon. But if you legitimately have the item for its original use and, when confronted by an attacker, it's the nearest thing that comes to hand to defend yourself, you are within the law – as long as the injury inflicted is what the police recognize as 'proportionate'. For example, if you find someone rummaging around your house, you creep downstairs, are then confronted by the burglar, fear for your safety and the only thing to hand is a baseball bat to whack him with – no problem. However, if you come downstairs and he's on the way out of the window, the law doesn't treat you kindly if you then crush his skull with a bronze statue found nearby.

FURTHER INFORMATION

Freedom of Information Act 2000: See the Information Commissioners website for details on the right to request information held by a public authority at **www.ico.co.uk/whatwecover/freedomofinformation/thebasics**.

For landlord, tenant and neighbour disputes try the Citizens Advice Bureau Advice Guides on **www.adviceguide.org.uk**.

Secured by Design at **www.securedbydesign.com**.

To add information on stolen property to the National Stolen Equipment Database or register your mobile phone visit **www.immobilise.com**.

Get general security advice at **www.met.police.uk/crimeprevention**.

The National Security Inspectorate is an independent, not-for-profit approvals body that inspects companies providing home security, business security and fire protection services. Find them on **www.nsi.org.uk**.

Sold Secure is a non-profit making company which assesses security products, **www.soldsecure.com**.

If you want some more ideas, a good range of crime-prevention products can be found at **www.c-p-p.co.uk**, **www.property-marking.co.uk**, **www.tomsgadgets.com** and **www.securityvillage.co.uk** but once you find what you need, it's worth shopping around for the best price.

If you are a witness to, or victim of, a crime the Victim Support Scheme is there to help, **www.victimsupport.org.uk**.

Find out more about Neighbourhood Watch schemes on **www.neighbourhoodwatch.net**.

For lots more crime-prevention advice and details of government initiatives which you could take part in try **www.crimereduction.homeoffice.gov.uk**.

For information about insurance see the Association of British Insurers on **www.abi.org.uk**.

Information on Smartwater and related products at **www.smartwater.com**.

If you're interested in design, the Design Against Crime website may be worth a visit on **www.designagainstcrime.org**. They hold exhibitions and competitions.

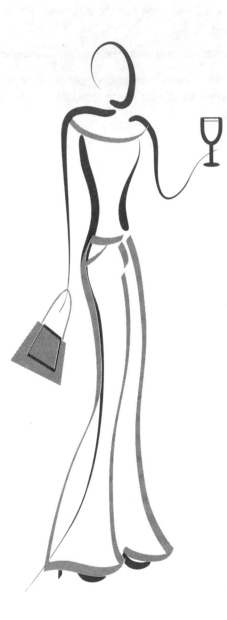

2

Let's Party!

WOMEN HAVE AT LONG LAST DISCOVERED WHAT MEN HAVE been experiencing for centuries: the joy of having the freedom to go out when they want, where they want and with whom they want. If we want to drink, we can, if we want to get down on the dance floor and fling ourselves about, we can, if we want to chat up the seriously attractive guy in the bar, we can (we were never quite that brave but good luck to you). But with all this newfound freedom there are new risks to consider. When you go out to that great new club in the centre of town, how are you going to get there and back? What will you do with your bag when you're there? When is it too late to travel safely on public transport? When you go to a restaurant, a club or a footie match, what should you be looking out for? If you feel threatened, are you able to defend yourself? And then there's the big subject – booze. We don't want to sound like killjoys (and God knows we've been there, done that, when it comes to drinking), but far and away the biggest issue surrounding your safety when you're out is alcohol. Drinking yourself to a standstill will take you to the top of the list in the vulnerability stakes. If you suddenly find yourself like Bambi on ice, you're probably not in the best position to judge the character of the man offering to buy you a drink, whether you should go on to another club, how you're going to get home or whether dancing in just your bra (because you're really, *really* hot) is a good idea.

I was out with a group of friends on a weekday night in a pub. One of my closest friends is called Jane. She's a good laugh but could never handle her drink and always got pissed very quickly. While the rest of us were drinking and talking, Jane was being chatted up by two guys a bit older than her. They were standing very close to her and kept putting their arms around her and being very touchy-feely. After a bit they went off to dance in the middle of the pub. They were all over her like a rash, but then I lost sight of her. After about half an hour, Jane staggered back to our table looking upset. She said the guys had left her on her own, she couldn't find them anywhere and now she couldn't find her handbag. We looked all around but couldn't find it either and Jane got more and more upset as it began to dawn on her that those guys who had seemed so interested in her had actually just wanted to rob her. She was seriously the worse for wear at this point and as we all looked for her bag, things began to go downhill fast – she started shouting over and over that she'd been robbed. I knew she'd completely lost the plot when she yelled at the top of her voice, 'They've gone and taken my car keys too – and it's only parked in Swinton Street!' By this time she had the attention of everyone in the pub and so, as quickly as we could, we dragged her out of there and set off to find her car. Sure enough, when we got to Swinton Street, there was no sign of it. If those two guys hadn't known where to find the car at the start of the evening, they were certainly left in no doubt by the end of it. ALISON, GLASGOW

A few things spring to mind with this particular story. Firstly Jane was a total wally. If she was planning on drinking, it was a bad idea to bring the car. She was lucky her house wasn't burgled as well. And, maybe Alison could have acted more responsibly towards her friend and stopped her from being dragged off by two strangers in the first place.

GETTING THERE AND BACK

One of the biggest decisions you need to make when planning a night out is how you're going to get where you're going and back again. The exciting bit is working out where you're going to go, who you're going to go with, what you're going to wear. But you need to think through both ends of the journey to make sure you won't be left stranded flagging down the nearest cab only to realize you've run out of cash or end up shivering at a nightbus stop with no idea if or when the next bus will come along. Always know your options before you go out. If you're going out with friends, make decisions and plans about how you're going to get home, and stick together – look after each other.

Public Transport

Certainly your cheapest and usually the most reliable option, 6 billion journeys are made by public transport each year. Depending on the time of night and who you're with, it can be a top choice. As you set out for the evening, consider whether the tube or bus will still feel safe and friendly later on that night. If it's late, we don't travel alone on public transport and we don't recommend that you do either. But everyone has a different view about what is 'late' and when 'late' turns into 'too late'. It depends on where you are, how well lit it is and how many people there are about. Some parts of the centre of London or Manchester, for example, can feel as safe at 3 a.m. as they do in the middle of the day, with lots of people about and loads of packed nightbuses, but other areas can feel dark, empty and menacing. If there are plenty of people around you and the area has good street lighting, you may justifiably feel secure and safe. There are no hard and fast rules; you have to work it out for yourself. Trust your instincts and past experiences.

But there's certainly safety in numbers – think about whether you could stay at your friend's house for the night and go home together rather than travelling on your own. And always know the time of your last train, tube or bus. Details of the public transport in your area will be on your local council website or, in London, on the Transport For London website (www.tfl.gov.uk). You can also call TFL on 020 7222 1234. Otherwise, you could end up walking home, as indeed we have – it's invariably cold, unpleasant and can take hours.

——————————————— BUSES ———————————————

Buses usually have CCTV, which doesn't always stop people misbehaving, particularly if they're drunk, but it does help the police to catch them afterwards and makes for some handy items for *Crimewatch*.

If you're walking to or from a bus stop in the dark, use the route that has the best lighting and the most people walking along it, even if it's not the shortest way to get to where you're going. If you have a choice of bus stop, wait at the busiest and brightest one. If you're on your own, stand near a group of people so that you look as if you're part of a crowd. Once you get on the bus, sit as near to the driver as possible and don't hesitate to ask him or her for help if you need it.

——————————— TRAINS OR TUBES ———————————

Confirm your train times and connections before you set off. If you're unsure (or very forgetful), double-check at an information point when you arrive at the station. Or you can use the local council website, which should have all the local public-transport details you need. National travel is covered by sites like www.transportdirect.info, www.the trainline.com, www.theaa.com/travelwatch/planner_main.jsp or www.nationalrail.co.uk.

Use the front or middle carriages; they're less likely to empty suddenly. Try to choose a carriage that has plenty of people in, though if the people in the carriage are all part of the same group, you might want to give them a wide berth. They could be harmless but they may feel like singing their entire repertoire of eighties hits at the top of their voices all the way home. 'Come on, Eileeeeeen . . .' Avoid compartments which have no access to corridors or other parts of the train. If you decide you don't like the look of a person in your carriage, or if he makes you uneasy for any reason (no matter how irrational it may seem), get off at the next station and get into a different carriage further along. If you think it's absolutely necessary, get off the train altogether, and take the next one. Check where the emergency cord or alarm is. Neither of us has ever had to use one, but it's reassuring to know where it is.

At the station, stay in well-lit areas on the platform. Many station platforms now have help points with both information and emergency buttons; make sure you know where they are. If you feel uneasy, stay near the ticket office or station staff until your train arrives. And talking of staff, will there be any there when you're travelling late at night? Unless it's a very busy location, the most likely answer is that they will have evaporated into thin air. A deserted station feels very different on your way home to the busy one you set out from, especially as trains run much less frequently late at night. If you check the train times before you head out and if it seems likely that you'll have to spend half an hour on a deserted platform in the dark, think of another transport option. If you're driving to and from the station, try to park in a bay near the exit if you know you're going to be coming home late.

And what about the walkways in the station? Are there long corridors or underpasses or stairways with no escape routes? We've shown lots of cases on *Crimewatch* where people have been assaulted or mugged in just such areas because it's very easy for an attacker to grab your handbag – or you – in a place where you are likely to be on your own, where no one will be able to see what's happening and it's hard for you to get away.

On *Crimewatch* we showed some CCTV footage from a camera that was mounted on a covered bridge that formed the walkway between one platform and another. A young man was loitering alone on the bridge, clearly waiting to see who might come his way. A woman commuter came into the vision of the camera and just as she passed the man he grabbed her around the neck with one arm and then got hold of her bag. He ran off with it across the bridge and disappeared from view. I never spoke to the woman involved but the police told me she'd been absolutely terrified and hadn't felt able to use that station since.

It was on the journey she made to work every day and she had to take a much longer route to avoid that station, but it was the only way she felt safe. It really makes you think about how secure those stations are when there aren't many people around. FIONA

Check if the stations you're going to be using have been accredited by the Secure Stations Scheme. It was launched in 1998 and is managed by the government and the British Transport Police. About three hundred stations are listed on the scheme and they have to meet a high standard of passenger and staff security. This might involve lighting on the platforms, in the ticket halls and station car parks and the provision of help points and alarms. For a station to be listed on the scheme a crime-prevention officer from the British Transport Police must have judged that the station does actually work to prevent and reduce crime, and make passengers feel safer.

When you arrive at your destination, you need to have already thought about how you're going to get home (always easier to do with a clear head). Is someone picking you up from the station or are you driving yourself? If someone is collecting you, make sure you know exactly where they are going to be parked. Some stations have several entrances, and wandering round an empty car park is no fun. Are you planning to get a taxi? Will there be a rank where you can expect a nice line of warm, inviting taxis to be waiting, ready to whisk you off to wherever you want to go? Or will you have to try to find the local cab number and then stand around waiting for it to turn up? 'We'll get there as soon as we can but it'll be at least half an hour, love, we're very busy.' (See p. 74 for more about using only licensed minicabs.)

I covered a story for *GMTV* last year where a young girl got off a train at about 10 p.m. on her way home late from work. CCTV footage showed her walking across the lit car park towards her car (the only one left), talking to her boyfriend on her mobile phone. Suddenly, another car drove into view and, leaving its engine still running, a man jumped out, ran over to her, grabbed her phone, knocked her to the ground and kicked her several times before running back to his car and disappearing. It looked like her attacker had been waiting for her to come along. She might not have been able to prevent it, but if she hadn't been on her phone, she might have noticed the car waiting there and perhaps would have had a chance to go back into the station to summon help. Keeping her phone out of sight or using a personal-attack alarm (I'd like to see alarms incorporated into phones) may have put him off. It's worth remembering that a busy car park at 8 a.m. can become empty and exposed at 10 p.m.

JACQUI

General Rules

What puts most of us off public transport is, frankly, the other people on it. It's all very well thinking that you'll do your bit for the environment and leave the car at home, or you don't want to drink and drive or, OK, you don't have a car in the first place and you can't afford a cab. But then you get on the bus and some bloke is working his way through a massive, smelly burger on the top floor, a teenager is playing loud, tinny and truly terrible music on his mobile phone, some old man is looking at you in a funny way or some City type is sticking the hard edge of his brief-case into you in the rush hour – or at least you think it's his briefcase . . .

Here are some tips for a more bearable and hopefully a more pleasant way to start or end your evening:

- ♀ **Don't listen to your iPod** when you're walking to and from a bus stop or station. And, if you can bear it, don't listen to it when you're on public transport either. You need to be aware of what's going on around you – sound is just as important as vision. Plan your route to and from the bus stop or station. Let other people know where you are going and when you expect to return. Have your mobile on you and make sure the battery is charged and your credit is topped up.

- ♀ **If you're using a car park,** try to choose a parking bay close to the station exit, particularly if you're going to be returning in the dark.

- ♀ **If you're going to use a cab from the station,** make sure it's licensed (see p. 74).

- ♀ **Watch your bag.** Keep it on your lap with the opening facing inwards to your body. Stick your arm through the strap, especially if you think there's a chance you might nod off, though try your best not to. Don't put it down on the floor by the aisle.

- ♀ **Watch out for other people's bags.** If you see a bag that is not obviously connected to a person, don't be embarrassed to ask loudly who it belongs to. If no one claims it, report it to the driver or guard.

- ♀ **Be careful** what information you are giving out when you are talking on your mobile phone, particularly if you are one of those people who can't help SHOUTING on it. Keep personal details to yourself. Saying, 'I can't wait to get home and put my feet up but it's a shame everyone will be out 'cos I'm desperate to fill them in on tonight's gossip,' probably isn't the smartest idea.

- **Always make sure you have cash on you.** We're not talking masses, but enough to get you out of trouble if you suddenly find yourself stranded and need to get a cab.

- **Have a back-up plan** if you get separated from the people you are travelling with – you never know when or under what circumstances this could happen. Arrange a secondary location to meet up or make sure you have a couple of mobile numbers on you.

- **If you suspect you're being followed** when you're walking home from the bus stop or train station, cross the road. If the person behind you crosses the road too, your suspicions are probably right. Go and knock on the nearest door or go into the closest pub or shop. Get help and call the police. Don't carry on walking home alone.

- **Think about wearing a pair of flat shoes** or having a pair in a bag with you if you've got a bit of a walk home. We hesitate to suggest this, because it's not always convenient or possible, but one idea could be fold-up or 'After-Party Shoes' – they look like ballet pumps and come in fab colours and designs by Redfoot (available from www.vivaladiva.com or www.pretty pinktoes.co.uk). Useful if those killer heels won't take you another step, and they could allow you to leg it quickly from a difficult situation.

I was followed home late at night by a man with a knife who had watched me park my car. I was trying not to be paranoid – but I was right to be. I lived in a basement flat – I took a gamble on my

upstairs neighbours answering my frantic knocking on their door. Luckily, they were in. As they answered the door, he melted away. After that, I never wore high heels and a tight, long skirt if I thought I would be coming home late. It restricts your ability to run away.
PENNY SMITH, PRESENTER, *GMTV*

Carry a personal-attack alarm. There are lots on the market: a search on the web produced over 3 million hits. However, if you want to support a worthwhile cause, the Suzy Lamplugh Trust sells a basic model for about £6.99. Locally, try B&Q, who have one you can clip on a belt while jogging for £5, but our advice is to shop around and find what suits you and your lifestyle best. Most are pretty small and can easily fit in your handbag or pocket. On the whole, it's just a case of pushing a button or pulling a pin and an ear-splitting din will ensue. Some are gas-powered, some electronic. The level of noise starts at around 126 decibels and goes up to 140 decibels, which can be heard up to half a mile away – so don't let them off for a laugh or to impress your friends. We are told 125 decibels is the average person's pain threshold. Ouch!

Make sure you have your alarm instantly accessible. It's no good it being at the bottom of your handbag – it needs to be in your hand so you can set it off in a split second. Some have additional features like DNA spray to mark your attacker, or an ultraviolet marking spray, a kind of thick, sticky-red-goo spray, and there's even one on the market that emits what it calls a 'repulsive odour'.

The Lucie Blackman Trust (a charity set up by the family of Lucie, who was murdered while working in Japan in 2000) launched the Buddy Safe, a personal-attack alarm with a difference, in December 2007. It is a key fob with a button which when pressed in an emergency 'talks' via a Bluetooth connection to your mobile phone. The phone then sends a silent message to the server which pinpoints the phone's location through mobile-phone-positioning technology. This information is then sent to pre-set contacts, through text message, voice call and an email which has a map attached. These friends can then contact the emergency services and also the holder, if possible, to ensure you are OK or haven't moved location. Its big advantage is that you can use it in situations when it is impossible for you to make a 999 call, and you don't have to try to explain exactly where you are, as the positioning system will do it for you. It's not cheap, at £15 initial set-up fee and £6 monthly subscription, plus 20p per message, but the trust is non-profit-making and has managed to negotiate a cheaper option for under-eighteens. See their website, www.lucie blackmantrust.org.

We think this is a great step forward from the good old audible personal-attack alarm, but see no reason why this system can't be integrated into a mobile phone itself, with a hot key setting off the alarm. Perhaps there's a mobile-phone company out there who'd like to take up the challenge?

In the meantime, take your pick of the personal alarms available. But don't go for mace spray (which is sold in the United States), as it's illegal here – you can be arrested for being in possession of it, as it is classed as an offensive weapon.

Think about texting a message if you're going out alone, to alert people to where you're going and what time you expect to get there, particularly if you regularly travel late at night or on your own in areas you don't feel particularly safe. That way, if something goes wrong en route, your car or the bus breaking down leaving you stranded, or in the unlikely event you get some threatening attention from a stranger, people will know to start looking for you and coming to help. (Read more in Chapter 3, 'On the Move'.)

If you're walking, avoid ill-lit or very quiet areas, even if they are the shorter route. Try to walk where there are plenty of people. If you know that it will be pretty deserted and dark, don't walk there at all, even if it's a route you use in the daylight all the time. Look confident and walk quickly and decisively. Walk on the side of the road that faces oncoming traffic – that way you'll be less vulnerable to kerb-crawlers.

I was travelling home on the tube one evening after a party at work. It was quite crowded, and most people were just sitting quietly or reading. A young woman was sitting a few seats away from me at the end of the row, looking through a newspaper. I'd noticed one man who seemed a bit agitated; he kept looking round at everyone and every now and again would mutter something quietly under his breath. I always dread someone like that being in my carriage because they can be so unpredictable and you never know if they are going to start shouting or being abusive. I was glad I wasn't sitting next to him.

Suddenly he jumped up from his seat and walked up to the woman at the end of my row and began to yell at her. He was being really aggressive and threatening and was shouting obscenities. No one knew where to look and it was clear everyone (including me) was too frightened to get involved in case he turned on one of us. It seemed to go on for an eternity and, as we pulled into a station, he leaned over, punched her in the head and got off. She was crying, but it was only once he'd left that any of us went up to her to help and comfort her.

I felt really ashamed of myself for being so pathetic and replayed it again and again in my mind afterwards. But I have a horrible feeling that if it happened again, I might be just as much of a coward. SHARON, LONDON

TROUBLEMAKERS

So what *should* you do if you see something like that going on in your train or on your bus? Be the hero? Or what if it's something much less dramatic but still unpleasant? Like when a few drunks get on and start talking loudly and obscenely about you? Or if someone is staring at you, clearly wanting to provoke a reaction?

There's no doubt that the right thing to do morally is to help someone in trouble. But few of us actually do help, for the same reason that we don't react when someone is trying to provoke us. We just want the troublemakers to go away and hope that by ignoring them they will get the message and clear off. Whether you want to be a hero or not is up to you and your conscience, but be clear about the risks. And when someone is threatening you, the key thing is not to put yourself in danger. Try not to react, don't make eye contact, move from your seat, if possible to a place of safety (possibly by the driver) and raise the alarm. Report it to the police as soon as you can while you can still remember the details clearly.

Gropers are our pet hate. Who do these neanderthal morons think they are? What gives them the right to grab any woman they want to and cop a quick feel? We would castrate the lot of them. Harsh but fair. So how can you protect yourself from them? Regular users of public transport have developed super-sensitive antennae to men who seem to be standing just that bit too close and so move away pretty promptly. Our view, though, is that you should shame them publicly. It takes a bit of chutzpah but it'll certainly make them think twice about doing it again. Below is one of our favourite stories, about a friend who decided to fight back.

I was on my way out to meet my boyfriend in the centre of town before we went off to the theatre. I'd dressed up a bit in honour of the occasion and was really looking forward to the evening ahead. It was rush hour and the train was packed. I felt something hard sticking into my bum and thought it must be the edge of someone's bag or briefcase. I tried to move away a little to give myself more room but was hemmed in on all sides. Then I felt it again, and this time there was no mistaking it. It wasn't someone's bag – it was clearly a man with an erection pressing himself against me. It was revolting. For a moment I felt slightly panicky and wondered what to do. I tried to work out who it was but there were so many people around me it was impossible. And then I thought, 'Sod this, why should some disgusting old lech get away with touching my body and ruining my evening?' So I took a deep breath and said very clearly and as loudly as I could manage, 'Would whoever is pressing their erection against my thigh please stop right now. You are harassing me, which is a criminal offence. If you don't stop this second I will reach over and press the emergency alarm button.'

There followed a lengthy and agonizingly uncomfortable silence, during which no one met my eye, not even the other women in the carriage. But, miraculously, a little space appeared all around me and whoever had been pressing against me stopped. I never did find out who it was and the carriage virtually emptied at the next station. No one spoke to me about it as the journey went on and I was torn between excruciating embarrassment and pride in having stood up to my harasser. In the end, pride won out and I went to the theatre that night and had a terrific time. And if a groper ever comes up to me again and tries to have go, I'll do the same thing again. JAN, HAMPSHIRE

Getting a Cab

If you're going out for the evening and you intend to have a drink or several, getting a taxi is your safest bet. It's your priciest option, but at least you know that, at the end of the evening, you'll be driven back to your front door and you won't have to stand shivering at a bus stop or dicing with the drunks on the last train home. But one important warning: ONLY use a licensed taxi or minicab. NEVER get into one that isn't licensed – EVER.

How can you tell the difference? Easy – it is illegal for mini-cabs to tout for business on the street. Only black-cab drivers can do this. They have undergone three years' worth of 'knowledge' training before being granted a licence. So, if someone offers you a lift on the street, you know they are not licensed or they are breaking the law. A licensed minicab may not have a distinctive vehicle like the black-cab drivers, but it will still have a registra-tion plate with an identification number and where it was registered on it. The driver should also carry a personal ID containing his photo and, again, his registration details.

So, why are we banging on about this? Well, each year two thousand women are sexually assaulted by unlicensed cab drivers; ten a month in London alone. In some cases it's too complimentary even to call them unlicensed cab drivers. What they are is predatory sex offenders looking for victims. What a gift for them: a tired, lost, possibly drunk woman getting into their vehicle voluntarily – none of this dragging them off the streets or thinking up some other excuse. Just say you're a cab driver – child's play!

Using licensed drivers has other benefits too. They have to go through rigorous checks, which means that they and their cars are safe. If they have an accident they are compelled to have insurance that will cover injury to you as well as to them or damage to their car. Without this you'd get no compensation for injuries sustained or loss of earnings should you find yourself caught up in a crash. Licensed drivers often have extensive training and operate under strict controls.

As a seventeen-year-old student I had embarked on fully independent socializing, and the feeling of freedom was fantastic. I was living in south-west London at the time and one night had been invited to a student party in south-east London. No one I knew locally was going so I had to travel alone using the bus, but I had been promised a lift home later, so all was looking good.

A fab evening was had by all – until I realized that my lift home was too far gone to be able to drive and had in fact passed out in the back garden. I decided to run the gauntlet of the nightbus. All was going well until we got to Brixton High Street. We had just reached the town hall when the driver was taken ill, and the service suddenly terminated. So there I was, stranded, about 8 miles from home, outside one of the biggest pulling places for prostitutes in the area. The vultures started to circle round –

'Hello, love, how much for a quick hand job,' and so on.

Panic started to overwhelm me and I could feel the tears welling up. I had very little money, so trying to find a cab didn't seem to be an option, until at last I had a stroke of luck. A black-cab driver had spotted me – I must have looked very pathetic by this time – and offered to help. Now, I remembered from the depths of my befuddled head that black-cab drivers were generally much more trustworthy than the minicab type, as they had to be registered and do masses of training. So I threw myself on his mercy and, bless him, he took me home and refused any promise of a fare, saying he had a daughter my age. What a great guy. JACQUI

If you remember nothing else from reading this book, just remember this one thing: do not ever, EVER, get into an unsolicited or unlicensed minicab, especially on your own. You know the blokes who drive up and down outside clubs and pubs at closing time and shout out to see who needs a ride? Well, NEVER GET IN. Would you in any other circumstances get into the car of a strange man? We doubt it. We know it's tempting. It's late, it's cold, you're tired, you don't know how else you're going to get home, and a man in a warm car drives up and says, 'Do you need a cab, love?' Ignore him.

We've featured many items on *Crimewatch* and on the news about women being abducted by bogus minicab drivers and we don't ever want to feature them again.

CAB-RANK MARSHALS

Cab-rank marshals are now starting to appear in some town centres, which is brilliant news. They're usually organized as a joint venture between the town council and the police. They tend to supervise a specific taxi rank and, although they have no powers of arrest, they'll maintain orderly queues and prevent any drunken scuffles. If the rank is empty they'll call a cab for you and if there are lots of cars there and it's busy they'll ensure you get into a licensed one. There are nine systems currently operating in London and several others in cities across the UK: find out what is available in your area. If there is not one in your town centre, why not lobby your local council if you and your friends use cabs regularly? This is what one person had to say about a taxi-marshal system in Edinburgh.

> I was out on Saturday night and went to the taxi rank on Lothian Road. The attendants were cheery even though it was 2 a.m., cold and they were surrounded by idiotic drunken people. They kept order in the line and made sure you ate your pizza before you got to the front of the queue! It was the first time I'd used the rank since their introduction. I'd definitely use them again. MARY, EDINBURGH

CALLING A CAB

Lots of nightclubs and restaurants will now order a cab for you from a known licensed company and allow you to wait in warmth and safety so you don't have to stand around on the street. But this may not always be the case and you need to leave home prepared. Charge up your mobile and top up your credit. Programme it with the numbers of two or three licensed cab companies – preferably ones that you or a friend has used before. If you can book it in advance, all the better: don't forget the name you have booked it under and never get into the vehicle until the driver tells you the name it was booked in. Then you know it is your driver and not some chancer. Do not say, 'Are you the driver for Cook?' That just gives your name away and the driver will just say 'Yes.' If you and your friends have to book separate cabs to go in different directions, consider taking one cab together and taking the onward cab from there or even staying over at one of your friend's houses.

Make use of one of a number of schemes that exist to make your journey in a cab as safe as possible. To find out if there are any in your area, contact your local council. One example is Cabwise, which was launched in London in 2005. You just text HOME to 60835 and, hey presto, the telephone numbers for one taxi and two licensed minicab companies which serve your area will pop up on your phone.

TIPS FOR SAFE TAXI TRAVEL

- **When you're in a cab, never get in the front** with the driver but sit in the back behind him, where it is hardest for him to reach you.

- **Only get into conversation on general topics;** don't give out personal information.

- **Always ask your cab driver to wait outside your house or flat** until you've actually gone in the front door. We always do it and, believe us, they won't mind. It will deter anyone who might be lurking nearby.

- If you do find yourself alone in a car with a driver who for any reason is making you feel uncomfortable or worried, **trust your instincts.** First take a note of the cab registration number, and where you are, and ask the driver to stop in a busy and well-lit area. If he won't stop when requested, use your mobile phone immediately to call for help from the police. If you carry a personal-attack alarm, open the window and use it. Or just shout for help. Try not to panic and, if possible, leave the vehicle at any opportunity when it has to slow or stop for any reason. Try to appear as confident as possible. This might sound ridiculous in the circumstances, but it can make a real difference.

Driving Yourself

Getting from A to B in your car can certainly be the easiest way to reach your party venue of choice. But then, if you're planning on drinking, it can be a real drag. The maximum you can drink before driving is 80mg/100 millilitres of blood – in plain English: two pints of normal-strength beer or one large glass of wine could put you over the limit. If you're slight or small, the legal limit may amount to even less. After a heavy night, you can still be over the limit the following morning.

If you're convicted:

- you'll have a criminal record
- you'll be banned from driving for at least a year
- your insurance will go through the roof
- you could lose your job
- you'll be hit with a fine of up to £5,000
- you could go to prison. It's not worth it, is it?

Plus, you could injure or kill yourself, or someone else. Could you live with that on your conscience?

So, be very careful about how much you're drinking or, if you're with a group of friends, make one of you the designated driver for the night. Of course it's a pain if it's you, but if you take it in turns it won't be so bad. And make sure the person chosen to stay off the sauce that night can be trusted to do so. It's no good if you're all relying on him/her and then you find your carefully selected driver curled up in a drunken coma in the corner.

WHAT TO TAKE WITH YOU

Your Handbag
A girl's best friend on a night out is her handbag. Have you got the right things in it?

- Keys (only the ones you really need).

- Purse with emergency cash secreted separately from the rest – why not slip a tenner into your bra or down your boot? But make sure you take no more money than you'll need, even allowing for emergencies. And don't take all your credit or debit cards; take just one or two, if you really need to.

- A couple of minicab business cards (licensed ones you've used before).

- Mobile phone programmed with numbers of people you can call in emergency (including minicab firms) – and don't forget to top up your credit and charge the battery. There was a campaign a couple of years ago to encourage people to put an entry in their phonebook of ICE (In Case of Emergency) and the number of someone you would like called if you were in trouble. Add it into your contacts. Keep your mobile out of sight unless you need to use it.

- Y **Condom** – well you never know your luck . . .

- Y **Personal-attack alarm** – this could save your skin in all sorts of circumstances.

- Y **Lippy, perfume, mirror** – you've got to have fun and look gorgeous too.

Make your bag a small one with just the essentials in it. Don't drag your Filofax and unpaid bills around with you – if your bag is stolen with your door key in it, you'll also have given the thief your address.

Keeping Your Handbag Safe

Things must be pretty desperate in New York because they go to some pretty extreme lengths there to protect their handbags. How about this for safety-conscious? We found this on a US website:

- Y **Anti-slash** – Line your handbag with chicken wire to avoid losing the contents if the bag is slashed.

- Y **Anti-dip** – Use a small travel padlock to keep your zips together in order to hinder/prevent pickpockets. (Not a bad idea, though a bit of a hassle every time you want to get a round in.)

- Y **Anti-lift** – Use a long wire and padlock to wrap around your bag and a table or chair.

- Y **Anti-grab** – Take a personal-attack alarm with a pull cord and attach the alarm to your bag and the cord to your wrist.

We're not recommending anything quite so extreme. But you're probably most at risk of losing your handbag when you're out and about in a crowded or ill-it venue, and it can cause you real problems. Even if you manage to keep hold of your bag, it's possible pickpockets will relieve you of some of its contents. So what can you do?

- **Choose a bag with secure fastenings,** to make it more difficult for someone to reach into it.

- **Use inner compartments with zips** for money and precious items.

- **Don't overfill it** so that you can't close it.

- **Ideally, choose a bag with a long strap** that you can wear diagonally across your body.

- **Keep your bag to the front of you,** where you can see it. Those little rucksacks that you can carry on your back look cute and are comfortable to wear, but it's far too easy for someone to open them up and reach inside without you ever being aware of it.

- **Don't leave your bag unattended.** If you don't want to take it with you when you're going to have a dance or nip to the loo, leave it with someone you trust.

- **If you do take it to the loo with you, don't put it down on the floor** by the gap between cubicles or between the door and the ground. Someone could easily just reach in and pull it out.

- **Don't place your bag under your chair or out of sight.** You might think that's making it safer but, if you can't see it, you may not see it being nicked either. If you place it in among a pile of coats, for example, it's easy for a thief to take while pretending to look for his jacket.

♀ **Be aware of your surroundings.** A nearby row might be fascinating to earwig on but it might be just a distraction while someone else nicks your bag.

♀ **Look out for pickpockets.** They will try all sorts of ruses and even disguises to relieve you of your purse or keys, including chatting you up while their mate dips his hand into your bag, knocking into you, spilling drinks over you or even asking a simple question like 'What's the time?' Anything to distract you from the fact that your purse is disappearing. They can work alone or in teams of two or three – men and women included, and it can be very lucrative.

I had my purse stolen in a club in London and ended up stranded at 2 a.m. with no cash to get home. I vowed that it would never happen again, so I started putting some cash and a credit card in my bra. My friend Sarah used to keep them in her knickers. I still carried a bag and tried to keep it safe, but it only had some cash in it for drinks and I knew I could still get home if it disappeared.
ANNE, LONDON

♀ **Beware of skimming.** So many of us like to keep our mobiles to hand when out and about and put them on tables or bars so that we're aware of calls and texts as soon as they come through. Well, thieves have developed a scam called 'skimming' whereby they approach you under false pretences (such as asking the time), lay something over your phone like a coat or newspaper and then, when they move away, hey presto, your phone has gone. Another regularly used ploy is for them to ask you for directions and place a map over the phone. So watch out!

There are some dinky gadgets on the market to help you keep hold of your bag and find what's in it when you need it. We've selected a few that particularly appealed to us:

THE HANDBAG HANGER

It's originally an Aussie gadget but you can now get them in the UK. We both love ours! If you're trying to avoid putting your bag down on the ground, this is for you. And we like it not just from a safety perspective, but it also means that if you've a beautiful light-coloured bag you don't have to put it on the floor where it will get dirty. And think about it: that same bag you put down on the floor in a pub, loo, office, etc., is also the bag you bung on to the kitchen worktop when you get home. The Handbag Hanger is a little portable hook that you can slot on to the back of doors, chairs and tables to keep your bag in sight but off the ground. For the fashion-conscious, they come in all colours and designs, including lovely jewelled versions, and most fold up into their own cute little bag. We found them on several websites with prices ranging from £5 on www.mybaghanger.com to £40 on www.brittique.com. (For more links see Further Information at the end of the chapter.)

Some cafés, bars and pubs are now fitting more permanent, functional-looking versions to the undersides of tables and on vertical surfaces such as pillars, walls and bars. Look out for them when you go in, or lobby your favourite haunts to buy them – they only cost about 50p each from www.handbagclip.com or www.selectadna.co.uk.

We also found a product called Keyfinders for about £7 to save you scrabbling about in your bag looking for your keys. It's a pretty little clip attached to your keys at one end and to the edge of your handbag at the other, and is available from www.purseangels.co.uk. A word of warning about these though, make sure they don't make it easy for someone to steal your keys. If you don't really want to fork out on gadgets then why not improvise yourself – if you're given an ID tag to hang round your neck at work, the lanyard can be used to attach your purse to your bag with enough leeway to stop it restricting use. Eat your heart out, *Blue Peter*!

HANDBAG LIGHTS

You can buy different types of these; it is just a small, flat square box with a light that you clip inside your bag. When you want to find something inside, you just switch it on and you can see what you need. Unfortunately, Jacqui's handbag would also need a floodlight and a metal detector.

TRANSMITTER

You can go really hi-tech and buy a transmitter that will sound an alarm if your bag is separated from you. The device comes with two components, a transmitter and receiver. Put the former in your bag, the latter somewhere on your person and set the distance anywhere up to 80 feet. Then, if the bag goes further from you than the designated distance, an alarm will sound. You can use this, incidentally, on anything you really value, or even on your child when you're out together, so it could be very useful. A slightly less extreme idea is the mini handbag alarm with separate built-in torch we found on www.securityvillage.co.uk for about a fiver. You attach the alarm to the bag and its cord to either yourself or a solid fixture. If the bag is suddenly pulled away and the cord is detached, a loud alarm is set off to encourage the thief to drop it asap. Finally, www.bagsafe.com have a small clip and coiled plastic-coated wire device which can be attached to a handbag, laptop bag, rucksack, etc. and then to either you or a fixed point. It can withstand up to 300lb of pressure should someone try to steal it.

Several years ago I was on a filmset for a crime drama in Manchester, recording some interviews with the characters playing police officers. It was set in an old prison building and we were offered the use of a room to leave our stuff in while filming in other areas. We were assured everything would be safe, so I left my large, heavy handbag in the room so as not to have to lug it around. We got back a couple of hours later to discover that my purse, which not only contained cash and credit cards but also my ticket home, was missing. Can you imagine how embarrassing, not to mention humiliating, it was as a serving police officer, on a filmset surrounded by uniformed police officers (albeit actors), calling the local police to come and report a theft? I still can't believe how stupid I was – but we all have lapses, and nine times out of ten probably get away with it. I've been really careful ever since and in similar circumstances have just taken my purse out, if nothing else. JACQUI

If, despite all your best endeavours, your handbag or purse is nicked, call the police straight away with as much information as you can: a description of the bag, who you think took it and where they might have gone next. Then you need to notify all your credit- and debit-card providers so that they can cancel your cards. This is important because from the moment you notify them that your cards have been taken, you should not be liable for any money that is withdrawn on them. Inform your mobile-phone provider, too, so that they can put a block on the phone.

Your Mobile

Having your phone nicked when you're out is a serious headache. As well as the inconvenience, you know that someone will probably be running up a bill on your phone as soon as they've got their hot little hands on it.

To make things harder for them, use your phone's pin-code lock if it has one, record the serial number and consider separate insurance. As soon as you buy a new phone register it with www.immobilise.com – all you have to do is fill in the registration form with your name, address, and phone details including what's called an IMEI number, which will allow the operator to disable the phone if it's stolen. To find out what your IMEI number is, type in *#06# and it will be displayed on your handset. Registering your phone means that if it is stolen you should be able to get it back, and more quickly than otherwise. It only takes a couple of minutes to do and could save you a lot of hassle if you lose your phone. It is an industry objective to get 80 per cent of stolen phones blocked within 48 hours. There are already over 16 million phones registered, and there are efforts to persuade suppliers to register them at the point of sale, which already happens in a couple of European countries. Remember, though, that blocking doesn't extend beyond the UK, so if you lose your phone while travelling abroad it won't be blocked, but do still report it as soon as possible.

DRINKING

So you're on your big night out and you want to have a drink or several. Alcohol may be the cheerful accompaniment to a pleasant evening or it may be the focus of the night. But be aware that one in five violent crimes takes place in or around pubs and clubs. If you are the kind of person who likes to get so lashed you can't remember how you got home, make sure in advance that a friend you trust will stay sober enough to look out for you. You are at your most vulnerable when you're drunk. Your guard is down, your judgement is impaired, your memory will be a bit dodgy, and that bloke sitting in the corner that you'd written off as a loser will suddenly look like Brad Pitt. So you want to be sure that you are in a safe place with people around you who have your best interests at heart.

And watch out for people adding more alcohol to what you're drinking when you're not paying attention. Looking at it kindly, it's sometimes seen as a bit of a laugh to spike drinks, even by so-called friends. This is incredibly irresponsible, as you can never be sure of the effect it will have, particularly if the person whose drink is being spiked is on medication you don't know about. Alcohol features in so many crime reports: it is the single most significant factor in making you more likely to be a victim of crime.

I worked for a couple of years as the office manager of the Serious Crimes Analysis Section of the National Crime and Operations Faculty. There we collected all the cases from throughout the UK of murder, rape and abduction – attacks by strangers or so-called date rapes (that's generally when the victim has only known the suspect for less than twenty-four hours). The majority of case files which passed across my desk had one or both of these things in common: the victim was walking home alone; the victim had been drinking. Please, please remember this. JACQUI

Stories of people binge drinking every week are probably a bit exaggerated but, to keep safe, you cannot underestimate the association between alcohol and crime.

Alcohol – The Advantages and the Risks

For most of us, alcohol is a relaxant: it helps us be more sociable, bolder, more outgoing. It can make a boring night into a pleasant one; it can turn a good night into a fantastic one; and it might even give you the courage to take to the dance floor. But it's not all good news.

Alcohol can be a depressant, so if you're already feeling down, it'll make you feel worse. Your speech can become slurred and your coordination can be affected. You can lose consciousness and run the risk of choking on your own vomit. Alcohol poisoning is no joke – we've seen it close up and it can kill, though that's rare. If you regularly drink a lot, you can become addicted. Even if you don't call yourself an alcoholic, regular binge drinking can cause serious damage to your internal organs. It can make you look older by dehydrating your skin (making all those expensive face creams a bit redundant), give you the shakes, mood swings, brain damage and, ultimately, cause death.

Heavy drinking is more likely to bring you into contact with crime in a number of ways. Over 70,000 facial injuries in the UK every year are linked to drunken violence. And most of them happen on licensed premises. You might take a swing at someone, or someone drunker than you may take the opportunity to deck you.

Eight out of ten pedestrians killed on Friday or Saturday nights have been drinking, and a third of all pedestrians killed on the roads have consumed alcohol. So, statistically, if you're staggering around paralytic, you're more likely to harm yourself by stepping out into moving traffic.

We showed a reconstruction on *Crimewatch* of the tragic case of a young man who'd been out drinking. He got separated from his friends and decided to walk home on his own. His journey took him along a dual carriageway and at some point he decided that he'd walk in the middle of the road. He then decided to lie down in the road. Maybe he fell asleep, maybe he was ill; there was no way of knowing. But a car came along the road at some speed and in the dark, and he was run over and killed. His family were heartbroken. There's nothing wrong with enjoying a drink, but make sure you know your limits so you don't put yourself in danger. **FIONA**

Alcohol is processed by your liver, and you place a big strain on this vital organ if you indulge in a heavy drinking session. Make it a regular fixture and you run the risk of developing a disease called cirrhosis. If it goes too far, there's no cure. Fiona has a number of friends who had to give up alcohol entirely in their late twenties because they had already done so much damage to their livers.

While one of the advantages of alcohol is that it's a relaxant, that positive effect can quickly turn into a negative one. What you considered to be carefully chosen words of wisdom to your boss can later turn out to be career suicide. Having the courage to make a move on the man you've always fancied can be a real ice-breaker. But you might not be in much of a state to follow through if he offers to take you back to his place.

When I first joined the Metropolitan Police at the tender age of nineteen I was by no stretch of the imagination a big drinker. It quickly became apparent to me that the accepted way of 'relaxing' or 'de-stressing' after a heavy shift or long inquiry was to get completely plastered. Initially, I was quite good at just having a few but gradually I too found myself well ensconced in the culture of drinking almost every night. When I progressed into the CID, as one of the few women detectives at that time I was anxious to be accepted as 'one of the lads' and also used drinking as a way of escaping the pressures of policing and some of the more difficult decisions and experiences.

I remember one evening going out to celebrate the end of a particularly difficult and long inquiry. We'd been working sixteen-eighteen-hour days for weeks and were ready to let our hair down. After a boozy lunch we toured several pubs and, after giving a drunken rendition of a selection of songs from *The Sound of Music*, I was apparently last seen asleep under a table cuddling a teddy bear.

Someone took me home and I was woken up the next morning by the sound of the telephone ringing and someone on the other end informing me I was needed unexpectedly to give evidence at Crown Court. Fortunately, I was given a lift, because otherwise I would never have made it – I felt horrendous, and not just then but for several days afterwards. Facing the judge that morning was a real feat of willpower and mind over matter and I'm not sure to this day how I managed it without throwing up all over the usher as I read the oath. It was a pivotal moment for me. Since then I've been very conscious about when I've had enough and switch to soft drinks or even alternate throughout the evening. I can still have fun, and feel OK the next morning. JACQUI

So here are our top tips for surviving a boozy night out:

☐ **Eat before drinking.** There is some truth in the old wives' tale that you can line your stomach to stop you getting pissed too quickly. Alcohol is absorbed into your body through the stomach and small intestine. Food slows down the rate of absorption, which is why booze affects you more quickly on an empty stomach. Choose starchy foods that take a while to digest, such as potatoes, pasta, bread and cereal.

Y **Set yourself a drinks limit.** Decide how much you're going to drink in advance and stick to it.

Y **Keep track of how much you're drinking.** You won't know your limit if you don't know how much you've had.

Y **Choose lighter-alcohol options.** When it comes to lighter beers, for example, the difference between a 5 per cent pint of lager and a 3.5 or 4 per cent one can be a whole unit.

Y **Don't mix your drinks.** The effect of mixing shorts, wine and beer can be unpredictable and much harsher on your system than if you stick to one thing.

I was filming in Scotland, making a fairly serious documentary about psychiatric hospitals and the availability of illegal drugs within them. It was a two-day shoot and at the end of the first day we had a decent meal and several glasses of wine. The Scottish cameraman was appalled that I, a fellow Scot, didn't like whisky, so he took it upon himself to convert me. Several whiskies later, I was beginning to come round to the stuff, and didn't get to bed until about 3 a.m.

I have never felt so ill in my whole life as I did the next day. My producer had a total sense-of-humour failure as I tried to carry on filming while feeling like I wanted to die. I kept having to absent myself to go to the loo in the vain hope that I might throw up and be done with it. It being a psychiatric institution, staff kept an eye out for anyone who'd been in the loo for too long, and every ten minutes or so, a nurse would come and knock on the door and ask if I was OK. I'd feebly reply that it was 'just the lady from the BBC' and then have to drag myself out of that loo and go off and find another one to crawl into until I was discovered again. It was a nightmare. In the end, I had to stop filming and go and sleep it off in the cameraman's car. I can say with total honesty that I have never, ever mixed the grain and the grape again. Or drunk those kind of quantities of either. FIONA

- **Drink some water.** A strategic glass of water or a soft drink can do wonders to keep you from getting too drunk too quickly. Try to get into the habit of having a quick glass of water or a soft drink after every glass of alcohol.

- **Pace yourself.** Peaking too early is no fun. Everyone else will be having fun while you're either incapable of sensible speech or asleep under the table.

- **Drink smaller drinks.** Sounds like a no-brainer but it's better to drink less and often in smaller glasses if you can. A large glass of wine can be equivalent to a third of a bottle.

- **Avoid drinking in rounds and drinking games.** You want to be drinking at your own pace and not trying to keep up with others. And just because someone offers to include you in a round, it doesn't mean you have to accept.

- **Coffee does not sober you up.** Big myth this one. Caffeine in coffee and fizzy drinks is a stimulant, so it might make you more alert but not more sober.

- **Beware of having your drink spiked.** If your drink tastes even slightly different to how it should, leave it. This brings us neatly on to . . .

DATE-RAPE DRUGS

Well, here's a subject that has been talked about a lot in recent years. While we believe it's a good thing to raise this issue and make women aware of the possibility, we can't help having concerns about the exaggerated level of fear it has raised.

To put the issue into context, there's no doubt that, historically, men have tried various means to get women to have sex with them, with or without their consent, whether it is the unreconstructed chauvinist who plies a woman with drink to make her more cooperative, or the predatory sex-attacker who administers a controlled substance against the will or without the knowledge of his prospective victim to make her compliant and therefore easier to rape. While these things do happen, they are certainly at the top end of the crime scale and are still quite rare.

The statistics around this are confusing. Some organizations claim that as many as one in four women who regularly go to pubs and clubs have had their drinks spiked. On the other hand, when the Association of Chief Police Officers did a survey of people who claimed to have had their drinks spiked, in most of the cases, they struggled to find strong evidence that any kind of date-rape drug had been administered. There could be a number of reasons for this, not least that the drugs don't last long in the body and can be very difficult to trace hours after they have been consumed. But also, most of the people who claim to have had their drinks spiked are usually tipsy or drunk at the time, and a number have taken illegal drugs of other kinds themselves. So it is hard to tell whether the claims the victims are making are the result of a date-rape drug or because of their own self-inflicted befuddled state of mind at the time. Nevertheless, date-rape drugs do exist and, even if they're not used very often, you should know enough about them to be able to protect yourself.

We've featured cases of assaults allegedly using date-rape drugs a number of times on *Crimewatch*. They can be hard cases to appeal to the public about because the victims generally remember very little about what happened to them and so we have few hard facts to give to the audience. But the stories are always heartrending, and the worst of it is that when the victim can remember so little, she can be left imagining untold horrors to fill the gaps in her memory.

One woman went out to a pub with friends and then woke up several hours later in a strange house where a party seemed to be going on. She could remember nothing except flashbacks of a man having sex with her. Most disturbingly, she had a hazy recollection of people being in the room watching them some of the time; at other times she was alone with the man, who was sitting up in bed watching her. In another case, a woman went out for a drink with friends and didn't remember getting particularly drunk. But then she woke up in a toilet with her trousers around her ankles and she was bleeding from her vagina.

In another case, which was captured on CCTV, a woman was again out with friends at a pub and remembered suddenly feeling very strange, dizzy and unable to talk. She had a foggy recollection of one or two men walking out of the pub with her and taking her along the road, half supporting her, half dragging her with them. On the CCTV you could see grainy images of what appeared to be two men walking along with a smaller figure between them. She couldn't then remember much about being assaulted until a few days later when she began to have flashbacks. FIONA

There are three major groups of drugs used in drug rape and other drink-spiking crimes: Gamma Hydroxybutyrate (GHB), Ketamine and Benzodiazepines (which include Rohypnol and Valium). They all act as a kind of anaesthetic and so reduce a person's ability to react, resist rape or robbery and can cause a victim to cooperate with the criminal. After a few hours the victim will fall asleep and have little or no memory of what happened while under the influence of the drug. The drugs tend to stay in the system for just a few hours, so it's difficult for the police to find evidence of what has happened. Promisingly, the police are now better at investigating these cases and react more effectively in the crucial initial stages. To detect a drug from a blood sample the test really needs to be done within eight hours, although with more sensitive tests being developed it is now becoming possible to detect it in urine over slightly longer periods.

GHB
This is a depressant that acts on the central nervous system and has been widely abused for its ability to induce euphoric and hallucinatory states. It's easy to make and difficult to determine a safe dose – which makes it very dangerous. The effects of an overdose can include deep sedation, seizures, a drop in blood pressure or heart rate, coma and death. Its effects are made worse when mixed with alcohol or other drugs.

Ketamine
Some street names for it are Special K, Ket, K and Vitamin K. It's popular with clubbers and is an anaesthetic used primarily by vets on animals. It can induce a kind of euphoria or a feeling of having your mind and body separated from one another. Too

much of it will cause deep sedation. It can also depress respiration and cause death.

Benzodiazepines

A class of drug used as tranquillizers and sleeping pills. The two best known are Valium and Rohypnol. Rohypnol is up to ten times stronger than Valium and is intended for use as a surgical anaesthetic, muscle relaxant or sleeping pill. It can cause sedation, dizziness, difficulty with walking and, when taken with alcohol, can cause confusion and memory loss. Its street names include roofie and roach.

There have also been reports about two new drugs, GBL and 1,4-B, which are sold legally as industrial solvents and cleaners but when swallowed have a similar effect to GHB. The Home Office's drugs advisory body has recommended that they be banned.

As we've said, the evidence about how widely these drugs are used is extremely patchy, but the police in some parts of the country take it seriously enough to have issued pubs and clubs with stoppers for bottles and drinks to prevent them being tampered with. Here's our guide to making sure you know what you're drinking:

- **Take it in turns to keep a look-out on your drinks,** and try to keep them with you until they're finished.
- **Don't leave your drink unattended.** If necessary take your drink to the loo with you.
- **If someone you don't know offers to buy you a drink,** either refuse or go with them to the bar and see what they're giving you.

♀ **If you're really worried, use a protective stopper to cover your drink.** There are quite a few different types on the market. One is called a Spikey and fits securely over the top of a drinks bottle, making it virtually impossible to add drugs to a drink without it being noticed. You can fit a straw through the Spikey but nothing else. Some clubs have been giving them out free to drinkers for some time now. There's another, called Safeflo, which has been tested by the police and is endorsed by Crimestoppers.

♀ **Or you can test whether or not your drink has been spiked by using a product called the Drink Detective.** It's a matchbox-sized test kit which will indicate whether a drink has been adulterated with Ketamine, GHB or Rohypnol. It's not practical to test every drink (though that would certainly slow down your alcohol intake) but you can use it if you have any suspicions. Look at the end of the chapter for suppliers.

♀ **Look out for your friends.** If you think their drink has been spiked, get them out of there and to a safe place as soon as possible. Don't accept help or a lift from anyone you don't know and trust.

♀ **If you think your drink has been spiked,** if you begin to feel unwell, or extremely drunk when you're not expecting to, or tired and dizzy after just a couple of drinks, get help straight away. If you have been given some kind of drug, it will probably kick in very fast. Ask a friend to take you home or, better still, to their home, where they can keep an eye on you. Do not accept help from anyone you don't trust, no matter how kind and concerned they seem. In extreme cases, go to the pub owner or security staff and ask them to call you an ambulance.

DRUGS

What can we say? Taking drugs is against the law and if you are reading a book like this one, we assume you want to make yourself less likely to become a victim of crime, not actually become a criminal yourself. But, realistically, plenty of otherwise law-abiding citizens do dabble in a bit of recreational drug-taking. So if that's your choice, you should know what you're letting yourself in for. The effect of a particular drug can feel very different depending on what environment you take it in. And drugs affect everybody differently. Mixing drugs makes for unpredictable results and mixing them with alcohol is dangerous. Booze is a relaxant and can slow down your nervous system. Combine that with depressant drugs and you might slow down until you stop for good. We in no way advocate taking drugs, but if you or your friends do partake on a night out, it's worth knowing a bit of drug first-aid if things take a nasty and unexpected turn.

Cannabis

Reduces your inhibitions. Too much can cause hallucinations and sensory distortions. If you're left virtually unable to speak, for example, that's not good news when you're out for the night. Combine it with alcohol and you may end up vomiting. Nice. In recent years a much stronger version than was previously normal called 'skunk' has become more widely available. It's proving very toxic and anecdotal evidence suggests it may trigger schizophrenia in some people.

> During my uniformed days in Brixton I was with a colleague
> searching the home of a prisoner I had earlier arrested for theft. As

I opened the loft hatch the pungent and instantly recognizable smell of cannabis hit me square in the face. I had smelt it many times before, but never so strongly. I climbed in and retrieved a three-foot-long log of herbal cannabis, which I showed to the prisoner and then deposited in the boot of our police car. As we drove away from the house the smell almost overwhelmed us. By the time we got back to the station all three of us were (metaphorically speaking) flying on the roof of the car. My head was swirling and I felt really sick – it was a really weird experience. We floated into the station and reported back to the station sergeant, who promptly sent us to the canteen to 'recover'. It took a couple of hours, a couple of visits to the loo to throw up and a lot of coffee before we 'came down' and started to feel back to normal, by which time I felt worse than I had after any hangover. The experience was enough to stop me ever wanting to try the stuff for real. I can't see what the attraction is. JACQUI

Ecstasy
Used to be the clubbers' drug of choice. Can give you great energy and warm feelings to those around you. Make sure you have a slow, steady fluid intake to avoid overheating – up to a pint of water or juice over an hour. If you have an adverse reaction it can cause death.

Poppers or Alkyl nitrites
Side effects may include coughing, nausea, headaches – you may even pass out altogether. They reduce blood pressure, so they are dangerous if you have any heart or breathing problems, low blood pressure or anaemia.

Cocaine

A very addictive stimulant and, the more you take, the more your body becomes accustomed to it, so you increase your risk of ultimately taking a hit that your body can't handle. And we've all seen the horrendous pictures of models and actresses without a septum. Yuck.

LSD

You can't be sure that the trip you have will be a pleasurable experience. A bad one can induce feelings of terror, panic and paranoia. Do you want that to happen to you when you're in a club surrounded by strangers? You need to have someone who is going to stay clear-headed to look out for you if things go wrong.

There are many other drugs and derivatives around and new substances turning up all the time, so it's impossible to list them all. But the main thing to remember is this: what is seemingly safe for your friends may not be for you. And you can never be sure that the drug you've bought is what it's claimed to be. Drugs get mixed and cut up with other substances (talc or concrete powder, to name just a couple) to maximize profits for the dealers, and you cannot know exactly what you are putting into your body. So why take the risk?

If It All Starts to Go Horribly Wrong

If someone gets seriously sleepy and you are struggling to rouse them, they may well be suffering the effects of tranquillizers or mixing drugs and alcohol. Call an ambulance, gently try to keep them awake and put them in the recovery position, which is basically lying on their side, upper leg bent, and remember to keep their head up and airway open. Don't give them coffee.

If someone gets too hot and dehydrated, they may complain of cramps, headaches or extreme tiredness. They may have overdone it on the dance floor or they may have overdone it on ecstasy or speed. Move them to a cooler area, remove any excess clothing and get them to slowly sip water or juice. If they don't show signs of recovering, call an ambulance.

If someone passes out, you need to call an ambulance straight away, as they are likely to have had a bad reaction to a drug or combination of drugs and/or alcohol. Check to see if they are still breathing. Put them in the recovery position. Keep them warm but don't let them get too hot. There are some simple and clear basic first-aid tips on the British Red Cross website – www.redcross.org.uk.

NIGHTCLUBS

For most of us, a nightclub is the place to drink, to dance, to shout at each other and lip read. Years ago, a few very exclusive clubs (or seriously pretentious clubs, depending on your point of view and on which side of the roped-off VIP area you were standing) began to employ bouncers. Now, even a club in an old Portakabin in the middle of a car park in Grimsby is likely to have bouncers. They stand like masters of the universe around the entrance and are notoriously fickle about who they will let in. The bad news is that they are entirely within their rights to refuse entry to anyone for any reason. But you do have some rights – so read on.

Fiona made a documentary a few years ago about dodgy bouncers who deal in drugs, have convictions for assault and take enormous pleasure in taking someone round the back of the club and beating the living daylights out of them. But now bouncers have to be licensed, trained and have undergone a criminal-records check. Anyone with convictions for drugs or violence can no longer do the job.

Bouncers are legally entitled to search you for weapons and drugs, and many clubs have them do this routinely. But you don't have to put up with being searched by a man if you don't want to. The club must provide women searchers too. If you refuse to let yourself be searched, even by someone of the same gender, you can be refused entry. They do not, however, have the right to strip-search you or feel inside your clothes without your explicit permission – that is assault.

If a bouncer removes any of your possessions, they must be returned to you when you leave. Obvious exceptions are weapons or drugs, in which case you'll be heading for an appointment with the local constabulary.

If the bouncers turn nasty or become threatening, you could start telling them that you know your rights and that they are breaking their code of conduct. But we wouldn't recommend it. Try to talk to them clearly but quietly. If that doesn't work, walk away as fast as you can. Report it to the club, the bouncers' trade body (the Security Industry Association) and to the police. Pressing charges is the best way to get even.

STAYING SAFE

You are most likely to become the victim of a mugging, sexual assault or rape by a stranger when you're out in the evening. But the fear we all have of such a terrifying ordeal is far, far greater than the chances of it actually happening. The most recent figures suggest that less than 1 per cent of women have reported a serious sexual assault. As for a stranger leaping out from behind a bush or a dark corner, that too is comfortingly uncommon. In nearly 90 per cent of cases, women know the person who assaults them. And most of the time it is a partner or ex-partner. But that is not in any way to downplay the seriousness of such an assault. Any kind of physical interference with your person against your will is traumatic.

As for the definitions of various types of assault:

✦ **Mugging** is a nasty, and in some areas, reasonably common type of street theft, often involving some form of assault.

✦ **Rape** is when a man intentionally penetrates the vagina, anus or mouth of another person with his penis.

✦ **Serious sexual assault** is penetration of those same parts of the body with a part of the attacker's body (like a finger), or with anything else, without the person's consent.

✦ **Sexual assault** is committed when a person intentionally touches another person in a sexual way and the other person does not consent.

The biggest thing you need to be aware of when you're out partying, and in particular drinking, is that your defences are down and you are altogether more vulnerable. That vulnerability increases in direct proportion to how drunk you are. A study carried out in 2006 for the Association of Chief Police Officers suggested that a woman could be expected to show 'marked intoxication levels' after drinking the equivalent of two bottles of wine. And it found that out of 120 cases of sexual assault examined by researchers, in 119 cases the woman had been drinking.

If you do find yourself assaulted or raped, judges vary in the view they take of a victim's ability to give consent. The law already suggests that a woman who is asleep or unconscious is less likely to have consented to sex. Since 2003, a man accused of rape has had to show he had 'reasonable' grounds for believing a woman had actively consented. Before then, he had only to demonstrate that he believed she had consented. But only 6 per cent of accusations of rape result in a successful prosecution. Many never make it to court. The government is currently considering a consultation document which would strengthen the law so that when a woman is seriously drunk, she cannot be said to have given her consent. The idea behind this is to prevent unscrupulous men taking advantage of a woman and telling a judge that she was gagging for it when she was in fact too drunk to know her own name. But at the moment, it's an area of law that appears to be unclear and is left open to a judge's interpretation. As a result, while some women are able to prove that they didn't consent to sex when drunk, other judgements surrounding rape are confusing.

In 2005 there was a landmark case in which a twenty-year-old security guard had sex with a twenty-one-year-old woman student while she was lying drunk and unconscious in a corridor outside her flat in a university hall of residence in Aberystwyth. The case hinged on whether the woman he was accused of assaulting had consented to sex. The woman said she didn't know the security guard and that there was 'no way' she would have agreed. But when questioned by the defence, she acknowledged she could not remember anything and therefore could not definitively say if she had consented or not. So even though the security guard was a stranger to the woman, a judge at Swansea Crown Court instructed the jury to bring in a not-guilty verdict because she could not remember whether she had given consent. The judge ruled that 'Drunken consent is still consent.'

It's a verdict that shows how complex this area of law is. It seems outrageous to me that a woman can be utterly paralytic and yet still judged able to agree to sex. But until an assault-free utopia finally dawns for women, we have to take some responsibility for ourselves. Just as I wouldn't lie down in the middle of the road and expect cars to swerve around me, I wouldn't get totally wasted and assume that all men will respect my personal space. I know they should but sadly, life isn't like that and won't be for the foreseeable future. FIONA

So be warned – drinking to excess increases the chances of a wonderful evening turning pear-shaped. And if the worst should happen, your chances of justice are greatly reduced. So be savvy – we're not saying you have to ruin a night out by being too careful, but you can make sure it starts and ends well.

FURTHER INFORMATION

If you want to find out more about what you've read in this chapter, here are some organizations and websites which will help.

For advice on personal safety visit **www.wiredsafety.org** or **www.thesite.org**, or the sites of the Suzy Lamplugh Trust at

www.suzylamplugh.org or the Lucie Blackman Trust at **www.lucieblackmantrust.org**.

For specialist advice on drug rape, go to the Roofie Foundation at **www.roofie.com**, or **www.rapecrisis.org**.

The Department of Transport, **www.dft.gov.uk**, gives travel advice as well as details of the Secure Stations Scheme – see if yours is included; see also the site for Transport For London: **www.tfl.gov.uk**.

For general safety and security advice, visit **www.crimestoppers.co.uk** or **www.homeoffice.gov.uk**.

For advice on alcohol safety go to **www.knowyourlimits.gov.uk** or **www.alcoholconcern.org.uk**, **www.thedrinkdebate.org.uk** or **www.drinkaware.co.uk**.

For help and advice on drug abuse see **www.talktofrank.com**.

Each police force now has its own individual site; you can find the Metropolitan Police site at **www.metpolice.uk/crimeprevention**.

Handbag hooks are available at **http://prettypinktoes.co.uk/handbag hanger.aspx**, **www.selectadna.co.uk**, **www.handbagclip.com**, **www.brittique.com**, **www.mybaghanger.com** or **www.purseangels. co.uk**.

Find handbag lights at **www.happybags.co.uk** or **www.coolest-gadgets.com** and the transmitter from **www.21stcenturygadgets.com**.

Other personal safety gadgets and ideas at **www.securityvillage.co.uk**, **www.bagsafe.com**, **www.selectadna.co.uk** and **www.maplin.co.uk**.

You can also find some interesting ideas at **www.designagainstcrime.org**.

To prevent drinks in bottles being spiked go to **www.safeflo.co.uk** or **www.spikey.co.uk**, and drug-testing kits for drinks are available at **www.drinkdetective.com**.

For information on private-security licensing go to **www.the-sia.org.uk**.

3

On the Move

THE UK IS A SAFER PLACE TO LIVE AND WORK THAN IT WAS TEN years ago, yet a recent survey suggests that over 70 per cent of women feel vulnerable on Britain's streets, with alleyways the places they regard as the most dangerous. About half of the women questioned said they feel uneasy on public transport and worry about being alone in car parks. Almost all believe that crime levels are rising when in fact the level of most crime is falling.

We found these statistics really shocking. Why are so many women scared of venturing out of their own homes and why are they living in fear of attack when going about their daily lives? By arming yourself with information about the area you live and travel in, and by taking on board some of our suggestions, we hope your fear of crime will be reduced and you'll feel much freer to move around. Generally, the streets of Britain really are safe places to be.

WALKING

Well, we're always being told we should do more of it, but you do need to think about where you're walking and at what time of day or night. The golden rule is always to walk confidently. It might sound a bit daft, especially if you don't know where you're going, but the woman who is striding along, head in the air, looking in control is a far less attractive victim to a would-be mugger or attacker than someone who is obviously lost, scared and vulnerable. Don't wander along with your iPod earphones on – while you're grooving along to your favourite sounds, you won't be able to hear what's going on around you or if someone is coming up behind you.

In an ideal world, you shouldn't walk along talking into your mobile phone either. OK, OK, we all do it, and we doubt that reading this will stop you doing it again, but what we would say is: if you are going to use your mobile when you're out and about, look around you and *think*. Is this a dodgy area? Do I need to keep my wits about me? It is the easiest thing in the world for someone to sneak up behind you while you're yakking away on your mobile, and the next thing you know, your mobile or your handbag will be disappearing down the road in the hand of some seventeen-year-old kid who can run a lot faster than you can.

Trust your instincts about where it is safe to walk alone. It's always best to stick to the busier areas. In the evenings, try to stay within well-lit areas. Don't take short cuts if it means you will be walking somewhere that is deserted or dark. Walk facing the traffic if you can – that way a kerb-crawler can't pull up alongside you and try to pick you up or drag you into the car. Walk near people with whom you feel safe. As we've mentioned before, if you think someone is following you, cross the road to see if they do the same. If they do, assume your suspicions are right. Go straight away to the first place you can to get help. Shops, restaurants, cafés, bars or an office can provide safe havens, or you could knock on someone's door and call the police from there.

JOGGING

If you're jogging, first of all, congratulations. Permission to feel fit and smug. But most of the above applies to you too. Running with an mp3 player makes all that exercise a lot more bearable and flattens out the hills a treat, but you are definitely more vulnerable if you can't hear what's going on around you and, unless you are jogging in a busy area, just don't do it.

All that lovely countryside or that picturesque path down by the riverside can be a beautiful place to run but it can also be pretty deserted. It's a sad fact of life, but all police officers know that any attractive stretch of woodland or common will have its fair share of weirdos lurking within. Most of the time you will have no problems at all – in all probability you may never encounter anyone – but be aware that such people are out there and that if you are alone and a shout for help won't be heard, you're at risk. Only you can weigh up the extent of the risk, and you don't want to end up so paranoid you spoil your enjoyment of your surroundings.

Think about carrying a personal-attack alarm; that way, even if your voice can't be heard, there's a fair chance that someone will come to investigate why an ear-splitting siren has suddenly gone off.

On *Crimewatch* we featured the case of an attacker who was targeting women joggers in parks. On one occasion he'd managed to kill his victim, and I went to the scene where the woman was killed. It was an ordinary urban green space used frequently by people walking across it to work, by mums with their children and, of course, by joggers. She had been running in full sight of the park but for just a few moments was out of sight as she ran along a little path beside some bushes. That's where he struck.

Some time later, he tried to kill again, but this time his victim managed to escape, even though she was stabbed several times. It's amazing what adrenalin can do for the human body – despite her serious injuries she carried on running and he gave up pursuing her. I hate to imagine how terrified and desperate she must have felt as she struggled to keep going.

After the programme, I tried to think if there was any way these women could have avoided being attacked. If a man is determined enough to find a victim, he'll probably succeed, and all you can do is significantly lessen your chances of finding yourself in his sights. I run myself and usually I'm so knackered that the last thing on my mind is to look around me for anyone who might be suspicious. But after that case, I made a real effort to become much more aware of my surroundings, to keep an eye out for who was around and to try to avoid any paths that look too quiet. FIONA

HITCH-HIKING

Easy one this: DON'T DO IT – NOT EVER.

PUBLIC TRANSPORT

This is covered in greater detail in Chapter 2, so have a look there, but it's worth going over some general safety points here.

- **Plan in advance.** Know where you're going and which stop you need. Make sure you know the time of the last bus or train. If you're in an unfamiliar area, you may want to arrange for someone to meet you at the train station or bus stop. Carry a tube map or bus timetable. Most are freely available on the internet.

- **Carry enough money to get you home** if you get stranded. Always have the number of a licensed cab company on you.

- **Stay near people you feel safe with.** If anyone is making you feel uncomfortable for any reason, get off or change compartments. Don't think, 'I'm being paranoid, I'm sure it's fine, there's only one more stop to go.' If you can, get yourself away from that person. It's always better to be safe than sorry, and your instincts are probably right.

- **Locate emergency or help points.** You'll probably never have to use them, but there's great peace of mind in knowing where they are.

- **Sit near the driver.**

- **Avoid empty compartments or carriages** that don't connect to corridors or other parts of the train. You might get in thinking, 'This is nice and peaceful,' but then when the lone man who gets on at the next stop starts shouting to himself and twitching and it's just you and him, you'll regret it.

- **Stay in well-lit areas** and try not to use isolated or dark walkways. Don't be too reassured if they have CCTV. It's very useful as evidence but it's not always a great deterrent.

I promise I won't mention *Crimewatch* too often, but I can't resist telling you this story. The police passed us some CCTV footage of a man spotted at several different points on the tube network around London. There are cameras all over the underground so he must have known he was being filmed. But undeterred, he would walk behind women or stand just below them as they were going up the escalator. The women all had one thing in common – they were wearing skirts. Then he would get out his mobile phone and hold it just by the hem of their skirt, filming up their skirt on his phone camera as the women carried on their way, most of them entirely unaware of what was happening. I'd long got past the point where I thought I could be surprised by anything, but I found that bloke's behaviour astonishing. I was torn between outrage at the violation of these women's privacy and laughing at how desperate and pathetic he was. FIONA

CYCLING

Bikes are stolen so frequently, you need to think hard about where you can store one safely before you buy one. But they're good fun, the cheapest transport available other than your own two feet and you don't have to rely on anyone else for a lift.

How good a cyclist are you? Most of us just buy the bike and set off. But it's a good idea to get a bit of cycle training in, and many local authorities offer free or subsidized training. Lessons can be customized according to your level of ability and they're useful for beginners, return cyclists and even old hands. You might want to learn the basics, learn about road positioning and how to handle busy multiple junctions or how best to tackle a route to work by riding with an instructor, especially if you're planning to navigate an urban route in the rush hour.

Keep your bike roadworthy. Check the brakes regularly, make sure there are no cracks on the wheel rims, that the frame is not rusting or weakening anywhere and that your tyres are fully inflated. And keep a note of the serial number on the frame – it may help reunite you and your bike a lot more quickly if it is nicked.

Preventing Your Bike from being Stolen

I had just bought myself a new bike (the previous one had been nicked from my garage) and set off on our first outing together to the shops. I couldn't find anywhere to chain it to, it was a very busy shopping centre, so I thought it would be OK just to prop it up against a wall and chain the front wheel. I was away for five minutes and, sure enough, when I came back it was gone. A week later, I was in the *Crimewatch* studio getting ready to present the programme when it occurred to me that what was the point of working on a programme that makes appeals to solve crimes if I couldn't appeal about my own crime? So in the last couple of minutes of the show, just as the end credits were beginning to roll, I said, 'And if you're the person who nicked my bike last week, you know who you are and I want it back!' Didn't get it back, of course, but at least I felt better for making the effort. FIONA

We're sure that you are a lot more sensible than Fiona when it comes to locking your bike. But just in case, here are a few pointers:

 Always lock your bike to a secure, fixed object, ideally in a well-lit, busy area. Proper cycle parking stands are best.

Avoid butterfly racks which only allow you to secure the front wheel. It's easy for a thief to detach your wheel and make off with the rest of your bike.

 Avoid railings with signs saying that a bike may be removed – it really will be.

 Don't use short posts to lock your bike to, or even long posts. Your bike may simply be lifted over the top.

 It's not ideal to leave your bike out in the street overnight. Many insurance companies will only cover you if you store your bike indoors at night. Parking your bike in a shed or garage can be risky, too, but you can have a tough anchor installed into the floor or wall which you can lock it to as additional security.

 If your workplace doesn't have secure cycle parking, you may be able to get something done about it. In London, for example, there is a scheme called Take a Stand, whereby your employer can apply for cycle parking for up to forty bikes.

 Aim to spend at least 10 per cent of the value of your bike on a good lock. There is a three-tier security-grading scheme developed by Sold Secure (a non-profit-making company), which is used by many insurance companies. The highest are the gold-rated locks, which give you maximum security and may get you a reduction in the cost of your insurance; they are pretty heavy and bulky, though, and it may take a superhuman effort to carry it with you and still get up that hill without being dragged back down again. The silver and bronze levels are lighter and cheaper but are still a reasonable defence against an opportunist thief.

Insurance

Your bike may already be covered on your household insurance, but check the small print. Separate insurance cover can sometimes work better to avoid large excess payments. When deciding on a policy look out for details such as the amount of the excess – sometimes it can be more than the value of the bike itself. Check whether your accessories will be covered if they vanish along with your bike, and whether the policy will pay new for old – you may be left minus a bike and with only enough compensation to buy one that is well past its best.

Security Tagging

Many insurance companies will ask you to security-tag your cycle. This will enable you to have a full record of your bike on file somewhere and will help you prove it's yours if it's ever stolen and recovered by the police. Some police stations will stamp your postcode and house number or your name on to your bike and keep an electronic record of the details. You could also use ultraviolet marking pens, which only cost about £1 each. Crime Prevention Products (CPP) has quite a good website for buying things like this, but once you know what you want, don't forget to shop around (see Chapter 1, Further Information, for more details). You could register your bike with a company called Immobilise (again, see Chapter 1), which is the property register used by some police forces to reunite stolen goods with their legitimate owners. Datatag is another, slightly more expensive, way of marking your bike with an electronic tag. It's a miniature transmitter (about the size of an aspirin) containing a unique code, which fits inside the frame of your bike and can be read by special scanners issued to the police. The owner's details are kept on a database which the police can access twenty-four hours a day. A marking kit can cost around £35–50, depending on size – although we have found them cheaper on the net. If you buy a bike which is already fitted with this system, it costs around £15 to get the owner's details updated.

If your bike is stolen, report it to the police straight away. You'll need a crime-reference number for your insurer – and you never know, you might just get it back.

DRIVING

This can be summed up in three golden rules:

 Drive safely.

 Lock your doors.

 Keep your handbag off the seat.

Your car gives you ultimate independence, and it feels a lot safer than taking your chances on public transport. You are less vulnerable to people around you in one sense (you are physically separated from them) but, remember: you are far more likely to be involved in a crash in a car than a crash on a bus or a train. We're not going to attempt to give you advice on how to be a good driver (we've got too many bumps and scratches notched up between us for that), but we are going to try to help you to be a safe driver.

The key things are:

 Plan your journey.

 Know where you're going.

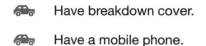 Have breakdown cover.

Have a mobile phone.

The Highway Code is hardly the most exciting read, but it does actually contain some good advice and tips about driving. It is available online at www.direct.gov.uk/en/travelandtransport/high waycode, so you don't even have to buy it, and if it is some years since you passed your test, the latest version may surprise you.

Before You Set Off

You don't want to be pulling over every five minutes to look at the map or, worse, trying to balance it on your knees and look at it as you drive along. Look at the map beforehand and write directions down in such a way that you only need to glance at them to remind yourself of the route. Or key the address into a satellite-navigation system if you have one. You want to avoid stopping to ask for directions along the way if at all possible.

If you're going on a long journey, let someone know where you're going and when you expect to arrive.

Have you got enough petrol? Top up as soon as you can if the tank is running low – don't be left stranded by an empty fuel tank.

Take your mobile phone and make sure it's charged (and has enough credit). In-car chargers that just plug into your cigarette lighter are quite cheap and can be a life-saver – especially on a long journey, when you may need to make lots of calls and you don't want to run down your battery in case of an emergency.

I was driving with friends in a convoy to the pub in my first ever car. It was a maroon Austin Allegro – with a square steering wheel (who ever thought that was a good idea?). We were three cars in all, chuntering along an A road, and I noticed that my car seemed to be smoking a bit. It was raining, so at first I wasn't sure if the smoke wasn't just condensation as the rain dried on the warm bonnet. But then I realized the car was feeling a bit sluggish too and wasn't responding particularly well when I pressed down on the accelerator. I was at the back of the convoy and I noticed that the other two cars were pulling further and further ahead. Gradually, the car stopped responding at all, I could hardly change gear and, eventually, I just slowed to a stop. When the AA turned up, they told me it wasn't surprising the car wasn't going anywhere as it had completely run out of oil and the whole engine had seized up. Believe me, that is a costly mistake to make and not one I've repeated. FIONA

- **Check the oil and tyres.** If you don't know how to, get the manual out and look. As a rule, you want to make sure that your car is regularly serviced and is in good running order. Your sure-fire way of getting home won't seem quite so failsafe if it's ground to a halt for lack of basic maintenance.

- **Make sure you are a member of a breakdown organization.** And ensure that the company prioritizes lone female drivers for call-outs. Being a woman has its advantages, so do not hesitate to tell them when you are on your own. They want to make sure you are safe, just like we do.

Once You Have Set Off

Lock your doors. Make sure that it's the first thing you do and make it a habit. The chances of someone getting into the car (to steal your bag, your car, or even you) when you're waiting at the traffic lights are slim, but it does happen. If you need to get out in a hurry, your car door should unlock automatically when you open it from the inside. If it's an old car, it may not do that, so it is best to double-check.

Keep your bag, your mobile and anything of value out of sight. It's so handy to pop your bag on to the passenger seat. Don't. Stick it in the footwell instead.

Open-top cars. The sun's shining, the roof's down, you're whizzing along with the wind in your hair – what could be better? We will sound like real killjoys now, but open-top cars make you a lot more vulnerable. Think about it – how hard is it for someone just to jump in beside you? Or reach in and grab your bag? Convertibles are fabulous, but think twice before you buy one. What sort of areas are you most likely to drive around in? Will you feel safe sitting so exposed in your car? If you do have one, you might want to put the roof up if you are in an area where you don't feel safe – no matter how sunny it is. And will it be safe parked outside your house?

When I was working as a presenter a few years back, I was lucky enough to be offered a free MG to drive around in. I guess it was good publicity for the car manufacturer and I got a lovely car out of the deal. I remember the exact day it was stolen, as it happened when I was doing an early news shift for Sky television on the day of the Hatfield rail crash. I came out of work ready to drive home and the car had gone. There was no sign of broken glass and I

Don't use your mobile unless you have to and even then only with a hands-free kit. You know it's against the law; we don't need to tell you. But other distractions might get you into trouble with the police too. The new Highway Code stipulates that if you are eating or smoking in such a way that you are not paying sufficient attention to the road, you can be prosecuted. We didn't see any mention of putting on make-up at the traffic lights though . . .

Don't indulge in road rage; you're quite likely to come off worse. If you feel threatened, try not to make eye contact with whoever is giving you hassle and ignore them. Make sure your windows are up and your doors locked. Do NOT retaliate. Keep driving or drive on if possible. If the driver gets out of his, or her, car to approach you, drive off past or reverse with your hazard lights on and your hand on the horn. If he pulls over in front of you and forces you to stop, keep the engine running and reverse. Remember: short of smashing the windows with a heavy implement, he cannot get at you. If you are being followed or tailgated by an aggressive driver, keep going until you come to a busy place, such as a garage, a supermarket car park, a police or fire station. Most bullies won't attack if they think it's going to be a public spectacle.

I was waiting for a parking space outside a department store. I was parked up alongside and just ahead of it, ready to reverse in when the occupant of the space had pulled out. But just as the car drove away, leaving the space all nice and empty for me, a van appeared out of nowhere and zoomed into it. I know I should have turned the other cheek and just driven off, but I was fuming. So I got out of my car and started remonstrating with the van driver, telling him that I had been waiting five minutes for that space, it was my space and he should let me have it. Well, the van driver got out, effing and blinding and brandishing a big metal crowbar. I couldn't believe that he would attack a woman with something like that, but he looked as mad as a snake and I decided not to take any chances. I dashed back to my car (shouting a few choice words over my shoulder) and scarpered. It was a completely pointless exercise and I nearly got my head stoved in. FIONA

If a police car tries to get you to pull over, you don't have to stop if the car is unmarked. Even if it is using a siren, the people inside may not be legitimate police officers. There have been cases where drivers have stopped for who they believed were officers in an unmarked car, only to then be robbed by the roadside. If you are in any doubt, keep going until you get somewhere there are other people, like a petrol station, and then stop. If, however, you know you are clearly breaking the law and doing 100mph, it's likely they are police officers and you have been rumbled. Not stopping probably won't do you any favours. But you are within your rights to only open your window a crack and ask for ID and the reason you have been stopped before you get out of the car. Remember: keep the engine running until you are 100 per cent sure who you are dealing with.

Beware of other drivers who try to signal to you that you need to pull over because there's something wrong with your car. If you can't see the problem yourself, keep going until you come to a busy area where you can stop and have a look.

If you break down, pull off the road as far as you are able, switch on the hazard lights and phone for help. Make sure you tell your breakdown service if you are a lone female driver. You should then be put at the top of the call-out list. If you're on the motorway, try to make it in the car to an emergency phone – they are situated every 1,000 metres, and a marker post every 100 metres will point you to the nearest one. The phone is free and will connect you to the police-control centre, which will be able to clearly identify your location.

Do not sit in your car on the hard shoulder waiting for help, because you have a reasonable chance of being hit from behind by a car. But if you sit on the verge, you are also advertising the fact that you are a woman who is stranded helpless by the road. It may sound like a cop-out but only you can make the judgement about where you feel safe. If you do decide to wait beside your car, keep your car keys on you and the left-hand door wide open so you can get in quickly if you need to. If someone pulls up offering to help, be conspicuous about taking their registration down and say you are expecting the police within minutes. It's best not to accept their help, no matter how tempting.

Do not give lifts to strangers. They are unlikely to be a Brad Pitt lookalike as in *Thelma and Louise*. And remember: Brad Pitt ended up robbing them. If you want a bit of company on a long journey, stick the radio on.

Last year I was interviewed on *GMTV* about a woman who was lost on a motorway on her way to a work do over Christmas. She saw a police vehicle on the hard shoulder and pulled up behind him to ask for directions. Unfortunately, he promptly gave her a ticket for illegally stopping on the hard shoulder and sent her on her way – still with no directions. Whilst it's true that it's illegal to stop on the hard shoulder unless it's an emergency, I do feel that the officer could have used some common sense and discretion. It was late in the evening, she was lost and a bit panicky, and it wouldn't have hurt him to give her a warning, some directions and just send her on her way. Police cars are supposed to be beacons of safety when you're in trouble and I hope will continue to be so. If you do get lost on the motorway it's probably best to pull into a service station and get your bearings. Even if the counter staff can't help, they invariably sell maps, or you could ring someone for help. It's better to arrive at your destination late and get there calmly and safely. JACQUI

Using a Satellite-Navigation System

You're driving, not the sat nav. You can't blame the sat nav if you commit an offence or have an accident. It's your fault.

Here are a few things to remember, courtesy of the AA:

- **What you see must take priority over what the sat nav says.** If the road looks wrong, don't take it. People have been marooned in fords, driven into rivers and down railways because their sat nav told them to go that way.

- **You know what you're driving, the sat nav probably doesn't.** If you have a large vehicle, or a trailer, you can't be sure that the road is suitable for you just because the sat nav tells you to go down it. Watch for signs.

🚗 **Watch the road – not the sat nav.** A sat nav can give all sorts of information about where you are going, much of which you don't need.

🚗 **Put the sat nav in a sensible place.** It should be in your line of sight but should not create a blind spot. Put it where it won't injure anyone in an accident.

🚗 **Don't try to programme the sat nav while driving.** You know it will take one hand from the wheel, two eyes from the road and a brain from driving. Pull over to adjust the settings.

🚗 **Use all the sat nav's features.** On a complicated, busy round-about, it is unwise to take your eyes off the road to look at the sat nav, and much better to receive spoken instructions. Some have features which show you a simple diagram of the road ahead and only need a quick glance.

🚗 **Check the route is practical before you start.** Is the sat nav taking you to the right Farnborough, Hampshire, Warwickshire or Kent? If you put in the wrong destination, it will take you to the wrong destination. Does the route look right?

I had been invited to the prime minister's country house, Chequers, for a charity evening reception. I was pretty excited as I'd never been there before and I knew it was going to be a swanky do. But the house is not listed on any map, for security reasons, so I tried programming it into the sat nav. It worked a treat and it looked like it must be the right place, as it was in the right county. I set off with plenty of time to spare and the sat-nav directions took me near to a pub called The Chequers. As I was half an hour early I decided to stop for a quick drink to kill a bit of time. After twenty minutes or so I got back into the car and carried on following the sat nav. About a minute later, the disembodied voice announced that I had arrived at my destination, but there was no sign of any big mansion suitable for a PM. I tried to find out where I was and then realized the sat nav had directed me to the Chequers Pub, Chequers Lane. Total nightmare. Now I was stuck with no idea where the real Chequers was, how long it would take me to get there and no map could help me. I was beginning to panic slightly when I saw a police car driving slowly by. Being on *Crimewatch* has its uses and I leapt out of the car, waved madly at the two officers and told them of my predicament. Fortunately, they knew where it was and directed me there. I turned up slightly flustered but fashionably late. FIONA

- **Update the sat nav regularly.** It needs to know about new roads, new one-way systems and generally keep itself up to date.

- **Remember: thieves like sat navs too.** If it's detachable, always take it out when you leave the car. Thieves know that when people remove them they tend to keep them in the car, so mounts or suction cap marks also attract thieves.

Parking

- **Hide away anything of value,** including your stereo and your sat nav. If it's the kind that you attach to the top of the dashboard using suction cups, wipe away the suction marks. Thieves have been known to look for those marks, as they are a dead giveaway that a valuable little bit of kit is stashed away inside somewhere.

- **If you can, reverse into spaces** so that you can pull out quickly if you should need to.

🚗 **Don't ever leave your vehicle documents in the car** as they will make it child's play for a thief to sell it.

🚗 **When you get out of the car, always have a quick look to see who's around.** If there's someone loitering who makes you feel uncomfortable, especially at night, don't get out. Wait, or move on, drive around for a couple of minutes and then see if he's still there when you come back. If he is, drive around for a bit longer. If he's still waiting and you think he's waiting for you, call the police or a male friend for help.

🚗 **Always have your front-door keys in your hand as you approach your home** – there's no fumbling about, you can get inside quickly and you can use them as a weapon if necessary. Same goes for when you're going to get into your car – have the key at the ready.

🚗 **When choosing a car park, make sure it's well lit** and, ideally, manned by an attendant. 20 per cent of all car crimes take place in car parks. You might want to check if a car park you use has been registered with the Safer Parking Scheme. It was launched in 1992 by the Association of Chief Police Officers, and then revised in 2004, with the aim of reducing crime in all types of car park. If you feel safe and secure in a car park, then a thief probably won't. On the other hand, if you don't feel safe, the thief probably will. So don't park there.

I'm sure some cars are jinxed! A few years ago I bought a new car and it was broken into five times in one year. The first time, they drilled out the driver's door lock and stole a £20 bottle of Miss Dior perfume left in the middle console – it cost £600 to get the car repaired. The next time, someone put a rock through the window and I'd stupidly left £150 cash in the glove compartment. Then I parked near a theatre in the West End one evening. I returned to the car after seeing the show to find someone had smashed a window and bled all over the back seat. All they'd stolen was a bog-standard pair of court shoes.

Next, one evening I'd parked under a street lamp in Covent Garden, thinking it would be safer for me when I returned to the car later, and someone smashed the window (again) and stole my mobile phone, which I'd foolishly left in its holder on the dash. Then, when my car was parked outside work one evening after dark, I came back to it and found the aerial had been snapped off and someone had used it to scratch obscenities (beginning with C – you can guess the rest) on the doors, so I had to get it repaired asap, as you can imagine. This time it cost £2,000.

Well, you'll be relieved to hear I finally learned my lesson. First, I got rid of that car, and now I never ever leave anything in my new one. I leave the glove box open so anyone looking in can see it's empty or contains nothing of value, and if I have to put something in the car, even shopping, it goes in the boot, out of sight.

CAROLINE, MANAGING DIRECTOR, CAROLINE MILNE INSURANCE BROKERS

Useful Things to Keep in Your Car

You should always keep a few basic items in the boot or glove compartment in case of emergencies.

🚗 Full petrol can, in case you run out of petrol. Regulations say you can keep up to 10 litres in a can in your car. How often have you been driving along with the fuel indicator on red, praying that a garage will appear out of nowhere?

- An ice-scraper

- Coins for meters

- Details of your breakdown service

- A warning triangle to put out on to the road to warn other road users if you break down

- A torch

- A blanket in case you break down

- A first-aid kit

- Spare screen-wash

You can even buy 'dummy passengers' to sit next to you when you're taking long trips on your own – they're a kind of blow-up doll and, frankly we reckon they could be a bit pervy – but at least they'll listen intently to all your stories, favourite music and won't give 'useful' driving advice at the most inopportune moments.

Preventing Your Car from being Stolen

─────────── CAR ALARMS AND IMMOBILIZERS ───────────

There are about 2 million car thefts every year. According to the Home Office, vehicle crime is falling, but it still accounts for about a sixth of all crime. A car alarm is a valuable tool to stop it happening to you. New cars generally have alarms and immobilizers fitted as standard. Older cars are less likely to, and as a result are much more attractive to thieves. You might wonder who on earth would want your old banger, but it's an easy target and there's a good market for spare parts. So if your car doesn't have an inbuilt security system, consider forking out for one. Most important is the immobilizer, which will stop someone from being able to drive your car away. Ideally, it should be supplemented by an alarm. It's generally recommended that you buy a Thatcham-approved system. Thatcham is another way of saying the Motor Insurance Repair Research Centre, which tests and approves security systems on sale since 1992. It publishes lists of approved products and systems. Some insurers insist on a Thatcham-approved system as a condition of offering cover, others offer discounts if you install Thatcham-approved systems. To get it installed, choose a company or individual approved by the Vehicle Systems Installation Board (VSIB).

REGISTRATION PLATES

Recent figures show that over 30,000 number plates are stolen every year. According to the DVLA, they are used by criminals to change the identity of stolen cars so that they can then be sold on, to disguise cars that are used in criminal activities or to avoid paying fines and congestion charges (maybe that last one's not such a bad idea . . .). You can buy plates that are made to withstand attack for at least three minutes, but they cost about twice the price of usual plates. If you're buying a new car, ask the dealer to fit theft-resistant number plates when the car is first registered. The DVLA has undertaken to oversee the standard of these plates and to compile a list of registered suppliers. At the moment there are two main suppliers, with a small but growing network of agents across the country:

Hills Numberplates Ltd: Telephone 0121 623 8050 or visit their website, www.hillsnumberplates.com.

Secureplate: Visit their website, www.secureplate.com, to find suppliers by county/region.

<hr>

RINGING

If you should be unlucky enough to write off your car, you need to inform the DVLA, so that if it turns up on the road again, they can then check it is roadworthy and is still the same car. By that, we mean check that its identity hasn't been used to cover up the theft of a similar car, commonly known as 'ringing'.

I was surprised one morning to receive a parking fine through the post from the Borough of Hillingdon. The correspondence clearly showed that my vehicle (accurately detailing make, model, colour and registration number) had been parked in a public car park without a parking permit or ticket. What made it even more odd was that I couldn't recall ever having been in that particular car park, and on the date in question I was visiting a friend (in my car) who lives in Highgate, in north London. I wrote to Hillingdon, with my explanation, and expected to hear nothing more. Just over a week later, I received back a further letter, this time with an increased fine, accompanied by a photograph of a car which looked exactly like mine!

Before I had a chance to respond, a further letter arrived, this time from Hammersmith, with a parking fine for 'my' car, in a residents' parking area. I wrote back to Hillingdon, to say that although the car looked like mine, it had a different bumper (and repeated the fact I was elsewhere on the given date) and I wrote to Hammersmith – having first checked my diary to confirm that I was not in the area at the time of the alleged parking infringement.

The next letter came from Ealing Borough Council, accompanied by a photograph of my car driving in a bus lane! On closer inspection, it was clear that this was not my car (the bumper was different, and the tax disc also was different), so once again I wrote a letter to Ealing with my whereabouts on the day and the explanation that it was not my vehicle. This was the first time I had ever come across what I now know to be a 'ringer' – a cloned number plate – and, frankly, I had begun to feel targeted and vulnerable. How did they know what make and colour of car to clone the registration number to, how did they know that I worked in the Ealing area and it could therefore have been feasible for these crimes to have been committed by me? It made me feel very nervous.

In the end I received ten separate fines, totalling over £1,000, and because I delayed responding to some, I finally received a summons to appear in court. On all the documentation I received from the various councils and boroughs, it stated clearly that I should make any representation in writing only, and that no telephone calls would be possible.

Finally, in such a horrible situation, I decided to ignore the warnings, and called Ealing Borough Council. After being passed through a couple of members of staff, I got a sympathetic listener, who ran through all the numbered fines with me, along with the correspondence she had received, and said that she would ensure that all the fines were cancelled. A couple of days later I received a letter explaining that the outstanding offences had been scratched from all records. Fearful that the 'ringer' was still on the road, I took myself off to Halfords the next day and bought and registered a new number plate, so that if the old one was seen parked in a residents' parking spot, driving along a bus lane, or neglected in a public car park, the fine wouldn't come back to me.

If your plates are stolen, report it to the police immediately. You might not feel like bothering, but it's not much fun to start receiving parking or speeding fines for a car you don't own. And it can be a real palaver to prove that the plates no longer belong to you if you haven't reported them as stolen.

SATELLITE-NAVIGATION SYSTEMS

While these are a brilliant help in finding your way about, as we said earlier, they are also attractive to thieves. The latest figures show there were more than 1.5 million thefts from vehicles in 2006, but while most car crime is falling, thefts of sat navs are bucking the trend. In some areas, police and motoring organizations have reported that up to half of all thefts from vehicles involve sat navs.

Another new trend is for thieves to steal sat-nav systems from cars so they can go and burgle the owner's house – they find out the address by using the details stored on the sat nav. Many systems automatically ask the owner to enter their address and, even if it doesn't, an awful lot of the time we're going to be navigating either to or from our homes.

GPS SYSTEMS

If you have a posh car, it might be worth getting a GPS system installed so that, if it is nicked, the police can track it. Pricier cars tend to come with this as standard now (it's sometimes called an in-vehicle telemetry system). There are tracking centres which can follow vehicles across Europe and sometimes even further afield. Less sophisticated systems, such as illegal-movement detection, are also available.

For every new anti-theft device on the market, thieves will spend time and effort to get round it, and there is a constant upgrading on the part of manufacturers to increase the security of these systems, almost equally balanced by villains' ability to overcome them. In my view, law enforcement is slightly ahead at the moment, but only just. JACQUI

─────────── SECURE YOUR WHEELS ───────────

Locking wheel-nuts are cheap, easy to fit and stop thieves from taking your wheels – especially if they're alloy ones. Actually, we just threw that last bit in. We've never been sure what alloy wheels are or what the point of them is.

─────────── STEERING-WHEEL LOCKS ───────────

Most of the time we can't be bothered with these – they can be so unwieldy and such a hassle to lock and unlock (especially when you're in a rush) – but they are a terrific visual deterrent. Imagine you're a thief wandering along a line of parked cars. Would you steal the one with a clearly visible steering lock or the car next to it which doesn't have one? They are quite useful for older cars which don't have modern locks and safety features and might attract some idiot looking for an easy 'joy' ride.

─────────── ETCHING ───────────

No, not that old line about, 'Would you like to come upstairs and see my etchings?' You can have your vehicle registration number or the last seven numbers of your vehicle identification number etched on to all the windows, both front and back windscreens and headlamps so that if your car is nicked, it can easily be identified as yours. Or you can do it yourself – etching pens are cheap and easily available.

CAR KEYS

Always keep them out of sight at home and don't be tempted to leave them by the front door. You might as well leave them on the welcome mat for any crim to pick up.

Since 1995 the fitting of electronic immobilizers has become mandatory on all new cars manufactured after October 1998 (this is designed to prevent a car starting without the key). While this has been a brilliant method of reducing the theft of new vehicles, anecdotal evidence suggests that some criminals are now concentrating on taking those vehicles by stealing the keys from handbags and homes instead.

For cars registered after 1997, keys were used in 85 per cent of thefts. The most common methods of obtaining keys were through burglary or owners leaving the keys in the car.

So . . .

Remember to keep your keys safe at all times. Hide a spare set away in your home and never leave them by the front door or window. Also, remove the ignition key every time you leave your vehicle when you are filling the car up with petrol or popping into the newsagent. If you warm your car up in the winter, do not leave the vehicle at any time. It only takes a few seconds for someone to jump into your car and drive away.

And . . .

Never leave car keys near a door or window at home. Some thieves have been known to use a fishing rod or a magnet on a stick to steal them through your letterbox. Burglars will break in to steal the keys of high-value cars, so take care of them and, if you have a garage, keep your car in it rather than on the drive.

My first car was an Austin – a green 1300 and I was very proud of it. Unfortunately, one of my colleagues at Clapham Police Station, where I was working on the Crime Squad, also had the same car, same colour, and even the same year reg – what a coincidence. One night I had been working for sixteen hours and was exhausted. I got to my car to go home at 2 a.m. and realized I'd forgotten to lock it. Thanking my lucky stars that it hadn't been stolen, I opened the door to get in and found a tramp asleep in the passenger seat. From the smell, he was obviously sleeping off a drinking binge, and had in fact relieved himself in the footwell. This was not boding well for me getting to bed for my four hours' sleep before having to be back at work. After some coaxing (and not a little swearing on my part) I eventually woke him up and got him out of the car and on to the pavement. After persuading a passing probationary PC to take him into the cells to let him sleep it off, I spent the next half-hour cleaning up the wee and spraying the car with perfume to try and get rid of the smell.

Eventually, with all the windows open, I drove off towards a warm bed at last, only to be stunned by a series of shudders from the engine before it slowed to a stop and then flatly refused to start again. Horrors. Despite my bleary eyes, after a minute or so I realized the problem was that there WASN'T ANY PETROL! UGHHHH. So after a nice walk to the petrol station (thankfully open), I finally got on my way again.

Feeling a little peckish, I remembered some old mints I'd left in the glove compartment and so reached in to grab a few. Imagine my shock as the latest issue of *Playboy* fell out, together with other bits and bobs which definitely were not mine. You'll have guessed by now. No, it wasn't my car. I'd got into my colleague's car and, for some strange reason, the ignition key had worked. Thankfully, these days car-door and ignition locks are a lot more secure, but I've never forgotten to lock mine since. JACQUI

Buying a Car

Whenever you buy a car, take a moment to check what security features it has. It's undoubtedly the least exciting part of the purchase, but since cars cost so much, you should probably do your best to hang on to it for as long as possible. Get a copy of the *Car Theft Index*, published by the Home Office. It lists those cars with the highest levels of theft in the last year, so you can get an idea how long you and your new car are likely to stay together. After your home, it's probably going to be the most expensive thing you'll ever buy, and your pride and joy – so why not spend a few minutes making sure it's as difficult as possible to steal or break into?

Check what insurance group your car falls into. All models of car are placed in one of twenty groups according to a number of factors, including its security features. The group your car is in can have a significant effect on the insurance premium you'll end up paying.

If you're buying a new car make sure it has the following: an alarm, an electronic immobilizer, doors fitted with deadlocks or double locking, a central-locking system, a visible Vehicle Identification Number (it can be bonded to the dashboard), etching, security glazing (which makes it much harder for a thief to break in), lockable fuel cap and lockable wheel nuts. This may seem like a long list, but most cars will have all these as standard.

If you're buying a used car, the security features are still important, but you may have to get some of them installed once you've bought it. Check to make sure you're not about to buy a stolen car, because if you do, the police are perfectly entitled to take it from you and, even if you bought it in good faith, you'll never get your money back. You can check at one of several private companies that hold information on vehicles whether the car you have your eye on has been reported stolen, seriously damaged or is still subject to finance. Check out the website www.direct. gov.uk/en/motoring/index.htm. And look to see if the Vehicle Identification Number (usually found on the chassis), including any number etched on to glass surfaces, matches that on the documents.

FURTHER INFORMATION

CYCLING

For good all-round help and other links go to **www.bikeforall.net**. And, if you're based in London, also try the London Cycling Campaign at **www.lcc.org.uk**, which also has details of the Take A Stand scheme. There is also a registered charity for cyclists' safety; you can find its site at **www.brake.org.uk**.

DRIVING

For an online copy of the Highway Code go to **www.direct.gov.uk/ en/travelandtransport/highwaycode**; the car-theft index is available on **www.homeoffice.gov.uk/documents/car-theft-index**.

For general motoring advice go to **www.theaa.com** or **www.rac.co.uk**, and for the government view, **www.thinkroadsafety.gov.uk**.

For general road safety advice visit the Royal Society for the Prevention of Accidents (RoSPA): **www.rospa.com**.

VEHICLE AND PERSONAL SECURITY

You can find the Motor Insurance Repair Research Centre at **www.thatcham.org**, and car parks which are certified at **www.secured carparks.com**.

For vehicle-security products go to **www.soldsecure.com**; Datatag Security systems are available from **www.datatag.co.uk**.

For property-marking products try Crime Prevention Products on **www.c-p-p.co.uk**.

VEHICLE HISTORY CHECKS

The following are some of the organizations that provide this service:

Autotrader (Trader Data Systems, TDS): **www.vehiclecheck.co.uk**, 0844 470 3708

eBay: **www.ebay.co.uk/motors/services/vsr/**

Exchange and Mart: **www.exchangeandmart.co.uk/iad/car/info/historycheck**

Motors: **www.motors.co.uk/buying-advice.php**

Experian AutoCheck: **www.autocheck.co.uk**

HPI Limited: **www.hpi.co.uk**

4

The World is Your Oyster

So, you've decided to take a holiday – hooray! Or maybe you have to travel for work – which can sometimes turn into a good excuse for a holiday – hooray as well! Thanks to the explosion of cheap flights, more and more of us are travelling abroad. Wherever you're going in the world or whether you are working, sunning yourself on a beach, travelling on a gap year or having the adventure of a lifetime, you're likely to encounter some common hazards, which we can help you navigate safely.

Being a woman, travelling around the world can be tricky. Different countries have very different views about a woman's place in society. In Saudi Arabia a woman cannot drive, cannot vote and must cover herself from head to foot. In Brazil, the bum is considered the most attractive and the most sexual part of a woman's body (we know – total nightmare). Everyone there wears a thong on the beach and casts care about cellulite to the wind. If you venture out in a slightly more modest bikini or, God forbid, a one-piece, all in all, it's considered a pretty poor show. In some Muslim countries a woman cannot shake a man's hand, even in a business setting. So if you're left standing there with your hand proffered while your host keeps his firmly in his pocket, you'll know why.

It's important to know something about the culture of the country you're visiting before you set off. When you think you're giving a friendly smile in one country, in another you may be signalling, 'How's about it, big boy? Why not make it a quickie round the back?' Words lost in translation can make for some classic marketing errors. Take the American milk board's campaign, which used the slogan 'Got milk?' When they extended their advertising into Mexico, it was soon brought to their attention that the Spanish translation read, 'Are you lactating?' If you get your words mixed up when you're venturing further afield you can end up in some unexpected situations.

I was filming in Argentina and kept getting the Spanish phrases *'no entiendo'* and *'no entendo'* mixed up (well, you can see how it could happen) and I couldn't understand why everyone kept shouting at me. It turns out that the former means 'I don't under-stand' and the latter means 'I can't hear'! FIONA

A couple of months after the end of the first Gulf war I was working on the BBC's *Panorama* programme as a junior researcher. We were about to make a programme in Kurdistan – not the safest of places – but I begged to be allowed to go. It was an amazing experience and I learned a lot there. One problem we had was ensuring that the Turkish military (who were in control of the partic-ular area in which we were working, Diyarbakır) did not seize the footage we had so carefully shot. There were all sorts of political sensitivities at the time and in the past they had taken footage when they were unhappy with what the camera crew were filming. To avoid this, my producer decided that I should take all our tapes to the Turkish capital, Ankhara, and have them flown back to London by courier. Only problem – Ankhara was an entire day's drive away right across Turkey. Looking back on it, I can't quite believe that I agreed to do this, but in the end it was decided that I would go in a car with a local driver (a complete stranger) and that he would drive me and the tapes across Turkey.

As we set off on the thirteen-hour journey, I did begin to wonder what I would do if he turned out to be a) a thief, b) a pervert or c) a mad axeman. Fortunately, he was none of the above, but he did have a massive black eye from a fight he had been in the night before. He couldn't see out of that eye and he was struggling to keep the other open. After an hour or two, I could see we were in serious danger of crashing so, in sign language, I gestured to him to pull over and took over the driving myself.

Two thirds of the way there we broke down in the middle of nowhere but, as if by magic, a man happened to be passing who had a soldering iron, so he welded some bit of the car back on and we carried on. I made it to the airport with about five minutes to spare. So far so good. But then I had to get back to the town where I'd left the camera crew by the next morning. I arranged to hire a Land Rover with a driver (another strange man), and half an hour later we set off back across Turkey through the night. I remember lying on the floor in the back trying to get some sleep and hoping that this man didn't fit into the a, b or c categories either. The journey was uneventful, except for a pause in the small hours for a cup of sweet tea in some kind of truck stop in the desert. All men and not a women's loo in sight. We rolled into Diyarbakır at about 6 a.m. and my epic trip across Turkey and back was over. I was twenty-six years old and had entrusted my safety to not one but two strange men. I had nothing to protect myself, not even a mobile. It was one hell of a journey but I can't help feeling with the benefit of hindsight that it was pretty damn reckless. It's not something I would do now, that's for sure. FIONA

So that's how NOT to do it. Read on to learn about some basic precautions you can take to help you travel safely as you make your way around the world.

BEFORE YOU GO

The key thing is to make sure people you trust know where you're going. Make copies of your travel itinerary and leave a copy at work with friends or family – particularly if you're travelling alone. Include hotel numbers and addresses if you can. If you don't speak the language, it's definitely worth going armed with a phrasebook and some useful phrases by the time you reach the airport. Have some local currency ready for when you land, preferably in small denominations so you're not flashing your cash.

Documentation

Make sure your passport is valid for six months beyond your return date of travel. Some countries are absolute sticklers for this, and you can be left stranded even though your passport is still officially within date.

Make photocopies of all important travel documents, such as passports and visas. If your passport is nicked while you're away, having a copy available will make getting a replacement one much easier. If you have any medical problems, make sure you also bring a copy of your medical history with you. Leave one copy at home and pack a spare in your luggage. You might want to consider emailing copies to yourself which you can access abroad should you need to get replacements in a hurry.

> Make sure that you keep your passport safe at home. A friend of mine has just spent three days turning her house upside down looking for her passport before trying to jet off for a quick week in the sun. If you can't find it, the passport office will not issue a replacement without a crime report being lodged with the local police, not to mention extensive form-filling. JACQUI

Medicine

Depending on where you're going, you might want to take an emergency medical pack with you. Whenever Fiona travels for the BBC to a developing country, she is given a pack containing painkillers, rehydration tablets and a few other basics. More importantly, it also contains sterilized needles, canulas and sutures. In some African countries, for example, AIDS is a major problem, and you never want to find yourself in a bush hospital worrying about whether or not the needle that's about to puncture your vein is infected. You can get them at big chemist's, or your GP will be able to point you in the right direction.

Frightened of needles? You're out of luck. If you're venturing far afield, you have to make sure you have the right vaccinations. They vary from country to country and what you need may change from year to year. Your local hospital may have a special surgery for vaccinations or, again, you can get information from your GP. Don't assume that just because you've had a particular jab in the past that you'll be OK. Many only last a few years.

I had a brilliant holiday in Sharm el Sheikh, Egypt, this year. We were warned extensively about not drinking the local water, which we did avoid, but despite this we did succumb to tummy bugs. However, none were too serious and they didn't disrupt the holiday for more than one day. Strangely, though, about two weeks after returning I came down with a different tummy bug (I won't go into details in case you're eating, but it had most of the usual symptoms and a few more besides). I went to the doctor and it took almost three weeks to work out what was wrong (by this time I'd lost loads of weight – hooray! – but felt terrible and was having trouble getting through the day). Finally, a lab test came back positive for a bug which is found in water, *Cryptosporidium*, which you can pick up from a contaminated swimming pool or drinking water and can stay in your system for several weeks before symptoms appear. Thankfully, no one else in the family got it, but it made me realize that you can bring bugs and germs back to the UK with you and have no ill effects for some time afterwards. JACQUI

Find out if you're travelling to a country where the water might be a problem. If you are, it's worth being very strict with yourself – clean your teeth with bottled water, don't have any ice in your drinks and avoid foods such as salad, which may have been washed in tap water.

Crime
Do your homework about what kind of crime you're most likely

to encounter where you're going. Naples: jewellery and bag-snatching. Guatemala: armed robbery in the hills outside towns. India: backpacks stolen from hostels. Colombia: shooting and knife attacks, not to mention kidnapping, drug-gang killings – in fact: just don't go there. Check out your destination on the Foreign Office website (see p. 184).

Packing

Baggage handlers aren't going to like this, but it's fair to say they don't have the best of reputations when it comes to stealing. We've both had valuable items stolen from our bags somewhere between checking them in and taking them off the carousel at the other end. If you want to take something valuable, firstly think whether or not you really need it. If you absolutely insist on taking your Tiffany necklace and matching earrings, don't pack them in your suitcase; you may never see them again. Anything small, portable and electronic, such as mp3 players and digital cameras, are also tempting to a thief as they're so easy to sell. If you absolutely must take it with you, stick it in your hand luggage.

Incidentally, you may think it's the last word in chic to have matching Louis Vuitton cases, but have you seen how those bags get chucked on and off the plane, left on the tarmac in the rain, crushed in baggage carts under twenty other bags? They will get trashed. And how many times have you stood by the luggage carousel watching the bags go round, at least five of which look just like yours? It may look naff, but that lime-green suitcase will come into its own when you're trying to pick it out. And if you can't face anything quite that unstylish, just tie a ribbon on the handle or put a sticker on the case to make it stand out. There's nothing worse than getting home with your bag to unpack someone else's dirty undies. Yuck.

—————————— BAGGAGE RESTRICTIONS ——————————

When it comes to what you can or cannot take on to a plane, we throw in the towel. Just before writing, we were slaves to the transparent plastic sandwich bag with all liquid items held within. But that has since changed in some airports and will undoubtedly change again, as will the rule concerning the size of hand luggage you can carry on. So, check with your airline or the British Airports Authority (www.baa.com), and stick to the rules religiously. While some customs officials are prepared to let the odd extra lippy slip through, others approach the rules with incredible jobsworth zeal.

Never, ever agree to carry something for someone else. It sounds so blindingly obvious, you may think that you'd never be so stupid. But it is surprisingly easy to be lured into forming a friendship with someone while you're away who then just can't quite fit a particular souvenir into his/her suitcase, and there seems no harm in putting it in your roomier case instead as a favour. And it might not just be drugs or some other illegal substance you're unwittingly carrying. It could be a bomb.

Accommodation

Book at least your first night's accommodation, especially if you're arriving after dark. On arrival, you're likely to be tired, disorientated and potentially at your most vulnerable during the whole trip.

Travelling Alone

Women can get an extraordinary amount of hassle when travelling alone. Some men, even in European countries, seem to assume that your solitary status means you are available and gagging for it. Relentless and unwanted attention from the opposite sex can make your trip abroad thoroughly miserable.

Fiona had one particularly grim week in Egypt when she was a student. A local man pretended to be a legitimate holiday rep and organized a camel trip for her (it turned out he was the camel driver and couldn't wait to get her out into the desert on her own). After that, Fiona decided that in future she would wear a fake wedding ring whenever travelling on her own or with girlfriends. It did seem to put a lot of men off. Now she has the real thing. If you're not there yet, just get a cheap fake wedding band and flaunt it.

Insurance

The most seriously ill I've ever been was when I was in bed with flu. I took to my bed one day and was unable to get out of it for another three weeks. I could not believe how bad I felt – too ill to eat, or read or watch television. I survived by drinking squash by my bedside and sleeping most of the time. At one stage I seriously began to wonder if I was developing ME, I felt so lousy and weak. I had a skiing holiday booked and was determined to get better for it but just couldn't shake off this wretched flu. By a minor miracle I had inadvertently booked holiday insurance that paid for the cost of the trip in the event of illness. So when I couldn't go, I was minus a holiday but at least I wasn't minus a couple of grand.
FIONA

Travel insurance is not a luxury, it's a necessity. Make sure it covers the basics – you'd be surprised how many policies don't.

- ☀ **Your cancellation:** It will pay out if you can't go because of illness or jury service.

- ☀ **Their cancellation:** It will pay out if the holiday firm goes bust or the hotel goes up in smoke.

- ☀ **Delays:** If you are held up by a faulty aircraft or staff illness.

- ☀ **Vehicle rental:** See more on p.162 under car hire.

- ☀ **Dangerous sports:** Skiing, parasailing, climbing, parachuting are just some of the activities for which you'll need extra cover.

- ☀ **Medical cover:** See p. 174.

COME FLY WITH ME

Let's face it, deciding what to take with you on a trip is always tricky, and discipline is needed to ensure you don't take the entire contents of your bedroom with you. As we said before, our golden rule is: if you would be devastated to lose it, don't take it with you. That beautiful pendant and the gorgeous silk dress may well look stunning with a tan, but save it for when you get home, it really isn't worth taking the risk – particularly when you realize that around 26 out of every 1,000 British Airways passengers arrive at their destinations to find their luggage has gone somewhere else on holiday. Reassurances that almost all baggage is reunited with its owner within forty-eight hours is all very well – *but what on earth are you going to wear for two days?* BA is one of the worst in Europe, but it's certainly not the only one and, across the board, over 16 out of every 1,000 passengers will arrive baggageless.

So what do you do? Firstly, if you are taking something of value with you, make sure you have a receipt to show the airline so you can prove it existed in the first place, and if you do have to take lots of stuff other than the basics, keep a list of what's in there. Check the airline's terms and conditions: some include a list of items they won't take responsibility for if lost, for example camcorders, in which case it's best to take them on to the flight with you. It's definitely worth finding out in advance where the lost-/missing-luggage counter is located in the airport, because you can guarantee that if *you've* lost something, then so have others on your flight, in which case there'll be a queue. And unless you want to spend a couple of hours watching one or, if you're lucky, two harassed members of staff spending, on average, fifteen minutes dealing with each report, get into the queue as soon as you think there are no more bags coming on to the carousel. You can always re-check it again later. And remember: just because you have one of your bags, it doesn't necessarily mean the other will follow.

If you are one of the unlucky ones, don't panic if you have travelled on more than one flight. The last carrier is the one responsible for finding your luggage, so go to the counter for the airline you last flew with.

Now, the best scenario is that your bag has been delayed, which means that it has missed your flight but will be put on the next available flight to your destination. Make sure you are not being misled and fobbed off with this explanation; they will need to find your baggage number on their computer screen, so ask to see it. Then you need to decide whether to wait for the bag or have them send it to you. If you decide to stay and wait, ask the airline rep to give you a meal voucher for an airport restaurant – after all, you're saving them money by not having a courier deliver it to you.

If you are told that your bag is actually missing, i.e. they don't have a clue where it is, don't panic: 98 per cent of all bags are recovered within four to five days at this stage, and most within twenty-four–forty-eight hours. If it does eventually turn out that your bag has gone for ever, then you'll have to claim reimbursement from the airline. How much you can claim varies according to the airline policy. There is no point trying to claim thousands for a Chanel suit when you are on a £150 last-minute budget beach holiday, but if you are on a business trip and you have important meetings to attend, then asking them to pay for a suit is not unreasonable. Remember, most airlines will require a twenty-four-hour delay before you start to seek reimbursement, but it's worth asking them if they have any overnight kits or would give an immediate cash advance to help you get over the first night. This initial help from the airline will often be at the discretion of the staff member on duty, so keep your cool and be as nice as possible. It's tempting to have a go and let off steam, but good manners and a hard-luck story can only help your situation.

You can claim for the loss of your luggage later, but it has to be declared 'officially lost' and, with most airlines, this is after twenty-one days. Under the Montreal Convention you can claim up to a total of £850 from the airline. Some insurance companies cover you for your luggage as well: check your holiday-insurance small print before you go.

If you're not happy about the way the airline or insurance company deal with you, you can complain later to the Air Transport Users Council, www.caa.co.uk/auc, or the Financial Ombudsman, www.financial-ombudsman.org.uk.

WHEN YOU GET THERE

Did you know?

- ☼ In the Solomon Islands, swearing is a serious offence (and they speak English).

- ☼ In Japan, it is rude to blow your nose in public.

- ☼ In Barbados, you should leave trendy camouflage clothing at home. It is an offence to wear it there.

- ☼ In Brazil, when you have a drink in a bar, you are expected to use a glass, not drink out of a bottle or can.

- ☼ In Bulgaria, shaking your head means yes and nodding means no.

- ☼ In Belarus, don't eat mushrooms, as they contain high levels of radiation.

Be aware of local customs – from tipping, to clothing, to religious observation, to food. Do a bit of homework and make sure you know that when you let off a satisfying belch after a good meal in China, you're paying your host the ultimate compliment, whereas in the United States, you are likely to be considered more trailer-trash than Britney.

Personal Safety

I'm a very keen traveller and have often gone on trips abroad alone. In January 2006 I decided to spend six months travelling around South America. One day, in Venezuela, I found myself at a bus terminal awaiting my next connection, which wasn't for several more hours, so I decided to go into the ticket booths to sort out tickets for another section of my trip. While there I got chatting to a man in another booth. He was very friendly and asked me if I needed any help. He flashed what I took to be a police badge and explained he was a plain-clothes detective. Everyone working in the ticket booths knew him and said hello. After getting my ticket I sat down and he followed me. His English was OK, my Spanish wasn't great, but we were able to communicate. He showed me his badge again; this time there was a family photo with it showing his wife and two kids. I started to trust this guy and believe what he was saying. I told him what I was doing, and he knew I had about three hours to kill before my bus arrived. I decided to go and find an internet café to email a friend for her birthday and he offered to take me in his car. I felt at that stage that he was OK, so I did. I had received help once before from a uniformed policeman in Brazil, who'd walked me back to my hostel when I'd been feeling a bit worried. I got into the front passenger seat of his car and he drove around the city pointing out the sights like a guide. Then we started travelling into what appeared to be a park, and I realized we were going away from the city. I asked him to turn around, but he stopped the car in a car park on the outskirts of the city. He got out and said he was going to the toilet before driving me back to town. I didn't know what to do – I still half trusted him and still thought he was going to drop me back at the bus station. While he was behind a tree I heard a bottle smash. As he walked back towards the car I could see he had something in his hand. I started to panic and grabbed the door handle, but before I could get out he got back in and suddenly swung a broken beer bottle to my neck. I opened the door and fell out, and he ran round the car shouting 'Dinero, dinero' – 'Money money'. I ran up a hill to try to get away while trying to get cash out of my money belt to give to him, but doing this was slowing me down and he was getting too close. I started to fear for my life – he wasn't waiting for me to give him money, he wanted more: I felt he wanted to kill me. Luckily, a car came down the hill towards us, and I threw myself on to the bonnet to make it stop. Inside was a family, who let me in, while the man ran back to his car and shot off – with my luggage. The family took me to the police station, where I reported the incident. Fortunately, they had a translation system, where you typed in English on a computer and it translated it into Spanish, so the police were able to get my story really quickly. I also contacted the British Consulate but, as I still had my passport on me and access to money (my family could wire me some), there was nothing else they could do or offer me. The man told me that it was very common to hear stories from tourists about being attacked by police officers, both real and fake, but I still don't know which this guy was.

Within two days I was back home in the UK – I just didn't feel up to continuing my trip. EMMA, LONDON. (See Chapter 8 for what happened to Emma when she got home.)

When you're on holiday or in a foreign country, you want to let go, relax, let your hair down, let your guard drop, forget about all those things you have to worry about at home. We know, we feel exactly the same. But the reality is, the things that make you at risk at home are mostly the same on holiday but with a few extra things thrown in for good measure. When you're enjoying tequila in a beach bar, you still have to look out for your handbag. When you're taking a taxi to the shops in the centre of town, you still need to make sure the driver is legitimate. When you get your money out to buy something, don't flash your cash. When a friendly local guy offers to buy you a drink, you still need to check what he's actually giving you, particularly as many foreign countries don't have the same measuring system – you could end up drinking quadruple measures. Boring, we know, but a fact of life, so you may as well face up to it now. All the safety tips in Chapter 2, Let's Party!, apply to you when you're abroad or on holiday. We won't spell them out for you all over again here, but take a look before you hit the road.

You may need to consider how women in particular are regarded in the country you're visiting. In the Middle East, for example, women are not allowed the same freedoms as in Europe, and within regions there are differences: in Saudi Arabia, you cannot drive or drink, whereas just over the border in Oman you can. Think about what kind of clothing the local women wear. You may think it's too hot to wear anything but a vest top and shorts and what the hell, you're on holiday. But if you dress like that in some of the world's more conservative countries you could be thrown in jail, beaten with a large stick by the religious police or thought to be a prostitute and treated as such. Bear in mind that, while you may not have to wear a headscarf in some Muslim countries – Turkey or Egypt, for example – you will be expected to dress modestly, covering your shoulders and your knees.

Do not wander about casually in places where you will be in the minority as a woman, especially at night. Be careful and cautious. Ask your hotel for advice as to the safety of particular areas.

If you're travelling alone, keep it to yourself. Don't announce it to the man you've struck up a conversation with in a shop or bar. And if that man seems friendly and asks you out, you may think you're just saying yes to a casual drink but he may think you're agreeing to a drink, full sex and no pillow talk afterwards. In many countries, western women are thought to be of easy virtue, loose morals and enthusiastic and athletic sexual prowess.

Recently, I was walking in a town in Andalusia, Spain, with my husband. It was daytime but there weren't many people around. A man approached us holding a map and asking for directions, so we stopped to talk to him. The next thing we knew two policemen in uniform surrounded us and started demanding we show them our passports or credit cards for identification. They were very aggressive and we felt very intimidated. Initially, we couldn't understand why the police would need to see our ID and we tried to find out why, although my Spanish is non-existent, and then it dawned on me that they weren't real. I can't really explain why – I'd never come across the police over there before and didn't know what they were like anyway, but something wasn't quite right. I started shouting the first thing that came into my head, which turned out to be, 'Help, it's a heist,' for some strange reason (watching too much American TV probably) and, luckily, they ran off. I'm just so glad we didn't show them our wallets as, clearly, they were going to rob us and the first guy had been some sort of decoy. It was really upsetting and it's made me a lot more wary about automatically trusting what appear to be authority

figures when I'm abroad, the way I would at home. JULIE PEAS-
GOOD, ACTRESS, TV PRESENTER AND AUTHOR

Your Hotel

Again, don't broadcast the fact that you are a woman travelling alone. Use only a first initial when checking in, not Ms, Miss or Mrs. Don't be afraid to ask to see the room first – try to avoid rooms at the end of long corridors and on the first or ground floor. If you do end up with the latter, never leave the window open. Check that there is plenty of lighting in the corridors during the hours of darkness and that the door to your room has a security peephole, door chain and a deadlock.

If you aren't travelling on a pre-booked package it's worth trawling the internet for hotels so you have a good idea of what you're getting, and you'll probably find some good deals. Most hotels are reputable and when checking you in will ask for basic details plus an imprint of your credit card – if the receptionist wants more than that, it's worth checking why with the manager, just in case. The same goes for checking out: go through your bill and query anything that you feel you're not responsible for, if necessary, with the manager – that will usually resolve any problems.

A lot of countries ask you to lodge your passport with them upon arrival as a customs requirement. It's probably best to verify the reason with them, confirm where it will be kept and pick it up as soon as it becomes available. Keep a photocopy with you in case of problems.

My aunt was on holiday in Rome. She had booked a room in a
hotel near the Vatican and was pleased to have been given one

with a view and a balcony on the first floor. She wasn't so pleased when she woke up one morning to find her window wide open and her bag gone. She was pretty shocked and frightened that someone had been able to get into her room in the night while she'd been asleep. When she reported the theft at the hotel's reception, she discovered that the rooms on either side of her had been targeted in the same way. In all cases the doors had been locked and entry seemed to be through the windows, left ajar because of the heat. The police assumed that the thief or thieves had climbed up to the first room with a ladder and had managed to go from one room to the next using the balconies and got in through the windows. CLAIRE, LONDON

While sitting by the hotel pool on a beach holiday in Kenya we noticed clothes falling from a room balcony on the top floor. We looked up and saw several items being thrown over. A couple next to us started laughing (obviously not their room) and we asked what the joke was. Apparently, the local monkeys regularly patrolled the balconies looking for open doors or windows to climb into. Once inside the room they would rifle through belongings, stealing food or anything which attracted them, such as jewellery. Thieves come in all shapes and sizes and I've never forgotten to shut my balcony doors and windows since – wherever I am. JACQUI

☼ **Always lock your bedroom door** and use the safety lock if there is one. If not, use a door wedge or chair for extra security.

☼ **Avoid rooms near the lifts.** As well as being noisy, they are often the first ones a thief will target.

Never open your door to someone without being sure who it is. If it's someone unexpected, ring reception to check. Try to use hotels that have peepholes in the doors.

 Be careful with your room key. If it has a number on the fob, don't leave it where others can see it.

 Check connecting doors. Some rooms are designed to inter-connect to accommodate families or groups. If you do have a connecting door, make sure it is locked from your side.

 Use the hotel safe for your passport and valuables – but it's worth checking what the hotel's insurance policy is for stolen items. If the maximum limit is significantly less than the value of what you're storing in there, it won't be much use.

 Check where the emergency exit is in case of a fire. There should be a map on the back of your door. Walk the exit route and check that it works and that the door to the outside isn't locked. If it is, demand that the hotel staff unlock it and keep it unlocked at all times. They will almost certainly be breaking the law otherwise.

 Ask if the lighting in the corridor is on twenty-four hours a day. If it's not, ask them to switch it on. It'll be a lot easier to see where you're going if there's a fire, and it will deter any suspicious characters from creeping down the corridors.

Car Hire

When you're paying up front to hire a car, don't sign a blank receipt for a credit-card deposit. You may only find out how much you've actually paid for the car (or how much you've been fleeced) when you get home. You can often get cheaper deals locally on the ground than with the big international car-hire firms at home, but you can't be as sure of the honesty of the staff and the roadworthiness of the car. If you want to save yourself a few quid, shop around on the net with reputable companies before you go. It can be a big expense in some countries, particularly the States, where you seem to be quoted great deals but there are so many compulsory 'extras' they can add hundreds of pounds to your budget.

- ☀ **Make sure the insurance covers you adequately,** and go through with the agent what is and isn't included.

- ☀ **Inspect the car before you sign on the dotted line.** Tyres worn smooth? Rust? Dodgy brake lights? They are all a real pain to sort out once you've set off.

- ☀ **Book a portable sat nav if you can as part of the car hire.** Or buy an international one before you leave home and take it with you. They are absolute lifesavers when you're lost on a never-ending dirt track, the only person you've spotted for miles is the local goatherd and he doesn't speak English.

- ☀ If you're going somewhere seriously remote or into a wilderness, **think about taking a guide with you.** As well as preventing you from getting lost, a guide will be able to help you if you find yourself in difficult terrain, caught in unexpected weather conditions, or are injured.

- ☀ **Finally, think about whether the car you're hiring is suitable** for the terrain you will be covering.

I was in Ivory Coast in Africa to do a story for a current-affairs series I was presenting on BBC1 at the time. The camera crew and I were staying in the capital and we thought a big family car with a decent-sized boot for the camera gear would be fine. So we hired a pretty comfortable Audi saloon. But we hadn't bargained for two things: the monsoon and the fact that only a few roads in the capital are surfaced with tarmac. The rest are dirt tracks.

It soon became clear that our car, laden down with camera gear, was struggling to get along the tracks, which were either deeply rutted or liquid mud.

On one journey, the driver decided to take a short cut across a junction, and the car got completely stuck. It was pivoted on a rock protruding out of the ground and was wobbling backwards and forwards. About twenty men appeared out of nowhere, shouting, excitable, anxious to help and earn a few dollars for their trouble. While we were all sitting in the car, they started to rock it back and forth to try and dislodge it off the rock. I was terrified they were going to end up piercing the petrol tank.

The energetic rocking didn't work and I thought we should get out of the car to try to lighten the load, but our driver warned us against it. The crowd grew bigger. By now there were about fifty men trying to push the car, shouting advice, shoving each other out of the way to get nearer. I kept thinking of the thousands of pounds' worth of camera gear in the boot and how long it would stay in our possession if the men around us began to wonder why the car was so low at the back. We were completely stuck – it wasn't as if there was an AA we could call, or any kind of pick-up truck. And leaving the car there wasn't an option either. It certainly wouldn't have been there by the time we got back.

After about ten long minutes in which I was torn between fear and laughter at the sheer absurdity of our situation, the men heaved the back of the car as high as they could (a Herculean feat) and managed to push it forwards off the rock. Throwing dollar bills out of the window, our driver sped off, leaving our valiant helpers to scrabble for the money. Hiring a proper offroad vehicle in the first place might have been a lot easier. **FIONA**

You'll also need your driving licence and some knowledge of the local drinking and driving laws. In many Eastern European countries you can't drink a drop and then get behind the wheel. Mixing alcohol with driving in a foreign country is not the best idea, even if you stay within the limit. Not only are you unfamiliar with the roads and driving customs, but driving on the other side of the road and the different speed limits are things that need complete concentration. These factors all add up. And you may be surprised by how little you can legally drink in much of Europe, for example. There are wide variations from country to country but, for most, the limit is the equivalent of one small glass of beer. It may be less if you've got passengers in the car with you or if you're a new driver with less than two years since passing your test. In many parts of Europe, the police don't need a reason to stop your vehicle and breathalyse you. They're permitted to make random stops and checks, so you could easily find yourself being pulled over for no apparent reason.

Don't expect leniency if convicted of drink-driving abroad. The penalties differ greatly from country to country, but at the very least you're going to receive a large fine. You can, for example, receive a six-month sentence in the UK and Ireland, and anywhere from one day to three years in Luxembourg. In all cases, your licence will be suspended or you'll be banned from driving in the country. There is a facility on the AA website (www.theaa.com) which allows you to select the country you're visiting from a drop-down menu and then gives you details of the relevant driving requirements and regulations.

──────── HOW THIS AFFECTS YOU ────────

If you're banned from driving in one country, that doesn't stop you driving elsewhere in Europe. Attempting to return to that country and drive a vehicle, though, will lead to your arrest. According to the AA, drink-driving convictions abroad do not affect your UK licence. Even if your licence is confiscated abroad, the foreign government will simply send it to the DVLA, which will then return it to you without a penalty. It seems pretty incredible in these days of EU-wide regulation, but there it is.

Taxis

Getting a cab abroad can give the phrase 'taking the scenic route' a whole new meaning. You often end up feeling fleeced and with the sneaking suspicion that you've just been taken on a trip all round the city when you were sure your destination was only a couple of miles away. It's hard to know what to do about it when you may not speak the language and the location is unfamiliar to you.

 If you've booked your trip with a tour operator, ask their advice about what you should expect to pay for local cab journeys, the price of a cab from the airport, how safe the local cabs tend to be and whether you're expected to tip. Find out if cabs are licensed in the area and how you can recognize them.

 You can also ask at the airport tourist-information desk how much you should expect to pay for a cab to your hotel.

☀ **It's never a great idea to flag down a cab off the street** unless you're in a familiar city, such as Paris or New York, where it is easy to recognize the licensed cabs. Instead, ask your hotel to book them for you or give you the number of a reputable local cab firm.

☀ **Try and get some idea of the currency conversion rate** in your head before you arrive. It's so easy to hand over what feels like monopoly money and only realize hours later you've spent the equivalent of fifty quid on a five-minute journey.

☀ **If the cab doesn't have a meter, ALWAYS agree a price** before you set off.

☀ **The advice about using taxis at home applies abroad too.** For example, if you book a cab, get the driver to tell you what name it was booked in. Have a look at Chapter 2 for more details.

☀ **If you hire a cab driver to take you round the sights** for the day, be aware that he will probably be on a commission to take you to particular bars/restaurants/tourist attractions where he will get a kickback. Be prepared to be very firm about what you want to see and what you don't.

Piracy

What, in this day and age? Well, yes. It's pretty specialist and confined to certain parts of the world, but those parts are very, very large – think the South China Sea, Red Sea, Indian Ocean, Malacca Straits. Piracy is worth bearing in mind if you are the adventurous type and are venturing far afield by boat in these areas. There are websites that will give you the latest information on maritime piracy reports and what to do if you come under attack. Check them out at the end of the chapter.

Drugs

When you enter Malaysia, you can be in no doubt about the severity of their approach to drugs. There is a ten-foot-tall hoarding depicting a massive noose. If you carry drugs in or are caught taking drugs while you're there, that hoarding is there to tell you that you risk finding yourself hanging at the end of a rope. Or, hey, you could catch a lucky break and spend the rest of your life in jail instead.

According to the Foreign Office, at the end of 2005, 2,500 British nationals were detained overseas, over a third of them for drugs-related offences. In Spain, possession of all recreational drugs is illegal and can lead to imprisonment. In Cyprus, being caught with any drug will usually end up with your being imprisoned or made to pay a hefty fine. In Venezuela, arrests for drug trafficking are common and lead to severe penalties, including a lengthy time in harsh and dangerous prisons on remand awaiting trial.

Remember the story of Sandra Gregory? In 1990 she went on holiday to South-East Asia and ended up living in Thailand. But she ran out of money, fell seriously ill and was desperate to return home to the UK. She accepted a heroin addict's offer to smuggle his supply of drugs from Bangkok to Japan, in exchange for the money to buy a plane ticket home. She was arrested at Bangkok airport and convicted of drug trafficking. The sentence carried a jail term of twenty-five years. After four and half years in Lao prison, which Sandra described as traumatic and terrifying, she was repatriated to a British jail, where she did time until 2000, when she was released thanks to a rare pardon from the King of Thailand. Sandra has said she will live with the shame and consequences of what she did for the rest of her life.

Don't get involved in drugs abroad. And make sure you keep your luggage with you at all times when travelling to the airport and when you're in the terminal. If drugs are found in your bags, you will be held responsible, even if you have no idea how they got there.

Embassies and Consulates

You may be labouring under the comfortable illusion that if it all goes pear-shaped when you're abroad, the good old British Embassy or consulate will step in to help you out. Think again. There are limitations to how much they will do, so you need to be able to protect or help yourself as far as possible.

What they will do:

- ☀ Send you money from your family if you are stuck without funds.

- ☀ Issue replacement passports.

- ☀ Provide appropriate help if you have been raped or assaulted or are a victim of crime.

- ☀ Visit you if you are in prison, and tell family and friends that you have been arrested. Offer you information about the legal system and supply you with a list of local interpreters and lawyers.

- ☀ Visit you after you have been sentenced – though in some countries only the once. Don't expect to form a lasting and beautiful friendship.

What they won't do:

- ☼ Pay any bills or give you money (except in very exceptional circumstances, in which case they will lend you money but you will have to pay it back).

- ☼ Get you out of prison or interfere in criminal proceedings.

- ☼ Give legal advice.

- ☼ Make travel arrangements for you.

- ☼ Find you accommodation.

- ☼ Help you get into the country if your passport or visa isn't valid.

IF YOUR HOLIDAY GOES WRONG

If you discover that your trip isn't up to scratch – building works not completed, planes cancelled, room doesn't have the promised sea view, the kitchens give you salmonella, that kind of thing – there are some things you can do to maximize your chances of getting some or all of your money back.

Firstly, speak to the holiday-company rep, at your location or back in their head office. Get their name, make your complaint clear and ask what they intend to do about it – give them a deadline. If the problem isn't resolved straight away, start making a written record of what happens. Log any phone calls with the name of the person spoken to and the time of the call. Take photos if you can or use a video camera.

If it's a problem that affects other travellers, get them on side with you. The more people complain, the stronger your case. A company will find it much harder to ignore twenty people than you on your own.

Use the media. The local or national press love a story about a spoilt holiday, about children who didn't make it on the promised trip to Disneyland, about the hotel from hell. It will almost certainly encourage the holiday company to cough up, as they will want to avoid the bad publicity.

Once you get home there's no time limit on how quickly you should lodge your complaint but, obviously, the sooner you make your feelings known, the more seriously you will be taken by the company.

If your plane is cancelled or you get bumped off because the plane is full, the European Union has given passengers new rights. The fulsomely named EU Denied Boarding Regulation came into force in February 2005 to ensure that you can get compensation if your flight is cancelled or delayed – but it's being widely ignored. So make sure you know your rights so that you can insist on them. The regulation applies to all flights where you have a confirmed reservation, you've checked in on time and you are leaving from an EU airport (or from a non-EU airport but using an airline that has its HQ within Europe).

☀ **If the flight is cancelled,** you should be offered either a refund or another route to your destination. While you wait for this to be arranged, and depending on how long that wait is, you should be offered free food and drink, free hotel accommodation and transfers to the hotel and back. You may also be entitled to some financial compensation, too, depending on the length of the delay.

☀ **If your flight is delayed,** you are entitled to free food and drink and an overnight stay if necessary.

☼ **When an airline overbooks** and then has to bump passengers off (one of the evils of the modern world in our book), it must first call for volunteers who will agree not to fly in return for 'benefits'. Usually that means cash, and it can be quite a large sum. But you have to weigh that up against the hassle factor of having packed, got to the airport, being mentally all ready to go – and then suddenly ducking out at the last minute. If there aren't enough volunteers, the airline can chuck off whoever it chooses. If that happens, you are entitled to immediate monetary compensation for the same amount as if your flight had been cancelled.

But, we repeat, this kind of information is not always something the airlines offer up freely, so know your rights and don't let them take advantage of you.

I had booked about thirty seats on a flight from the UK to South Africa for staff members of the company I worked for. We were all going to the company's head office in Johannesburg for the annual general meeting. We were all rather excited about going to South Africa and looking forward to the trip. The flight out was uneventful and we spent about four days in Jo'burg either in meetings or seeing the sights. We turned up at the airport for the flight home and I made sure that everyone else checked in before me so that, if there were any problems, I would be around to help. Everyone went through, and it looked to be very straightforward. But when it came to my turn, the person behind the check-in desk informed me that the flight was full and I couldn't get on it. 'What do you mean, I can't get on?' I protested. 'I've personally booked thirty seats on this flight, the rest of my colleagues are getting on, what do you mean, I can't?' The woman at the check-in was completely unmoved and said that there was nothing she could do about it, I'd have to stay behind and get the next flight the following day. She offered me nothing in the way of compensation, meals, accommodation, not a thing. I was so outraged, I rang home to speak to my boyfriend and asked him to quickly check on the internet what my rights were. He had a look at a few websites and found out the airline had a duty to offer me all sorts of compensation and should have asked for volunteers to bump off before it started picking passengers at random. I went back to the check-in desk armed with my facts and, lo and behold, the woman at the check-in decided to let me on the plane. What it meant, of course, was that some other poor bugger got booted off instead. But, to be honest, I was just relieved to be going home.

EILEEN, ROCHESTER

There are two organizations that guarantee your holiday should your travel agent or airline cease trading. ATOL (Air Travel Organizers' Licensing Scheme) is part of the Civil Aviation Authority and is a protection scheme for flights and air holidays. It prevents you from losing money or being left stranded if an airline or air-tour operator shuts up shop. If you are already on holiday when the operator ceases trading, you can finish your holiday and get your flight back home courtesy of ATOL. To qualify, you must get an ATOL receipt from your travel agent when you book.

ABTA (Association of British Travel Agents) is a trade body that represents travel agents and tour operators responsible for most package holidays and about half of independent travel arrangements sold in the UK. If your holiday involves a flight, ATOL will be your first port of call for help. If it doesn't, then you need to turn to ABTA, who (as long as you are using an operator registered with them) should help you continue your hols and get home, even if the travel company goes under.

MEDICAL COVER

When you book your travel insurance, make sure you are getting good medical cover. If you aren't properly insured you could risk your life and it could cost you your savings. Just to give you a rough idea what you could be letting yourself in for:

- ☀ Two days in a general ward in a European country: £600

- ☀ A broken leg in the USA: £10,000

- ☀ A heart attack in the USA: £20,000–30,000

- ☀ Bronchitis, requiring a week in hospital in the Far East : £15,000

Pricey, isn't it? Don't get caught out.

I had just over a week left until the end of my year in Paris, part of my foreign languages course at university. My health insurance had run out, but I didn't bother renewing it with so little time to go before I was due to leave. I woke up one morning with what felt like period pains and rang some friends I was in a band with to say I wasn't up to coming along to rehearse that morning. (I use the word 'rehearse' in the loosest possible sense. We were rubbish and no amount of practising was going to change that.) They came over to see me and suggested I see the doctor at their local hospital. That seemed a bit over the top to me, though I had exaggerated my symptoms a little (well, quite a lot), including telling them I'd thrown up when I hadn't.

We trooped off to consult the doctor (who turned out to be a surgeon – my French wasn't that good and I hadn't fully understood who I was being taken to see). He asked me about my symptoms in front of my fellow band members, so I had to keep up the exaggerated version. After examining me in a sideroom, he announced – to my utter horror – that I had acute appendicitis and needed to be operated on that night.

This was obviously the cue for me to confess that I had exaggerated my symptoms and that although I wasn't feeling very well, it wasn't as bad as all that. To this day, I don't know why I didn't do just that. Call me stupid or just too embarrassed to admit I'd lied, but I just couldn't. The next thing I knew I was in a ward, awaiting the operation, and all I could think was that this was divine retribution for lying and, on top of that, my insurance had run out.

I managed to persuade the surgeon to wait until the following morning in case I suddenly made a recovery. But the next day he would brook no further prevarication by yours truly and my appendix was whipped out. My mum came to my rescue while I convalesced in hospital for the week and my dad forked out for the cost of the op – and, most importantly, they forgave me for being such a complete idiot. FIONA

When you book your medical insurance, check it covers you for any particularly risky activities – if you're thinking of hanggliding or bungee-jumping, for example. Even something like scuba-diving can be exempt, so read the small print.

If you're travelling in Europe you should also have a European Health Insurance Card (EHIC). This has replaced the old E111 and entitles you to free or cheaper healthcare during a temporary visit to a country within the EU or Switzerland. It basically gives you the same rights to treatment as the residents of the country you are visiting. Remember: this might not cover all the things you'd expect to get free of charge from the NHS in the UK. You may have to make a contribution to your care. It won't cover you at all, though, if medical treatment is the main purpose of your trip. The EHIC can be obtained easily online at www.dh.gov.uk/travellers; you just need to supply your NHS number, which can be found on your medical card.

You're advised to take out comprehensive private travel insurance for visits to all countries, regardless of whether you're covered by the EHIC. The insurance will cover any contribution which is not reimbursable, as well as other eventualities not covered by the EHIC. Further information, including a list of countries covered, along with details of their health systems, can be found online at www.dh.gov.uk/travellers or in the booklet 'Health Advice for Travellers', available at the Post Office.

I went to Crete with a couple of girls on a cheapo package when I was about nineteen years old. We ended up sharing a very basic hotel room containing beds, and a wardrobe with sliding doors. One night we'd decided to go to a pyjama party being held by the holiday company, and my mate decided to go in her favourite all-in-one sleep suit (her daytime dress sense wasn't much better, but she was huge fun). While changing she slid shut the wardrobe door, which was raised, with drawers beneath it. The next thing we heard was an almighty scream as the door came off its track and landed across her toe, cutting it almost to the bone. There was blood everywhere, so I wrapped her toe in a pillow case and applied pressure (yes, the Hendon police training finally paid off) and our other friend got the reception staff to call an ambulance.

After some time this hadn't arrived, so eventually the duty manager drove us to the hospital. We must have been quite a sight: 7 p.m. in the evening, two women wearing short night-dresses and fluffy slippers helping a third in a giant babygro. The hospital was deserted and eventually a big grubby-looking guy in motorcycle leathers turned up and said he was a doctor – well, at least that's what I think he said. After a quick exam and an X-ray he said it was just a cut, patched her up with a plaster and sent her back to the hotel a couple of hours later, and we were dispatched to find her one request – a cup of tea (not as easy as you may think).

She hobbled around for a couple of days before we went home but was still in so much pain we took her straight to the hospital. They were horrified. The cut hadn't been cleaned and stitched properly, the bone had actually been broken, which we weren't told – it was a complete mess and took months to sort out properly. I so wish we'd been more persistent and enquiring at the hospital, but we felt out of our depth in a foreign country where we didn't speak the language, and just accepted whatever we were told. Not any more. **JACQUI**

If you are injured or fall ill, check your insurance policy to see what you are covered for. Also contact the holiday rep, if there is one, to see what help you can get with access to the best medical treatment and possible repatriation. If you don't have a rep and you need to get back to the UK quickly, you could contact British consular officials. They may be able to arrange this for you, though you'll still have to pay for it. Keep the receipts and labels of any drugs you pay for, as you should be able to claim for these on your insurance afterwards.

GAP YEAR

God, we wish we'd had gap years! They sound just great. A whole year to wander around the globe, bum about and see the marvels the world has to offer with the only downside that you might get a bit smelly and contract some ghastly intestinal disease. But then at least you'd be whiffy and *thin*. There are whole books devoted to gap years and how to get the best out of them, the places to go and the companies to use. But from a security perspective, if you're about to set off, much of what is already written in this chapter applies to you. Plus, there are a few extra items we think you should add to your checklist.

- ☼ **Money:** work out how much you'll need on a daily basis (don't kid yourself with an unrealistically meagre budget) and make sure you have enough to last the trip. The embassy won't bail you out if you run short. Never leave your money and passport in hostel dormitories. Keep them with you at all times.

- ☼ **Make sure your airline ticket is a flexible one** so you can come home or leave a country when you want without restrictions.

- ☼ **Tell friends and family as much as you can** about where you're going. Make plans to keep in regular contact, especially if you change your plans. Take a mobile and text to keep in touch.

- ☼ **Set up an email account** such as Hotmail that you can access from anywhere in the world to help you keep in touch. You can use internet cafés in most cities around the world. That way you can let family and friends know you're safe. Give them a rough idea when you're next likely to be in contact then, if need be, they can raise the alarm if you go missing or fall ill.

☀ **Always make sure at least one person** other than yourself knows where you are. There are sites like www.tripit.com which help you organize your trip, including planning itineraries, which you can share with family/friends. This one's free but look around at others as well and see what suits you best.

☀ **Get a good guidebook** and try to stay in recommended hotels – always book ahead if you'll be arriving at night. The Rough Guides and Lonely Planet books are very good, but there are loads of others. Spend half an hour in your local bookshop finding one that suits the type of trip you're taking. Don't forget the net – it's full of useful info and personal anecdotes which allow you to go fully pre-warned and pre-armed to meet all eventualities.

☀ **Exchange contact details with people you meet.** It's always nice to know there are fellow travellers around if you need help – or get a little lonely!

I didn't have a gap year but I did take three months to travel around South-East Asia when I was a student. I was travelling on a bus from Malaysia to Thailand and fell into conversation with a man and his wife who were returning home from visiting relatives. We were driving past field upon field of palm-oil plantations and, rather grandly, he told me that his family owned them. As the journey went on he told me more and more about the family business and he seemed to be pretty wealthy. At the time, I was surviving on a budget of £3 a day (for accommodation, food and travel), so when he asked me if I'd like to come and stay with him and his wife at their home for a couple of days, I was inclined to accept, particularly when he told me his house had a flushing loo. Never mind my personal safety and stranger danger – I hadn't seen a proper loo in weeks – the height of luxury. There were no mobiles then, so I had no way of letting anyone know about my change of plan.

My new best friend asked the bus driver to pull over by some bedraggled shacks with tin roofs and a run-down market, and we got out. Well, it turned out that the grand plantation house I was expecting was actually a hairdresser's hut with a bedroom above. The flushing loo belonged to the man's brother-in-law across the main road. The sitting room was the hairdressing salon, so we perched on its three plastic chairs and, when it was time to go to bed, I slept on the floor while my new friend and his wife slept on a mattress upstairs. When I needed to go to the loo in the middle of the night, I tried to creep outside to pee behind a bush, but my host woke up and insisted on taking me over the road, waking up his brother-in-law and his entire family so that I could use the flushing facilities. I tried to leave the next day, but it was obvious that there was some kudos to be had by having a foreign visitor and that I risked mortally offending my host with a premature departure. So I stuck it out, sleeping on the floor for another couple of nights, but never managed to master my bladder, so the nocturnal visits to the brother-in-law continued. FIONA

BRINGING GOODIES HOME

We can safely say that the things we have brought home that have proved to be of real and lasting value are few and far between.

To be avoided:

- ☼ **Local jewellery** that looks brilliantly ethnic on holiday but just like old tat when you get it home.

- ☼ **The straw hat** that you bought from the hawker on the beach that looked so chic – it'll either get crushed in your luggage or you'll have to carry it in your hand all the way back.

- ☼ **The cooking pot** that you are going to use to rustle up some authentic local dishes in your own kitchen. Who are you kidding?

- ☼ **The little kitten** that looked so pathetic and clearly didn't have a home. You'll get fleas and it'll be taken from you at the airport.

- ☼ **The romantic bloke** of few words you fell for who worked at the local bar. So what if he doesn't speak English? This is love. Nooooo – he just wants a British passport.

There are a few things that could land you in trouble with the law if you choose to pack them in your suitcase. Are you aware of the Convention on International Trade in Endangered Species (CITES)? It is an international agreement between governments to make sure that the collection and sale of wild animals and plants does not threaten their survival. It offers protection to over 33,000 species, whether they are traded as live specimens, fur coats, leather belts, seeds or dried herbs. It's worth noting that no species protected by CITES has become extinct since the convention came into force back in the 1960s. Trading in banned plants or animals may be illegal in 164 countries, but that doesn't stop traders trying to sell them to you and, if you get caught with them at customs, you will be liable. As a general rule; it is illegal to sell you (and for you to buy) anything made from:

- ☀ fur from spotted cats or marine mammals

- ☀ sea turtles

- ☀ ivory (though there is some talk about allowing the sale of some legally harvested ivory, a thoroughly misguided idea in our humble view)

- ☀ feathers and feather products from wild birds

- ☀ live or stuffed birds from most countries in South America

- ☀ some crocodile and caiman leather

- ☀ most coral and shells.

If you want to bring back food of any kind into the UK, the rules vary, depending on where it comes from. Generally, it is illegal to bring meat and milk-based products into the UK from most countries outside Europe. And there are limits on other foodstuffs like honey, eggs, fruit and vegetables. The rules differ depending on which country you're coming from or which country you're going to. Check with the Department for Environment, Food and Rural Affairs – www.defra.gov.uk or www.importdetails.defra.gov.uk.

As far as duty-free allowances go, by and large you can bring into Britain pretty substantial quantities of booze and fags from most of the countries in Europe. There are restrictions still for some of the Eastern European countries so check at www.heathrow-airport-guide.co.uk/dutyfree.html to find out exactly where you stand. If you're bringing in duty-free from outside the EU, you're entitled to considerably lesser amounts. Again, look on the website. If you're unsure about the allowances, you can either check with the airline you're travelling with or the airport you're travelling from.

TERRORISM

Where to start? This is a massive subject not only in terms of the kinds of terrorism perpetrated in the name of a higher calling but also in the countries where you are at risk of experiencing it. You have to work on the basis that you are at risk everywhere – with the possible exception of Sweden (Osama Bin Laden happened to mention in one of his home videos that he thought the Swedes are a rather good thing and not prone to wage wars in foreign territories on behalf of the infidel. So they're OK then). But what about the rest of us? And how far do we want to allow our behaviour to be influenced by the fear of terrorist attack? Our view is that, while you can reduce your risk, that shouldn't mean you should limit your freedom to roam wherever you want to. That freedom is hard won and we're damned if we're going to let some misguided zealots bomb us back to the Dark Ages.

So how do you reduce your risk without being so paranoid you don't venture out of your front door? Firstly, be aware of things around you. If you see a lone bag or package, check who it belongs to – don't assume someone else will do it. If you see someone acting strangely when you're on public transport, at an airport, or in a busy shopping centre, take a closer look at them. Try to assess what it is about them that is making you uneasy. Do they seem nervous, sweaty? Or do they appear to be out of it, cut off from what is happening around them? There can be a hundred and one reasons why they might be acting like that – but don't write off the option that they may be a terrorist just because you're British and it's not cricket to overreact. If you are seriously concerned, get hold of a police officer, security guard or the nearest person in authority.

Don't think it will never happen to you. It is statistically *extremely* unlikely, but in recent years there have been attacks in London, Glasgow, Madrid, Bali, the Maldives, Kenya, Morocco, Turkey and Egypt, to name but a few. Nobody can guarantee to protect you from terrorist atrocities, but the one thing you can do to best protect yourself, the people around you and the society you believe in is to be alert at all times.

FURTHER INFORMATION

You can find useful information at the site of the Air Transport Users Council, **www.caa.co.uk/auc**, the Financial Ombudsman, **www.financial-ombudsman.org.uk** or that of the Civil Aviation Authority, **www.caa.co.uk**.

Take a look at the Foreign and Commonwealth Office's Before You Go campaign advice on their site at **www.fco.gov.uk/en**.

The Association of British Travel Agents are at **www.abta.com**, and the Civil Aviation Authority, which has details of ATOL, which protects you from losing your money or being stranded abroad, is at **www.caa.co.uk**.

The Citizens Advice Bureau, **www.citizensadvice.org.uk**, provides legal advice on lost luggage and insurance claims, as does Legal Claim Advice, **www.youclaim.co.uk**. Global Bag Tag, **www.globalbagtag.com**, is a service to trace lost baggage worldwide and Fly My Case, **www.flymy-case.com**, will fly your bags to your destination for a small fee.

For the EU Denied Boarding Regulation see **http://europa.eu/scadplus/leg/en/lvb/l24173.htm**.

For further information about CITES (the Convention on International Trade in Endangered Species of Wild Fauna and Flora) go to **www.cites.org**.

For restrictions on the import and export of animal- or plant-derived goods, visit the site of Department for Environment, Food and Rural Affairs at **www.defra.gov.uk** or **www.importdetails.defra.gov.uk**.

SAILING

The Royal Yachting Association website, **www.rya.org.uk/KnowledgeBase/boatingabroad/**, contains useful information and guidance, and for Maritime Piracy Reports try the International Maritime Bureau on **www.icc-ccs.org**, **www.yachtpiracy.org** or **www.noonsite.com/General/Piracy**.

GAP-YEAR ADVICE

There are many websites offering advice and information, among them **www.gogapyear.com**, **www.carolinesrainbowfoundation.org** (particularly for safety during your gap year) and **www.lucieblackmantrust.org**.

You can plan your trip online and share details with friends using **www.tripit.com**.

5

It's Not Who You Know...

THE WORLD OF ROMANCE USED TO BE SO DIFFERENT. WOMEN held the balance of power. In the eighteenth century, if a man wanted to woo the lady of his dreams, he had to visit her at her house, listen to her play the piano (no matter how excruciating), watch her do needlework, and read to her – all under the wary eye of her mother or a chaperone. The woman would decide if she wanted him to visit her again and she would choose who could take her to balls and dinners. Obviously, if a man didn't want to visit her or take her out she was a bit stuck, but if she was a reasonably attractive proposition, physically or financially, she was in the driving seat.

Courting progressed to dating as, by the early twentieth century, women started to experience life outside the home. They wanted their wooing to take place in private, away from the home and the gimlet eye of a watchful parent. The balance of power began to shift as men took control in the relationship by paying for the dinners and theatre tickets. And, now, books like *The Rules* tell us that the way to get a man is to be subordinate, not to challenge his authority and never to question his position as the alpha male.

Well, bugger that, we say.

We need to assert control over our relationships, not by becoming a caricature of a dominating harridan but by keeping our eyes open and not being afraid to question things which don't feel right. When romance sweeps us off our feet we need to make sure our brains don't fall out of our ears at the same time.

One Christmas I was staying with friends who live in a lovely farmhouse in Lincolnshire. I was with my husband, two children, our hosts' family and the other friends that came to join us. We were just over twenty in all – a real houseful – but we'd all known each other for years and got on very well and had a laugh together. There was one new addition to the group, a new boyfriend. Alice had brought him along and it was a real sign of how close they were becoming that she felt comfortable introducing him to such old friends.

From the start, I didn't take to him. I couldn't put my finger on it; there was just something about him that was a little bit creepy, not quite genuine. He was very affable and good company, and Alice was besotted with him. I'd not seen her so happy for a long time, and they were about to move in together. When he wasn't within earshot, I would ask her more about him, and it became clear that, although he claimed to be loaded thanks to a private income, he wasn't actually paying for anything, and Alice had to keep lending him cash to tide him over until he could get his money out of some kind of trust. It seems so obvious now that alarm bells should have been deafening Alice, but she was in love with him, he appeared to be in love with her and was incredibly kind and caring towards her. And not everyone in our group thought he was odd, it was mainly me that was suspicious.

But the more I heard, the more I became convinced that he was a conman. I rang an old mate who is a police officer and asked him to just check if the new boyfriend had a criminal record. It was totally against the rules – he shouldn't have done it but he helped me out as a favour. That was on the Christmas Eve. The day after Boxing Day some of us were out for a walk, and Alice and her man were back at the house. My copper mate called me on my mobile and told me that the boyfriend had done time on two separate counts of fraud and that he'd fleeced a woman in the past who'd eventually gone to the police when he upped and left with several thousand pounds of her money.

I was glad I'd found out but now I had to tell Alice. It was awful. She was furious with me, and she and her boyfriend left after a massive row. She split up with him a few days later and you'd think there might be some part of her that is grateful that I intervened. But she's never forgiven me and sadly we're no longer friends. ANNA, TUNBRIDGE WELLS

Where to start? Where do we meet new boyfriends or partners these days? One survey suggests that over 60 per cent of new relationships are formed in the workplace. Meaningful looks over the water cooler, snatched romantic moments by the photocopier, drunken abandon at the office Christmas party. The same survey found that a third of women have had sex in the workplace. *Really?* We salute your enthusiasm, stamina and ability to ignore that stapler sticking into your back.

There is a story about a bit of hanky-panky by a very

well-known television presenter at the BBC. She had finished doing a voiceover for her programme in one of the recording suites and then went on to have sex in there with one of the producers. Unbeknown to her, the microphone had been left open, so the rest of the staff could hear. We have no idea if the story is actually true but if we told you who it was, you'd be surprised, to put it mildly.

Other than the office, most of us meet prospective partners by going out to bars and clubs with friends. A few drinks, a relaxed atmosphere, a bit of a dance maybe, all combine to make it a lot easier to talk to the man you fancy in the corner by the bar.

We don't want to be killjoys but, even if things are going really well with the man you've only just met, you need to keep your wits about you. Nine times out of ten, he is putting his arm around you because he fancies you, not because he wants to slip your mobile out of your pocket *but* . . .

STAY SAFE WHILE FLIRTING

Don't get drunk. That is so BORING, we hear you cry. OK, OK. We're not saying don't have a drink, we're not even saying don't get a bit squiffy, if that helps oil the wheels of romance. But don't get paralytic. This is the first rule of successful and safe dating. Your common sense will disappear along with any instinct for self preservation. And if he does invite you back for coffee, you'll probably just fall asleep face down on his living-room floor and start snoring. Attractive.

Think about what information you're giving him. You know next to nothing about him, so what do you want him to know about you? Do you want him to know where you live? If things go pear-shaped later on, you might be very grateful that he doesn't know where to find you.

Don't leave your bag with him while you go to the loo. You wouldn't do that with anyone else you hardly knew, would you?

Watch your drink. There's little hard and fast evidence about date-rape drugs (see Chapter 2), but you should be careful about leaving your drink with someone you don't know or trust. It's easy for someone to slip a substance into your drink and you may know nothing about it until you come to hours later. Finish it before you go to the loo or dance floor. Or just leave it and order another when you get back.

Leaving with him. We might as well 'fess up now: we cannot pretend that we have abided by all the rules we are setting down here. But we are older and wiser now, so learn from our mistakes. If you spend a couple of hours getting to know someone in a pub or a bar, you're getting on really well, things are looking promising and he then suggests you leave your friends behind to go off to a club with him, what do you do? Before you set off, ask yourself if you trust this man. What kind of feeling do you have about him? Follow your instinct (which is why it helps not to be too pissed) and, if you're at all unsure, suggest an alternative that doesn't involve you going off alone with him. If you're with friends, they can look out for you; once you leave them behind, you're on your own.

I was out one evening with a couple of girlfriends. It was the usual Friday-night scene: we went to the pub near where we live for a few drinks and then got a taxi to a pub in the centre of town which stays open until the small hours. There were loads of people there, the music was good and we had some more drinks. We got chatting to some blokes who seemed like a good laugh, and one of them was pretty good-looking.

Then I got into an argument with my friends over something stupid and we had a bit of a row. I decided to go outside to get some fresh air and, while I was standing outside, the bloke I'd been talking to in the pub, the good-looking one, came out and asked if I was OK. I told him I'd had a row with my friends and that I was feeling a bit pissed off and wanted to go home. He said he'd walk with me to the nightbus stop and keep me company until the bus came. We walked off through a small alleyway and he stopped to kiss me. I was up for it and we had a bit of a snog but when he started to put his hand up my skirt, I didn't want to take it any further and pushed him away. He suddenly turned really angry with me and said I'd been leading him on, that I was stupid and ugly, and he pulled me down the alleyway and dragged me along the street by the arm. No one seemed to notice what was going on and I was too frightened to shout out. He took me to a park a couple of streets away and raped me. YVONNE, LONDON

Think about what signals you are sending. The above anecdote obviously describes the worst possible outcome of a bit of flirting in a bar, but you do need to be aware of the possible consequences of your actions. Is he mistaking your friendliness for a come-on? When you say yes to the offer of another drink, is he thinking yes, I'll definitely be getting into her knickers later on? Blokes are simple creatures and you don't want to confuse them by giving out mixed messages.

If you do decide to go home with him, remember, you are under no obligation to have sex. You can change your mind at any time – it's your body and that is your right. If he tries to force you to have sex against your will, it's rape, pure and simple.

Be prepared. You're not a slapper if you go around with condoms in your handbag. You're sensible. Unprotected sex isn't funny or clever.

MEETING PEOPLE

If scrabbling up the greasy pole is limiting the amount of free time you have available to use the usual routes to meeting a prospective mate, or if you've moved to a new area and don't know anyone, or just want to be a bit more selective when it comes to finding a new man, then you may need to take a more proactive approach. Dating is a huge business growth area and this can give you much more choice and opportunity to meet a wider range of people. It also comes with the same risks you face whenever you meet someone new – but magnified many times over.

There are all sorts of dating options out there. You can meet people online, in chatrooms, over dinner, at specially arranged weekends, for an hour or for three minutes. There is something to suit pretty much everyone looking to find that significant other. But there are major differences between the various options and it's worth knowing what they are before you embark on the road to romance. Let's start with an option that seems to have been around for ever . . .

Small Ads
Otherwise known as the lonely-hearts column, these are perennially popular if you can work your way through the acronyms WLTM, GSOH, SWF, etc. The first newspaper ads appeared in

the nineteenth century, and many newspapers and magazines have had thriving personal-ad sections for decades. They make for compulsive reading: some are brutally businesslike and some are poetic perfection. Here's a selection of a few of the most brilliant – and absurd – from *They Call Me Naughty Lola* by David Rose, editor of the *London Review of Books*.

'I've divorced better men than you. And worn more expensive shoes than these. So don't think placing this ad is the biggest comedown I've ever had to make. Sensitive F, 43.'

'Employed in publishing? Me too. Stay the hell away. Man on the inside seeks woman on the outside who likes milling around hospitals guessing the illnesses of outpatients.'

'Ploughing the loneliest furrow. Nineteen personal ads and counting. Only one reply. It was my mother telling me not to forget the bread on my way home. Man, 51.'

'My ideal woman is a man. Sorry, mother.'

'Bald, short, fat and ugly male, 53, seeks short-sighted woman with tremendous sexual appetite.'

'Romance is dead. So is my mother. Man, 42, inherited wealth.'

If you think you might end up inadvertently dating any of that lot, you need to take a few precautions.

♡   **Think about questions to ask** before speaking to them on the phone. There's not much information to be gleaned from a small ad. Are they hiding anything? Ask about their lifestyle and family – it's not unusual for married men or women to go looking for a fling, and if they start being evasive when you ask these sorts of questions it may give you an indication that they're already attached.

♡ **Think very carefully about whether you want to disclose your address when answering.** Why not just use an email address or temporary mobile number until you're sure about the person you're contacting?

♡ **Even if you don't intend to have it published, write out a small ad for yourself;** it will help you understand how difficult it is to sum up your character and what you're looking for when reading others. It should also shed some light on the decisions the writers have made as to what to include and exclude from theirs.

Speed Dating

Working on the premise that most people make up their minds as to whether they are attracted to a potential partner within the first few minutes of meeting, these organized events offer the opportunity to speak to a range of people for a restricted amount of time – generally around three minutes. You will find small companies staging these events locally, or you can access larger companies and search for events across the UK on the net. Either way, check the rules before you attend. Most reputable companies insist that no contact details are handed over during the meeting. You will generally be issued with a card to make notes on as you go round, and at the end you can express an interest in someone. If they also do the same, the company then exchanges your details on your behalf – at least that way you're not under pressure to reject or accept someone to their face. It's generally a safe environment and you're unlikely to encounter an engaged or married man, or a dodgy character, as may happen in a bar.

Introduction Agencies

These seem quaintly old-fashioned in today's world of online matchmaking, but they are the only way to be reasonably sure that the person into whose eyes you are gazing fondly (or wondering how you can make a speedy exit without hurting his feelings) is who he says he is. They will have one of two aims: to find you a new boyfriend or, more ambitiously, to find you a husband. They are the priciest option, and can vary from £20 a month to a signing-on fee of hundreds of pounds. One company we found likes to boast that Mel Gibson met his wife through a dating agency – though given his erratic behaviour in recent years, we're not sure how much of an endorsement that is. What sets reputable introduction agencies apart from the variety you find on the internet is that many of them meet every single person they put on to their dating register. That helps them weed out the weirdos and get a sense of whether the person sitting in front of them is someone they would be happy to send off on a date with a client. They also conduct some background checks as to the person's identity, address and place of work. That should stop you spending an evening with a man who claims to be a movie director when he actually works in the local garden centre. It's worth noting that no agency will conduct criminal-record checks, because of the cost and length of time involved.

Ascertain whether the dating agency you've selected is a

member of the Association of British Introduction Agencies. That will offer you some protection from poor service or being ripped off. The ABIA has a code of practice which ensures that its members have been operating for at least a year, has an office dedicated to its business rather than just a PO box number and will offer you the services of a comparable agency should yours go under. Companies not adhering to the code can be expelled from the Association. It also conducts mystery-shopper-style investigations to ensure compliance with the code, will look into complaints on your behalf and mentors new businesses to ensure good practice is adhered to from the start.

I've been running the Sarah Eden Introduction Agency for the past twenty years. We hold extensive interviews and do background checks with potential clients before taking them on, to ensure we make as honest an assessment about them as possible. You can guarantee that men will nearly always lie about their height and women about their age, but it's also worth thinking about their emotional situation. We often turn down newly separated or widowed people – it can take a long time to get over major emotional upsets, and it really isn't fair on potential new partners to try and become involved again before you're ready. **KAREN, WINDSOR**

Internet Dating Agencies

More and more people are signing up to the hundreds of new and 'free' dating sites to be found on the net. If you're tempted, what you are really getting is a place on the web where you can post your details for strangers to read and be able to contact you. Anyone can set up a dating website – literally anyone. For most people, online dating is either a positive experience or, at the very least, it's harmless and doesn't cost too much. But you should be aware that the vast majority of dating sites do not screen their members at all. So sex offenders, con artists and former criminals can join and mix in with genuine people looking for a short cut to lurve.

So, if you're going to dip a toe into the shark pool that is internet dating, there are some important things you need to consider.

Does the website display the OISP (Online Introduction Service Provider) logo? If it does, that's an encouraging sign, because it means the company behind the website has signed up to the Financial Services Authority voluntary code of practice, which offers you some measure of financial protection. For instance, they cannot sell your details on to any organization without your permission, there should be no hidden fees and there is a mechanism you can use to complain if you feel the service hasn't come up to scratch.

Have a good look at the website. Does it look professionally put together or is it poorly constructed, with missing text or misaligned sections? If it looks a bit amateurish, it gives you a clue as to the state of the agency itself. If they can't get their act together to format a decent web page, the chances are they won't be running their dating services particularly professionally either. They may not have good safety features and your credit information may not be secure.

Look at the sample profiles before you sign up. Are the people described in them just a little bit too good-looking, too successful, too athletic? Many sites (especially new ones that have just started up) pad their membership database with photos of models or random people, 'bait' – to attract new members. They may also keep the membership topped up with people who haven't used the service for months, even years, to make the website look more popular than it actually is. Some of the biggest sites will now tell you when the person you're interested in last logged on. This can at least reassure you that the person you're contacting is still looking and available, even if it cannot guarantee his reply! It can also act as a warning if that gorgeous guy who's promised himself to you is still keeping an eye on the competition in case someone better comes along.

Do any of the profiles have nonsense in them or stuff that doesn't make sense? If they do, it means the dating site hasn't screened them out so probably has no screening service at all. Get out immediately, as you are logged on to a service where anyone can say anything, no matter how offensive or obscene. On the other hand, be cautious when a company says it does offer screening. What that will almost certainly mean is that it runs a series of analytical searches on phrases or words which could have negative connotations and possibly dip-samples every few hundred entries in order to weed out any dodgy daters. And that is all. In the United States, for example, there are companies that offer specialized searches as an accompaniment to an online-dating service. This usually means they have checked that the person's birth certificate tallies with the name given and that they have a reputable credit history. But again, that's all. The bottom line is: the only person who will conduct a reliable assessment of a person's character is you, so treat all potential Romeos you meet on the web with the same caution you would if you were hooking up with a complete stranger.

Does the site have a third-party, anonymous emailing address system? Reputable sites use double-blind email addresses to safeguard people's privacy and their true email address.

Does the site have a privacy link? Look at the bottom of the site's main page. You want a site that states clearly that it does not sell your email address and personal information to anyone. Otherwise, say hello to a deluge of spam and junk mail.

Fees. There have been many complaints about websites which automatically charge customers for a full membership after a trial period whether the customer is using the service or not. Some continue to bill customers even when they have asked specifically to be taken off the register. It's up to you to read the small print and check your bank statements for anomalies.

Does the site have a rules or terms-of-use page? You should only sign up to agencies that disallow racial, hate or overtly sexual material. You should avoid sites where anything goes. They're no fun, believe us: there is some truly weird and hideous stuff out there. It may be boring reading the terms and conditions small print, but the safety of your personal information could depend on it.

Is the agency a member of the Association of British Introduction Agencies? A new code of practice is being developed by the ABIA and Office of Fair Trading specifically for online dating agencies at the time of writing, so it's worth checking if yours is a member.

Of course the big drawback of internet dating is that you can never be completely sure what you're going to get until you meet the person in person, so to speak. Check out the toe-curling experience of this man.

Daniel Anceneaux spent six months talking to the 'girl of his dreams' on a popular dating site in France. The woman even emailed him poems and love messages. 'The conversations even got a little racy a couple of times, but I really started to fall for her, because there seemed to be a sensitive side that you don't see in many girls,' said Daniel. After exchanging dozens and dozens of notes on a dating site, they decided to meet.

Daniel who was called 'The Prince of Pleasure' and his sweetheart, 'Sweet Juliette', met on a secluded beach one summer evening in France. 'I walked out on that dark beach thinking I was going to hook up with the girl of my dreams', Daniel recalls, 'and there she was, wearing white shorts and a pink tank top, just like she'd said she would. But when I got close, she turned around – and we both got the shock of our lives. I mean, I didn't know what to say. All I could think was, 'Oh my God! It's Mother!'

And then it got worse. A local policeman noticed they were on the isolated beach and questioned them, and they blurted out the whole story. A local newspaper picked up the tale and then it was all over the news nationwide. 'People started pointing and laughing at us on the street – and they haven't stopped laughing since,' said a dismayed Daniel. In the days following the rendezvous, Daniel confessed he just didn't know what to say to his mother. 'The embarrassment was overwhelming for both of us. That is the last time I use the internet for dating.' FIONA

It's a good idea to ask to see your prospective date's picture before you actually set out to meet him. Even if he doesn't turn out to be a relative he could still be your boss/colleague/ex-husband . . .

───────────────── ONLINE SCAMMERS ─────────────────
Scammers can sign up to online dating agencies just like anyone else but will create a false profile. They will say they are seeking romance but they are actually seeking your cash. They can take

advantage of the anonymity of the internet to create the profile of your perfect match and make any number of promises to attract you and bring your defences down. The sure-fire way to know if you are being scammed is if you are asked for money. It may not happen straight away, but as soon as it does you should be on your guard. Scammers will ask for financial help for a whole variety of reasons and will almost always ask you to send them money using a method such as telegraphic transfer. Here, the money is transferred between accounts electronically and shows as cleared funds immediately. This means it can be withdrawn the same day. Some of the most common reasons a scammer will ask for the money are:

- I want to see you but I don't have enough money to travel.
- I've been robbed/beaten and my wallet stolen.
- I need urgent surgery.
- My mother/father/sister (you get the idea) is seriously ill and I can't afford the medical bills.

And on it goes. You need to ask yourself: why does this person claim that you are the only person who can help him when you've only just met? If you do send them money, you have very little chance of ever getting it back. If you are scammed, report it to the dating or chatroom site where you met the person.

YOUR FIRST DATE

For all dating, there are some obvious dos and don'ts when it comes to that crucial first meeting.

DO

♡ **Check him out first on Facebook,** Friends Reunited or any of those social internet websites. It might help you to research his background and find out more about his life and his interests. And it may give you a chance to double-check that he is who he claims to be.

♡ **Meet in a public place** where there are other people around.

♡ **Get together for a quick drink or a coffee** rather than a whole evening or a meal. There's nothing worse than being stuck with someone for hours when you know on sight that his comb-over is never going to grow on you.

♡ **Stay sober.** We're beginning to sound like a broken record on this one, but you know it makes sense. How are you going to work out if this man is right for you and trustworthy if you can't string a coherent sentence together?

♡ **Listen to your instincts.** If there's something odd about him but you just can't put your finger on it, don't think you're being paranoid. If he can only meet you at strange times or talks in hushed tones on the phone or has 'to go all of a sudden', he may not be quite as single as he makes out. If you can never call him at his place of work, maybe that's because he doesn't have one. You have to make a judgement about someone very quickly in a pretty artificial situation, so if something isn't right, move on.

♡ **Tell a friend or member of your family** that you are meeting someone and let them know where your meeting is taking place and when you expect to be back. You can always get them to

ring or text you with an 'escape' message after half an hour –
just in case!

♡ **Get as many details about the person as you can.** You're not
being nosy; it's what this kind of dating is all about. When it
comes to your personal safety, you have a right to snoop. Find
out as much as possible.

DON'T

♡ **Meet somewhere private or isolated, at his house or at
yours.** You know next to nothing about this man, and if he
doesn't instantly understand the importance of meeting in a
public place, then he's either a moron or of dubious intent.
Either way, he's not for you.

♡ **Lend him money.** Beware of someone who mentions how
broke he is. Be cautious if he mentions that he's just lost his
job or been the victim of some kind of scam. It's quite likely that
you soon will be too.

♡ **Give him your address.** If things are going well, give him your
phone number, but be very careful not to let him know where
you live until you know him better.

♡ **Let him give you a lift or even offer to give him a lift home.**
Arrange your own transport to and from the meeting so that
there's no uncertainty.

♡ **Take him back to your place.** If you're sticking to the game
plan of first meeting up for a quick coffee or a drink, then it
should be easy to make your excuses and leave. If you feel in
any way pressured to take him home, alarms bells should start

ringing in your head and you need to get away from him. Be especially careful about taking someone back to yours if you live on your own.

MEETING PEOPLE ONLINE

Chatrooms

An internet chatroom is just a virtual space where you can meet up with other people on the net. Users log in and type in messages which appear either in public (where the message can be seen by everyone in the chatroom) or through a private message that is seen only by the other person to whom you are directly chatting. It can be a bit more hi-tech than that, with users chatting via voice messaging and talking in real time through a microphone or chatting via video link and webcam. You can end up having conversations with people from all over the world.

The pitfalls are pretty obvious. There is a well known but probably apocryphal statistic that 70 per cent of people talking in chatrooms claim to be women but 70 per cent of users of chatrooms are actually men. One of the joys of a chatroom is that you can be whoever you want to be. The drawback is that you have no idea who you are really talking to. There is no way of verifying the authenticity of the other people in the room. For most people it's safe and harmless fun, but the stories of paedophiles using chatrooms to groom unsuspecting children are real.

You will learn a lot about a chatroom by watching the flow of conversation. Look for how friendly it is and what the topics of debate are. You'll soon be able to pinpoint identifiable characters – the one who's rude, the one who's more thoughtful or the one who makes jokes.

Don't use your real name; it really is OK to remain anonymous, unless you're happy for someone to find your life history from Facebook or Google. It's easy to link your name to an address and other personal details. Don't give out your email address, as that will also reveal more personal information. The less you say about yourself, the easier it is to keep your privacy. Every detail you give about yourself is a part of a puzzle that can be put together to form a clearer picture of who you are.

And watch out for the chatroom users who like to talk dirty. It might be tempting to indulge in a bit of filth and live out your fantasies behind a cloak of anonymity, but there have been reports of stalkers tracking down the whereabouts of someone they had an encounter with online.

Social Networking Sites

It's almost unbelievable to think that in just a few short years we have gone from having groups of friends gathered over years from school, work or the local neighbourhood whom we chat to on the phone and meet up with in clubs and bars to joining a network of millions just by sitting at our computers. Social networking sites such as Facebook, Bebo, MySpace and many others have, over recent years, exploded big time on the net, with registered users of up to 100,000,000 in some cases. Initially, it was a case of friends from schools, colleges or universities posting details of their lives to keep in touch with each other. Then they started linking up with others who had similar interests, but, nowadays, the list of things you can do on these sites is growing constantly and becoming ever more sophisticated –

blogging, chatrooms, discussion forums and photo albums, as well as the original use of swapping contact details with other users.

It is also worth remembering that these sites don't charge, so they have to earn money somehow. Your published personal data enables marketing companies and advertisers to gather data and focus campaigns on you, earning site owners millions.

We're sure that, around the world, there are academics, writers and journalists studying and agonizing over why this phenomenon has happened and whether it is the beginning of the end of life as we know it. But for many, this advance in socializing is exciting and liberating, and we're not about to try and dissuade anyone from taking part. However, we are, like many others, really concerned about the level of personal detail being posted. Because we're sitting in our own homes when we use these sites, we automatically feel lulled into a false sense of security and therefore have a tendency to reveal information to people which, if we'd just bumped into them in the street or even at a party, we wouldn't dream of doing. It's also easy to forget that the saucy pictures you're posting to show your friends how you've lost weight for your hols can also be accessed by that creepy pervert who lives in the next street, town or country.

And another word of warning: be careful when including your web address on your CV. A PA included her MySpace address on the CV she sent to a publisher in Scotland. When her potential employer looked at her profile they found the following illuminating information: 'I am the worst secretary in the world,' it read. 'I am a technological retard.' She didn't get the job, needless to say, and when we looked at the photos and comments posted on some profiles, we cringed to think that potential employers may use these sites as research for future employees.

Or what about these real-life stories?

A Texan driver was prosecuted after a fatal accident and arrived in court to find his MySpace posting – 'I'm not an alcoholic, I'm a drunkaholic' – used as part of the prosecution case.

Nineteen Northampton police officers are being investigated for comments found on Facebook after they posted messages of support for a colleague being investigated after a collision with a suspected burglar. Comments like 'Keep smiling, mate, you're a good hard-working copper' were deemed inappropriate while the investigation was ongoing.

A bank employee told colleagues he had to leave early because of a 'family emergency', but his Facebook page featured photos of him in drag at a Halloween party.

The Lawn Tennis Association suspended two gifted junior tennis champions after pictures of them partying and drinking were found on Bebo, together with comments that they liked to 'eat junk food and party hard'. One photo pictured the woman at a nightclub with her legs wrapped around a vending machine.

A recent survey said that 62 per cent of employers check Bebo, MySpace and Facebook for job applicants and that 25 per cent of those rejected the candidates for reasons such as excessive drinking, ethics and disrespect for the job.

The Information Commissioner's Office research states that 4.5 million web users between the ages of fourteen and twenty-one are leaving themselves open to ID fraud because of the relaxed way they disclose personal information on the internet, particularly on social networking sites. Two-thirds posted their date of birth, a quarter their job title and one in ten their home address. If you combine these bits of information with other disclosed details, such as the name of a pet, sibling and even their mother's maiden name in some cases, a fraudster has sufficient info to make an informed guess at your passwords and go shopping on your behalf, or even access bank and online accounts. More info is available from the Information Commissioner's website, www.ico.gov.uk/youngpeople, but remember their motto: 'If you don't think you'll want it to exist somewhere in ten years' time – don't post it.'

Here are our top tips for successful and safe online social networking:

♡ **Before you select a site, think about what you want from it.** Choose one which offers privacy and security options and restricts access to 'known' or trusted friends. Levels of privacy can vary from 'none' to 'restricted' to just one known group.

♡ **Read the privacy and safety tips published on each site** before deciding. For example, MySpace uses filtering software, and staff check for obscene photo posting, underage contributors and sexual predators, but it's unlikely that any of these checks will protect you from conmen and fraudsters.

♡ **Think very carefully about the implications** of your personal information and photos reaching a wider audience *before* posting. And speak to your 'friends' about what they are posting as well – there's no point in you vetting everything you post only to discover your best mate has published pics of you taking part in a wet T-shirt competition.

♡ **Remember that once the information is out there, you leave an 'electronic footprint' for the future.** While it may be a laugh to post naked or drunken pictures of yourself on holiday, when you go for that high-powered executive position a few years later, it may come back to haunt you. Some networking site users have already had difficulty in deleting their accounts.

♡ **Once you're logged on, be wary of making new friends too quickly.** Trust your instincts: if someone is coming on too strong, asking unusual questions or just doesn't feel right, don't get sucked into a relationship, albeit an electronic one, because you feel obliged to. Be firm. Conmen and fraudsters can be very persuasive and will try all sorts of psychological tricks to get you to disclose information. It is best not to accept anyone as a 'friend' on to your entry if you don't already know them.

♡ **Finally, remember you'll never feel lonely again if you give out your name,** address, phone number and email address – apart from setting yourself up as the perfect identity-fraud victim, you'll probably enjoy cold calls from call centres, spam messages, and junk mail by the ton.

STALKING

How would you describe your average stalker? A loner, a weirdo, an obsessive and someone you hardly know or don't know at all? Think again: women are much more likely to be stalked by a former partner than by some stranger off the street. There have been over 4,000 prosecutions each year under the Protection from Harassment Act since it was passed in 1997. And it's not just celebrities who get stalked; most cases involve ordinary people. Fiona has had unwanted attention from time to time as a result of her work on television – most notably from a man she'd never met before who turned up at BBC Television Centre claiming to be the father of her children – but thankfully nothing too serious or threatening.

Stalking is defined as a pattern of behaviours in which an individual inflicts upon another repeated unwanted intrusions and communications. The motives are complex, but most commonly it starts as a result of rejection, which causes the stalker to seek revenge and to become obsessed by his former partner. He or she will bombard their victim with emails, gifts, messages or abuse. He can persistently try to communicate via the phone or through letters and cards, or he may order gifts and services on his victim's behalf. It can go on for months or years and increase in intensity over time. The majority of stalkers do not physically hurt the object of their obsession, but even apparently harmless behaviour, such as following someone down the street or sending them flowers, can be intimidating if it is persistently inflicted on a person against their will. It is a problem that the police used to regard as a social issue which, while irritating to the victim, was not putting them in actual danger and therefore not worth much police time and effort. Not any longer. The police now take stalking very seriously – although that's not to say they always get it right.

In September 2005, in the glamorous London department store Harvey Nichols, a beauty consultant was shot dead by her former boyfriend. Clare Bernal was twenty-two years old and had had a brief relationship with Michael Pech, a former security guard at the store. When Clare broke off the relationship, Pech refused to accept it was over between them. He bombarded her with thirty text messages a day, watched her at work and followed her back to her home. On one occasion, when Clare spotted him in a tube carriage, she told him she would report him to the police if he didn't leave her alone. Eventually, Clare did go to the police, but Pech was classed as low risk. A brief timeline of his campaign of intimidation shows the threat he really posed.

28 February: Clare ended her relationship with Pech
5 April: Clare made a formal complaint to the police about Pech
6 April: Pech was arrested and released on conditional bail
10 April: Pech was arrested after breaking bail conditions by approaching Clare
11 April: Pech was charged with harassment and remanded in custody
19 April: Pech was released on conditional bail
31 August: Pech admitted harassment and was bailed pending sentencing
13 September: Pech killed Clare and then shot himself

When the inquest took place into Clare's death, a number of errors emerged in the way her case had been handled. For example, the lawyers for the Crown Prosecution Service didn't oppose bail for Pech on 19 April because they wrongly thought he didn't know Clare's new address. And, due to an 'administrative error', Pech was charged with harassment rather than making threats to kill. But above all, what the tragic case of Clare Bernal and Michael Pech illustrates is how hard it can be to protect yourself from a persistent and vengeful stalker. But, let us repeat, most stalkers cause psychological distress but not physical harm, although this is not to belittle the impact of a stalker on his or her victim. They can cause immense mental anguish and suffering to the victim and his or her family.

If you think you are being stalked, here's what to do:

♡ **Do not react to or communicate with your stalker.** Do not agree to meet him or talk to him. Asking him to stop won't necessarily make any difference; it is a form of communication, which is what he wants above all.

♡ **Contact the police and try to get it stopped** as soon as possible. Research has shown that the longer a stalker is able to carry on, the harder it is to get him to stop. Make sure you get the name of the officer dealing with your case, and a crime-reference number, if applicable. In the first instance they may just give him a warning, which often nips the behaviour in the bud.

♡ **Make friends, family and neighbours aware** of what is going on. They can be your eyes and ears and keep a record of any suspicious sightings and incidents. And they can support and help you.

♡ **Review your home security** (see Chapter 1) and update it if necessary.

♡ **Keep your mobile phone and a personal-attack alarm on you** at all times when you go out.

♡ **Rely on your instinct.** If you ever feel in imminent danger, call 999.

♡ **Record all the incidents** in which you come into contact with the stalker, including gifts, phone calls, emails, etc. Take photographs or use a video camera if you have one.

PHONE CALLS

If you are called by the stalker, do not have a conversation with him. No matter how tempting to yell or scream down the phone, don't do it. Try not to show any emotion, just put the handset to one side and walk away for a few minutes. Make a note of the time and date of the call as well as anything that was said by the caller. Then come back and replace the receiver, but don't be tempted to have a quick listen to see if he is still there. If he knows you are likely to come back and do that, he'll feel you have rewarded him for waiting, and all you do is give him an incentive to hang on the phone to try to have another go at talking to you. Record any calls that are silent too. Try dialling 1471 for the caller's number and note it down. Contact your phone service provider, because they should have procedures to follow in the event of nuisance calls. They may be able to put a trace on your line so that all calls to your number will be listed. Use your answer machine to screen unwanted calls. If you receive calls or texts on your mobile phone, don't tamper with or dispose of your SIM card; it may contain valuable evidence.

SIGHTINGS

Record dates, times and locations. Descriptions of what the stalker was wearing and what he was carrying will be useful too.

CARS

If you are aware of a particular car, note the date, time, and location, model of the car, colour, registration number and any other distinguishing features.

MAIL

Record any mail that is delivered to you from the stalker. If you are wary of opening it, give it straight to the police or put gloves on to open it to avoid putting your fingerprints on it.

COMPUTERS

Save information received on to a disk and print out a hard copy for the police. Do not delete the original. Only open emails if you know who sent them and make sure your computer virus protection is secure and up to date. It is possible for the police to trace a stalker through the internet; they can contact the sender's internet service provider and have the message traced on their records.

DIARY

Keep a daily record of events and how you are feeling about them. If you get to the point of needing to bring a prosecution, this will help the police investigation, not only in terms of gathering evidence but also to show the impact of the stalker's behaviour on you.

I have recently been advising on a case in which a lady called Jayne, a music student aged twenty-five living temporarily in Birmingham, had met a man through an internet dating site. They exchanged messages for a while and eventually agreed to meet. On the first meeting, at a café, the man, called Alfie, showed interest in her love of music and said he would like to hear her play the flute, as she specialized in wind instruments. Jayne took him back to her flat, which she shared with another female student, who was out at the time. Alfie's behaviour started to become weird and Jayne eventually got him to leave, but that took some persuading and she told him there would be no further meetings.

The next day, however, she received a number of texts from him (she had given him her mobile number) asking to see her again, and Jayne thought it would be a good idea to meet him and make her position clear. The meeting went ahead with Jayne strongly making the point that she wanted nothing more to do with him. This prompted a barrage of text messages over the next two weeks from Alfie, thanking her for arranging the meeting and asking if they could get together again.

Jayne, who was now staying with her parents in Newcastle and also playing locally with an orchestra in a concert, ignored these messages. She had, however, told Alfie about the concert, and on the first night thirty bouquets of flowers were delivered for her. Jayne was also told that a man answering Alfie's description had been making enquiries about her. Jayne was now very concerned and, when she told me the circumstances, she started off by saying it was all her fault that she had been through an internet dating site. Jayne went on, almost apologetically, to say she was a very busy person and thought this would have been a quick way to find someone. Obviously, it wasn't her fault at all. HAMISH BROWN, MBE, LAW ENFORCEMENT CONSULTANT AND STALKING EXPERT

Your Rights

The Protection from Harassment Act 1997 created an offence of what it calls 'unsocial conduct', where on at least two occasions, a person is subjected to persistent and often obsessive behaviour causing harassment, alarm or distress outside existing civil or criminal law. The two occasions do not need to be the same incident – for example, one could be a phone call, the other could be a visit. But they need to be reasonably close together in time.

A police warning might be enough to stop the harassment but the police do have the power to make an arrest straight away if necessary. They can also pursue the option of a restraining order. If you don't want to go through the police, you can take out a civil injunction to stop the stalker approaching you, though you'll have to pay for it. Breaching a restraining order or an injunction is an arrestable offence and those who do it are liable to up to five years' imprisonment. If you go to your local county court they will advise you on exactly what you need to do. To get an injunction yourself will cost about £150. Getting a solicitor to assist you can be expensive, but if you're on a low income, help is available, and often the first half-hour consultation is free.

You can also take action against a stalker under the Telecommunications Act (it is an offence to make indecent, offensive or threatening calls) or the Malicious Communications Act, whereby it is an offence to send indecent or threatening electronic communications to another person. So there are other options.

Remember: you don't have to put up with stalking. You're not lucky to have a man who is obsessively in love with you, sends you flowers and gifts and follows you around – not if he's doing it against your will. And the sooner you try to stop it, the more likely you are to succeed.

The victims of stalking that I've come across in the past always tend to have several things in common. Firstly, they feel embarrassed about reporting it – this tends to be because in isolation the events can seem quite trivial when related to someone else. They also often feel they are responsible for the stalker's behaviour – they brought it on themselves in some way – and, finally, it's not unusual for them to feel sorry for the stalker and they aren't convinced that involving the police is necessary or what he deserves – despite the fact that the stalker has brought this on him-, or in some cases, herself.

One of the key questions to ask someone who you think may be the victim of stalking is: 'What has changed in your life since this started?' Quite often the answer will be something like 'I no longer go to that shopping centre,' 'I'm thinking of moving house/job,' 'I don't feel like going out in the evenings these days.' If their life has been altered like this because of someone else's behaviour, then the warning bells should be ringing loudly. Please give them plenty of encouragement and support. JACQUI

Cyberstalking

Sadly, while the web has provided the facilities and opportunities to reach out and communicate in ways never thought possible just a few years ago, with every great innovation comes a down-side. Cyberstalking and cyberbullying are two of them. The main reason we are so emphatic about you being careful about putting your personal details on the net is because it is a gift to people already predisposed to stalking. At least if someone is hanging around, sending you notes and presents or calling you on the phone, you generally know when it's them. On the net when you're in a chatroom or exchanging messages through social networking sites, it's much easier for them to change identities, so if one tack doesn't work with you, they can just change their name or profile and try another. Before you know it, you have let slip bits of information in different places which a stalker can piece together and use to track you down.

There was a case recently where a woman wrote in her blog that she was to be a bridesmaid at a friend's wedding. A quick look through her profile list of friends narrowed down which friend was the one who was getting married, and guess who turned up at the wedding? It's also easy to let slip where you work. You may be really careful about not putting your address out there, but saying I can't go out on Friday night because I'm doing a shift at the White Lion in Muswell Hill is a bit of a gift to a stalker.

We feel strongly that no one should be put off using the internet for chatting, making friends or dating – it's a wonderful, exciting resource. Plus, for all our warnings, there are plenty of lovely stories about lives being enhanced and liberated as a result of this phenomenon. But, as with all our advice, please *take control of your own safety* and think carefully before meeting up with anyone you encounter online.

MOVING IN TOGETHER

So you've met that Jake Gyllenhaal lookalike, with the brilliant job, gorgeous car and exciting interests, what's the next step? Well, some of the above must have worked if you've reached the point where you want to shack up together. Congratulations! How exciting. So you're ready to see him in all his living-together glory. Are you ready for this?

Personal hygiene: cutting his toenails, examining his nose hair, leaving floaters in the loo, wearing his boxers two days in a row (inside out on the second day).

Around the house: leaving dirty clothes on the floor, leaving his jackets to pile up on the banister, feeling smug and virtuous after washing up but never actually putting the dishes away, believing he's done half the housework when he's flicked a duster around for five minutes.

We don't want to rain on anyone's romance but, even though you really believe you love this man, now is not the moment to throw all caution to the wind. No matter how committed you both are to making it last, no matter how much you trust each other, there are certain aspects of your life that you should keep separate in the early years. And if you should split up, you want to be sure that you can disentangle your affairs relatively easily. The most civilized of break-ups can end in acrimony when arguments surface about money and possessions.

Luke and I moved in together after we'd been going out for about six months – or rather he moved in with me. He had a well-paid job in the City; I worked for the local council. He had a flash car and used to take me to the best restaurants in London. He took me on amazing holidays too. I really loved him and trusted him absolutely. He was always too busy to work out where we would go on holidays, so I would look around on the internet and, when I found something, he would tell me to book it on my credit card and then he'd give me the money when the bill came through. And sometimes he did pay up – but often he just wouldn't have the cash on him or he'd be waiting for his bonus to come through. I ended up paying for a lot of the restaurants too. It sounds so stupid, looking back on it now, but he was such a lovely person and was so kind to me in other ways that it didn't occur to me that there was a problem.

After about eighteen months he told me he no longer wanted to go out with me and that he was going to move out. I was devastated as I hadn't seen it coming at all. About a month later I rang him about my credit-card bill, which now totalled about £20,000. I knew he earned way more than me and never suspected he'd have a problem paying. But he told me he didn't have the money and that I'd have to sort out the bill myself. I couldn't believe it. And when I rang the credit-card company, they didn't want to know; they said that since the debt had been run up on a credit card in my name, I would have to pay. I feel such a fool for letting myself be conned like that, though even now I still can't quite believe that he was fleecing me all along. MARIA, HERTFORDSHIRE

Money

Talk about your attitudes to money. It's not unromantic; it's important to have a similar outlook. If he's a generous, impulsive spender and you like to hoard and account for every last penny, you might end up having more than a few differences of opinion.

- ♡ **Ask him if he has any outstanding loans.** They will be a key indicator of his ability to live within his means and of what he can afford from now on.

- ♡ **Make an inventory.** Start out by making a list of what belongs to whom. You don't want to be rowing about the CD collection.

- ♡ **Buy big items separately.** For example, let him buy the washing machine, you buy the tumble-drier.

- ♡ **If you need to take loans out, for a car or an expensive item for the home, do it separately.** If you can't afford to pay it off on your own, make sure you have a get-out clause in the loan contract and can return the item without penalty if your circumstances should change.

I had been going out with John for five years, since I was sixteen. He was my first boyfriend and we got engaged when we were both twenty-one. We moved out of our parents' houses and started renting a flat together. We couldn't afford much and it was small and not in the nicest of areas, but it was ours and we felt like we were setting out on the start of our new life together. When we wanted a car, it seemed the most natural thing to buy it together. John already had a loan and couldn't get another one, so I bought a car on hire purchase from a well-known national car firm. There was 0 per cent finance for the first six months, and after that the monthly payments weren't too bad, as long as were both contributing. The lease ran for five years and, since we intended to be together for the rest of our lives, I wasn't worried about it. But after two years we split up. Although we were both very sad, we managed to stay reasonably good friends. For the first few months John kept up his payments for the car. But then he told me he couldn't afford it any longer and that I'd have to pay for it on my own or give the car back. The trouble was, the lease had another three years to run, and there was no way my salary was going to stretch to those monthly payments. I couldn't give the car back because I couldn't afford the financial penalty either. In the end I had to take out a five-year loan to cover the payments and ended up paying the value of that car several times over.
SARAH, ESSEX

♡ **Don't have a joint account.** It might sound loved up and homey but there's no real need for one. When it comes to the household bills, work out who is going to pay for what and take the money out of your individual accounts.

♡ **Share payments equally.** You don't need to be pernickety about it, accounting for everything down to the last tea bag, but make sure that you're splitting your costs of living roughly equally. Or, if you have very different salaries, share the costs depending on the ability of each to pay.

Don't Lose Contact with Your Friends

We all know people who've got so loved up with their new man they've lost touch with their old friends. But a good girlfriend is for life. No matter how brilliantly you are getting on with your man, who else can really understand your obsession with Daniel Craig, handbags or gossip mags? And she will be there to pick up the pieces if your relationship starts to turn sour or difficult.

DOMESTIC VIOLENCE

When we thought about writing this book, the one thing we were adamant about is that we wanted to put crime into the right perspective. The news and the papers are full of stories about crime and increase our fear of it out of all proportion to how likely we are to be affected by it. Most of us will not experience a serious crime directly against our person or by physical violence against us, despite what we read in the headlines. But when it comes to domestic violence, the chances of it happening are far more common than most women think. The figures speak for themselves. One in four women in the UK are hit, beaten or terrorized by a current or ex-partner at some point in their life. Two women a week die because of it.

According to the World Health Organization, for women aged between fifteen and forty-four across the world, domestic violence is the leading cause of death – responsible for more than cancer, war or motor-vehicle accidents.

Domestic violence can take many forms. Physical abuse can range from a slap or shove to a black eye, burn or broken bone. In the most extreme cases it can result in death. It doesn't always leave scars; having your hair pulled or things thrown at you is physical abuse too.

Many women experience domestic violence without ever being physically abused. Sometimes they're not sure if what is happening to them is domestic violence. They worry that no one will take them seriously if they complain about it. If you find yourself altering your behaviour because you are frightened of how your partner will react, you are being emotionally abused. Your home should be your sanctuary – fear has no place in it.

Your partner should not force you or use threats to make you have sex. He should not make you perform sexual acts with which you are uncomfortable and he should not criticize your performance.

Louise and I had been friends since we were at school. She was always such a laugh – the one playing the loudest music, the one who would take the wildest dare. We bought our first flat together and became very close. We told each other everything – or so I thought. Eventually, we sold the flat when Louise fell in love with a man called Mark and moved in with him. I was never particularly keen on him; he seemed a bit humourless and didn't seem to treat her very well. I was astonished when she told me they were getting married. I remember thinking that it was a mistake but that there was no point in telling her so because she'd obviously already made her mind up.

The day of their wedding, Mark's behaviour to Louise changed. As they left the reception in their car with all the tin cans trailing merrily behind it, Mark started shouting at Louise, telling her she looked ugly in her hat and that she was stupid. Louise was devastated – not only was it their wedding day, but no one had ever talked to her like that before. The months that followed were very difficult. Louise would tell me that people should warn newly-weds about how difficult married life can be, but would never be specific about what was going on within her own marriage. She went on to set up a successful PR company and, on the face of it, was doing really well in life.

It wasn't until she had been married for several years that she told me that Mark was abusing her. That he would kick her, shout terrible obscenities at her, throw things at her, push and shove her. I couldn't believe what I was hearing – and I was horrified that she had waited so long to tell me. She told me how she had tried to resign herself to it. She would think, 'As long as he throws things at the wall but not actually at me, it's OK.' Then he would throw a cup or a plate at her head and she would think, 'As long as it misses, it's OK.' Then one of Mark's missiles would finally make contact and she would think, 'As long as he only aims at me and not at the children, it's OK.' And that's how she put up with it for so long.

He controlled their finances, even though she was the bread-winner. She lived in terror of trips to the supermarket, because if she even bought a duster that wasn't on the list, she knew there'd be trouble when she got home. Most of the time she believed it was her fault, that if she could only learn how to deal with it better she would be able to stop it. She lost all sense of what a decent and loving relationship is like. When she saw me having a minor disagreement with my husband, she was surprised when it didn't escalate into a full-blown row and fisticuffs.

She left Mark several times and came to stay with me – but then she would go back. It's hard to say what the final catalyst was that pushed Louise to leave him for good. I think when she opened her eyes to the effect it was having on her two children, she realized that, for their sake, she had to end it. The day Louise told me she was getting a divorce was one of the best days of my life. FIONA

It's not always easy for women to realize that they are a victim of domestic violence. If you're having the living daylights beaten out of you, it's pretty obvious. But women who are constantly belittled or dominated by their partner can lose all sense of perspective; they may think that the problem lies with them and not the abusive man they're sharing their life with. If you have ever wondered if your relationship is a violent or abusive one and whether you need help, take a look at this checklist. Do any of these apply to you?

✦ Are you afraid of your partner?

✦ Do you feel isolated? Does he cut you off from family and friends?

✦ Is he jealous and possessive?

✦ Does he humiliate you or insult you?

✦ Does he say abusive or threatening things to you?

- Does he say you are useless and couldn't cope without him?

- Has he threatened to hurt you or people close to you?

- Does he constantly criticize you?

- Does he have sudden changes of mood which dominate the household?

- Is he charming one minute, abusive the next?

- Does he control your money?

- Do you feel dominated and controlled?

- Do you change your behaviour to avoid triggering an attack?

- Are you unsure of your own judgement?

Who Does It Happen to?

Domestic violence can happen to anyone. It is a myth that it only happens to people who are 'lower class', or to women who are weak or somehow invite it upon themselves. It strikes at the heart of relationships and families of all types and social class. And it's not always easy to see from the outside. A common syndrome is that the man can seem charming and extrovert in public but, behind closed doors, he can change into a very frightening character.

> It is very difficult to say that there are any warning signs before embarking on a relationship which could turn violent. I didn't see any signs, other than perhaps that he was like my mother and very controlling – but when you have been brought up in that atmosphere, then you don't see the same pattern in someone new, you

just accept or believe that that is how relationships work. It was after we had married that I found myself being the puppet in the middle of two very controlling people, which took away my confidence, as I was unable to please both and was constantly put in a position where I had to choose. I either upset my mother or my husband, and when he felt I was not backing him, he would become violent.

Once in that situation, you don't want to admit what is going on either to your mum or to others; by admitting it, you feel worthless and feeble. If there are children involved, it makes the situation worse. Had I been without children, I may have decided to call it a day much earlier on, but there is always the conflict of whether it is fair to deprive your children of a father, just because you are too weak to deal with the situation.

In my case, my husband was regarded, outside the home, as a loving and attentive father and the life and soul of the party. Although I did confide in a close friend, I was not believed. My daughter was daddy's little girl and they idolized one another so, rather than be cruel to the children, which is how I saw it at the time, I decided to put up with the problems and to do everything I could to be the perfect wife and mother.

Although there were several times when I tried to leave my husband, he was always so very sorry and would demonstrate his regret in really positive and romantic ways, which again is controlling, as he was able to manipulate me into believing that if I hadn't done this or that, then everything would be OK.

Eventually, after thirteen years, I went to a solicitor, who wrote to my husband saying that if he was ever violent to me again, then divorce proceedings would be started. For about five years after that letter, I have to admit that things improved, as the physical violence stopped, although the controlling of the mind was still there. But when I went to the solicitor I made a promise to myself that, no matter what, if he hit me again, I would follow through with a divorce. Well, five years later it happened. It wasn't as violent as before, but I had made that decision and had to keep to it, or I would be allowing him to treat me badly yet again and when would it stop?

Somehow, I found the courage to leave but, as the children were then sixteen and seventeen, I had to let them make their own decision as to what they wanted to do. At first they both wanted to leave as well, but my husband soon found ways to manipulate them and eventually got them to feel sorry for him. He told them he hadn't meant to be violent, that he would go to anger-management classes and really try to be a good father. I nearly went back, but I had heard it all before and finally found the strength to keep my promise to myself.

Once we had sold the house, the children came back to live with me. I think that was the hardest time. Before, I had felt that my husband had only been hurting me, as he had never struck me in front of the children, but that was when I learned how damaged they both were. And that is what really hurt. All those years, I had thought I was doing the right thing for my children, only to find that in fact I had not done the right thing. I thought I had always put the children first, but when talking to them after the break-up I actually found out that they hated me for staying with him. I felt physically sick when I realized this, and it has taken me many years to overcome the guilt I felt.

It took my daughter fourteen years and many, many hours of talking with her, never running her father down, for her to see that perhaps I had made wrong decisions but that I had made them believing I was making the right ones. My son was never as open with me about his feelings, and it has been hard for him, as I don't think he felt he could talk to anyone. They both had counselling, but I cannot say that it helped them much. The only good thing is that brother and sister became very close during this time and really are now the very best of friends.

You never know if the decision you are taking is right and, even to this day, when I see families who have had hard times but have stuck it out, I do wonder if he would have stopped being violent as he got older. Perhaps we could have become a close family and enjoyed being together as our children grew up into adulthood, married and had children themselves. When you divorce for whatever reason, you lose your history, and I believe the children lose theirs as well, and if that history spans eighteen years, then that is a lot of life to lose. You lose your friends, especially if your partner has always been regarded as a wonderful person outside the home. No one believes you because, so many of those years, you have been hiding the truth from them.

So what would my advice be? If you find yourself in a situation with a violent husband, don't hang around. Be up front with everyone and don't try to hide the fact that you are being abused. Don't live a lie. Don't feel ashamed. Remember that, no matter what you do, you do not deserve to be treated badly. Men who abuse their wives are either physically or mentally weak. They have little intelligence in understanding other human beings. The longer you stay, the harder it gets and you have so much more to lose. But, more than anything, don't leave believing that this is how you will be treated in the future if you find another partner. I met and married a wonderful man eight years later, and I have had fifteen of the most wonderful years with him. We have few material things and are not wealthy in that way, but I feel so rich. I have complete contentment in my life and now I also have two well-adjusted adult children who have both found their own way in life and are doing very nicely. There can always be a light even at the end of a very long tunnel. CHRISTINE, HAMPSHIRE

Know Your Rights

If you are a victim of domestic violence or suspect that you are in a relationship which is heading down that road, remember one thing: *it is not your fault.* Your partner has taken a decision to act in this way, he could stop it if he wanted to – but you alone cannot. It is not up to you to try to sort his problems out; it is up to him. Your only responsibility is to keep yourself safe – and your children, if you have any.

It is your right to live safely in your home, to be respected and to be treated kindly and with consideration. And, let's face it, that's no more than you would say for a pet, so it's not exactly much to ask. If you're not getting that, then you are in the wrong relationship.

The law regarding domestic violence changed a few years back, so the police can now prosecute an abuser even if his partner does not want – or is too frightened – to give evidence. It makes the police's job a lot easier if you do help them with details of the violence, but they can still act without you. Keep details of abusive incidents, including times, dates, names, what was said and what injuries were inflicted.

You can get an injunction from the courts to stop your partner using or threatening violence against you, or pestering, intimidating or harassing you. It is a criminal offence to breach the injunction and so the police can arrest him immediately if he does. Feedback from people who've used injunctions is generally very positive, with most noticing an immediate improvement in the abuser's behaviour. By obtaining the injunction they have managed to shift the balance of power from the abuser to the victim. It is also a very public statement that the authorities believe her story over his and that his behaviour is wrong.

Keeping Yourself Safe
If you are still living with your abusive partner, think about how to protect yourself (and your children).

- Be ready to call 999 if you are in danger.

- Keep some money and a set of keys in a safe place. You could leave them with a friend if you don't think there is anywhere you can hide them in your own home.

- Find out about your legal and housing rights through a solicitor or your local Citizen's Advice Bureau.

- Keep copies of important documents (passports, birth and/or marriage certificates and court orders) in a safe place.

- Investigate the possibility of going to a women's refuge. This is a place of sanctuary where you (and your children) can go and be sure that your partner will not find you. Their locations are kept confidential, and the people who run them will help you not only with somewhere to stay but will also provide the legal, psychological and practical help you need to get back on your feet. Walking out of your home to an unknown place like a refuge can be very daunting, so why not talk to one of the organizations that provides them, such as Women's Aid or

Refuge – and then you'll have some idea what you will be going to. Alternatively, talk to family and friends about staying with them in an emergency.

♡ **Carry a list of emergency numbers:** police, relatives, friends, a refuge.

♡ **Tell someone you trust about the abuse.** Don't keep it to yourself.

♡ **Report any injuries to your GP** so that there is a record of your abuse.

♡ **Think about escape routes from your home** if you are unable to get out through the front door.

If you have already left your partner, there are some precautions you may want to take, as you may still be in danger. Change the locks and put locks on your windows. You can get advice from the police about making your home more secure, and look for more details in Chapter 1. If you have children, make sure the school is aware of your partner's violence and that they are clear about who can pick up the children and who cannot.

If It is Happening to a Friend
If you suspect that your friend is being abused, it's not the easiest topic to raise. Your friend may be horrified at the suggestion and may want to cut off contact with you. It's incredibly upsetting to think that someone is hurting a person you care about, and your first instinct may be to intervene, but that can be dangerous for both you and her. You may also find it very hard to understand why your friend is putting up with the abuse and not just upping and leaving. It helps to try and understand what she may be

experiencing and feeling. She may be overwhelmed by fear and this is governing her every move – fear of violence, fear of the unknown, fear for her safety. She probably believes it is her fault and that, if she changes her behaviour, it will stop. She is likely to have conflicting emotions; she may love her partner but hate the violence. She may be living in hope that his good side will re-appear or think that it is worth tolerating the abuse because his good side is so wonderful. She may be dependent upon her partner emotionally as well as financially. She probably feels stupid, guilty and ashamed at letting herself get into this situation.

The best thing you can do is be the person she can trust and open up to. You will want to tell her to leave him, and it is very hard not to keep going on about that. But it may not be the most helpful thing for her, and she may begin to feel that she cannot confide in you if you keep on at her to walk out. Try not to judge her but prepare to be very frustrated if she keeps going back to her partner, even though you think it's the most obvious thing in the world that she should never see him again. The most important thing is for you to simply be there, to be the person she can talk to, the person she can turn to for help and be the person she can rely on completely.

And, as a friend, realize the limitations of what you can achieve. You cannot change your friend's situation for her. She has to come to the realization by herself that the relationship has to end. It may take her years to get to that point. You can point out that his behaviour is unacceptable or dangerous but you cannot physically remove her from her situation unless she is ready to go.

The hardest thing I found about seeing my friend Louise going through years of abuse from her husband was how helpless I felt. She would come round to my house and we would talk for hours about what was going on and what she could do about it. No matter how many times I told her that she couldn't change him and that she should leave him, she would always go back to him. At one point she was having counselling about how best to deal with her husband, and he would go along to some of the sessions with her. I couldn't believe that the counsellor was giving her advice on how to handle him rather than telling him in no uncertain terms that he should leave and try and sort himself out.

Louise would spout what seemed like cod psychology to me about why her husband behaved in the way he did and that she was the only person who could help him through it. All the evidence suggests that, once a man is abusive, his behaviour will not improve in the long term. Louise knew that but kept hoping that her husband would be different. She didn't tell me about the worst of his abuse until the relationship was finally over. I think she was ashamed and embarrassed at what I would think of her for putting up with it.

I came to realize that my telling her to leave him was pointless. She wasn't going to until she was ready, and she began to feel that she could no longer confide in me because she was worried I would be cross and frustrated with her for rejecting my advice. So I had to bite my tongue. The worst moment was when she told me she was leaving London, where we both lived, to move to the middle of nowhere in the Welsh countryside to give their marriage one last shot. All I could think was that she would be totally isolated from her friends, from me and that it would be even harder to get help when she needed it. And since when did moving to a different location resolve someone's fundamental behaviour problems? But she was determined and, sure enough, his abuse got worse not better.

She left him in the end, but it took years for her to give up on him. If I was going to offer advice to anyone who has a friend in a similar situation, I would simply say, realize that you cannot sort out her problems for her, you can only listen and support her until she comes to the right decision by herself. **FIONA**

FURTHER INFORMATION

DATING

You can find general information on dating at **www.thesite.org** and on online dating at **www.getsafeonline.org**.

The Association of British Introduction Agencies outlines codes of practice for both personal and online dating agencies, and complaint procedures, at **www.abia.org.uk**. For information on online dating scams go to the Office of Fair Trading at **www.oft.gov.uk**.

For an overview of the most popular dating sites see **www.internet datingguide.com**.

STALKING AND NUISANCE CALLS

Visit the Network for Surviving Stalking (registered charity) at **www.secure.nss.org.uk**. If you are a victim of malicious calls or would like to request further information on personal safety and security relating to malicious calls, you can contact British Telecom, who run a 24-hour recorded advice line on 0800 666777 or 0800 1692707 (Monday to Saturday 8 a.m.–6 p.m.) or visit their Support and Advice website at **http://bt.custhelp.com**, and enter 'malicious calls'.

West Midlands Police have a comprehensive guide to dealing with malicious calls; visit **www.west-midlands.police.uk/crime-reduction/ crime-victim-malicious.asp**.

If you are receiving persistent nuisance calls, contact specialist advisers at the Malicious Calls Bureau on 0800 661441 (24 hours, 7 days a week).

Also, Telewest: 0800 9533333 (Monday to Saturday 8 a.m.–6 p.m. excluding bank holidays), and NTL: 0800 0522000.

Telephone Preference Service (TPS): **www.tpsonline.org.uk**

For mobile phone operators, please contact your customer services.

DOMESTIC VIOLENCE

Call 999 in an emergency.

National Centre for Domestic Violence: **www.ncdv.org.uk** or call the Freephone 24-hour National Domestic Violence Helpline on 0808 2000247, run in partnership between Women's Aid and Refuge.

Northern Ireland Women's Aid 24-hour domestic violence helpline: 028 90331818

Scottish domestic abuse helpline: 0800 0271234

Wales domestic abuse helpline: 0808 8010800 or **www.wdah.org**

General information: **www.refuge.org.uk**

The Samaritans: 0845 7909090 or **www.samaritans.org**

Rape Crisis: **www.rapecrisis.org.uk** or **www.truthaboutrape.co.uk**

Shelter: 0808 8004444 or **www.shelter.org.uk**

Victim support: 0845 3030900 or **www.victimsupport.org**

Crimestoppers: 0800 555111 or **www.crimestoppers-uk.org**

Refugee Council: 020 73466777 or **www.refugeecouncil.org.uk**

Immigration Advice Service: 020 73576917 or **www.iasuk.org**

Rights of Women: 020 72516577 or **www.rightsofwomen.org.uk**

Get Connected (for 16–25-year-olds): 0808 8084994 or **www.get connected.org.uk**

ADDITIONAL INFORMATION

Crime reduction government initiative: **www.crimereduction.gov.uk/ infosharing00.htm**

Government women and equality unit: **www.womenandequalityunit. gov.uk/domestic_violence/projects.htm**

The Department for Constitutional Affairs: **www.dca.gov.uk**

ACPO (Association of Chief Police Officers): **www.acpo.police.uk**

Metropolitan Police Force: **www.met.police.uk**

Office of the Deputy Prime Minister (information and guidance on funding for domestic violence services via the Supporting People Programme): **www.spkweb.org.uk**

In memory of Penny Beale (a victim of domestic violence): **www.penny bealememorialfund.org**

6
Money, Money, Money...

IT USED TO BE SO SIMPLE. IF YOU WANTED TO BE SURE THAT NO one took your money, you just had to physically hang on to it. When the highwayman shouted, 'Stand and deliver!' (or was it Adam Ant?) you had two choices: hand over your gold bullion or risk losing your virtue, and probably your life into the bargain. Then came the advent of banks – we give our money to them and they look after it; it's up to them to protect our hard-earned readies and, on the whole, they do a good job of it. The biggest ever cash robbery, in 2004 of over £26 million in Belfast, was obviously a bit of a low point, but it was the bank's money that was stolen, not that of individual customers. Without doubt our money is a lot safer in a bank than stuck under the mattress.

However, with the internet and the instant flow of information around the world, theft has taken on a whole new dimension. A murky underworld of scams has grown like some vast fungus flourishing in the dark. We can't see the conmen who are so keen to part us from our cash but, make no mistake, they are out there. Every day the development of technology spawns new ways of taking your money.

If you like to do a bit of internet shopping, use a mobile phone, bank online or use a cashpoint, you need to know how to protect yourself and your money. The good news is that, if your money is taken fraudulently, you'll get it back (unless the bank believes you were so spectacularly negligent you brought it upon yourself). The bad news is that the bank has to cover that cost which means it will ultimately load it on to us. We all pay in the end.

CASH

Let's start with the lowest-tech of all – cash. Each chapter so far has had at least one section designed to help you hold on to your money. Our advice is always to carry as little cash as you can get away with – and it's a good idea to secrete a tenner on your person somewhere in case you get pickpocketed or mugged.

Using a Cash Machine

It is at the cashpoint that you are at your most vulnerable with your money. There are over 2 billion cash withdrawals every year and, according to the latest figures, cash-machine annual fraud totalled £66 billion. In the not so distant past, all you had to do was make sure that someone wasn't loitering behind you trying to copy down your PIN number. Now you have to be wary of 'skimming' or cloning (when sophisticated electronic equipment copies your card and obtains or films your PIN number as you insert your card into the machine).

One thing to do is to make sure you look around you before you use a cashpoint, and again before you take your money out. If someone looks suspicious or is standing too close to you, don't use the machine. Just go inside the bank or, if it's closed, use a cashpoint somewhere else. When you do use the machine, cover your hand when entering your PIN number. If someone tries to talk to you while you're using the machine or tries to help you, avoid getting into conversation. If you don't want to be rude you could just ask them to hold that thought until you've finished. Distraction at the cashpoint means someone could rob you or note down your details without you noticing.

I was at the cash machine in the high street one evening. I'd just started when I noticed that three guys were standing behind me. When I tried to put my card in, the machine wouldn't accept it for some reason. I tried again and it still didn't work. The guys behind me started getting impatient and began to sound a bit aggressive. I turned to them and explained what was going wrong. Their mood changed and one of them told me that he had had the same problem earlier in the week and that he'd been given a number by the bank to call to access his money. He said he'd kept the number and gave it to me. He sounded so genuine and I was quite relieved that they were no longer sounding so threatening, so I called the number.

A woman answered, giving the name of the bank and asking how she could help me. I explained and she asked me for my name and bank account details. I know it sounds stupid but I didn't like to refuse given that the three guys were standing quite close to me, not near enough to hear what was being said but near enough to tell if I was following their advice or not. She didn't ask me for my PIN, so I felt slightly reassured, and she said that I did have sufficient funds in my account but that she couldn't make them available to me through this particular cash machine as it had a fault. She advised me to use another one, apologized on behalf of the bank and hung up.

I told the three guys what had happened, they commiserated and I left.

As I walked away I began to sweat as the realization dawned on me that I had probably been the victim of a scam. I had horrible visions of my account being emptied that very minute. I ran home as fast I could, rang my bank and told them what had happened. They said it was definitely a fraud and put a stop on my account straight away. Fortunately, no money had yet been taken. The bank later explained that the men had tampered with the cash machine so that it couldn't be used and set up a person at the end of a phone so that I would then hand over my account details. I don't know why I was so gullible. I know now that I shouldn't have let myself get drawn into a conversation with those guys at the cash machine but I think I felt intimidated by them and worried that they might turn nasty if I didn't take their advice. I was lucky not to lose any money. AMANDA, LANCASTER

Most cashpoints have a notice telling you not to use the machine if there is anything unusual about it or if there are signs that it has been tampered with. But do you know what you should be looking for? The most obvious indication that something is amiss is the area around the slot where you put your card in. If it isn't flush and flat or looks as if it has had something added to it after manufacture, don't use it. It's difficult to be specific, as it depends on how the scammer decides to tamper with the machine. Fraudsters have used many different methods, from a simple insert over the card-entry slot, to completely bogus ATM machines.

The machine may also contain a device to 'skim' your card. In a typical skimming scam, fraudsters attach a device to the entry slot of the cash machine to record the details of the card's magnetic strip when it is inserted. A miniature camera is hidden overlooking the PIN pad which allows the criminals to capture the PIN number as well. Fraudsters can then build cloned cards which they can use in cash machines to steal from your accounts. Trust your instincts – if the machine doesn't look right, don't use it.

> About a year ago, at a cashpoint, I noticed something slightly different about the slot where I had to put my card in. It didn't look strange or out of place but I didn't think it had been like that before. I looked more closely, and it didn't seem any kind of a bodge job, so I inserted my card, my cash came out and I thought no more about it. I'm not great at checking my statements so it was a while before I realized anything was amiss. A couple of months later, I wondered why my account seemed to be so short of funds. I hadn't made any large purchases that I could remember, so I spent half an hour looking back over my statements. I discovered that about £500 had been mysteriously taken from my account. I put two and two together and worked out that it must have been connected to that cash machine. I told the bank and they paid back the money. But next time I'll be more careful.
>
> RHIANNON, EXETER

If You Have to Carry Cash for Your Work

If your work involves carrying cash, such as the takings from the till at the end of the day, you don't need us to tell you to be extra careful. Discuss the risks with your employer and only agree to undertake the job if you are satisfied that your personal safety is being taken seriously and all the potential dangers have been considered and minimized.

◈ **Record as many details as possible of where you are going** and when you expect to return. Make sure it's on a register that's available to your colleagues.

◈ **Always have a point of contact** for when the job is over so that your colleagues know you have returned safely and that they should raise the alarm if they haven't heard from you.

◈ **Know your route** and the entrances and exits in the buildings you are visiting.

◈ This may sound daft, but **try not to make it obvious that you are collecting money.** Be discreet.

◈ **Try to vary your route.** If you always go the same way at the same time, you are making yourself an easy target.

◈ **Carry the cash in a bag that looks inconspicuous** and, ideally, could be mistaken for a sports holdall or a large handbag. Try to ensure you're not advertising what you're up to by rattling coins as you walk along.

◈ **Go straight to your drop-off point** when you have collected the cash. Stopping for a Starbucks along the way may seem irresistible but it's also insane.

◈ **Carry a personal-attack alarm** and, as always, keep it within instant reach.

◈ **If someone demands your money, hand it over straight away.** It's never worth more than the value of your life.

In the Bank
We shouldn't really have to tell you this, as it should be up to the banks to make sure they give you your money in as discreet a

way as possible, but we thought we'd mention it because we have lost count of the number of times we've gone to take out a sizeable amount of cash and the teller behind the counter has said in a voice that could reasonably be heard five blocks away, '£500, YOU SAID? DO YOU WANT THAT IN FIFTIES OR TWENTIES? SHALL I PUT IT IN AN ENVELOPE FOR YOU?' No, we are tempted to say, why don't you just put your brain cell in an envelope and have done with it? It's so *obvious*, but the banks just don't seem to get it. So, dear reader, the onus is on you. If you want to withdraw a serious amount of cash, go to the counter where you can ring for help and ask to be seen in a side office. And when the bank staff ask you what it's about *before* you go into the side office (as they so often do and where everyone can hear you, thus defeating the point of the whole side-office thing), just say you would like to tell them in private. And then you can take your cash away without everyone in the bank knowing about it.

Forgery

If you are unlucky enough to be handed a forged banknote, you have just been robbed. At the risk of stating the obvious, even if you took it in good faith assuming it to be genuine, it is worthless. And it is a criminal offence to knowingly pass on a forged note. Over 90 per cent of forgeries are of £20 notes and the number of counterfeit notes in circulation is rising so rapidly that the Bank of England has urged people to be vigilant and learn how to recognize a fake. So, here's a quick lesson:

◈ **Real banknotes are crisp, not limp,** because of the special paper used.

◈ **The metal strip on the note,** which looks disjointed, is revealed as a continuous line when held up to the light.

◈ **If you look at the number 20 on a £20 note,** both letters and numbers in micro-writing can be found next to the portrait of the Queen.

If you think you've come across a forgery, resist the urge to pass it on to an unsuspecting shopkeeper with your fingers crossed behind your back. Hand it into your bank. You won't get your money back but, looking on the slightly brighter side, they may be able to stop a gang of counterfeiters.

Incidentally, if you come across a banknote that is stained, it's probably stolen. Most cash boxes in shops and banks contain a special dye that explodes all over the cash inside if the box is forced open. It permanently stains the notes and colours the robbers a nice shade of red or blue too. Again, you should hand it into the bank. They will send it to the mutilated-notes department (yes, there is such a place) of the Bank of England, who will refund you as long as the note is not a forgery. You may think it's a bit of a faff but it really helps the investigation into any large robbery to see where the notes are turning up.

CREDIT CARDS

There are more than 1,500 credit cards to choose from in the UK. If you can trust yourself with them, they can be an excellent way of minimizing the amount of cash you carry around and thereby your attractiveness to thieves. And they have added benefits such as extra protection if things go wrong. Under the Consumer Credit Act credit-card companies are jointly responsible, along with the supplier of the goods, for any breach of contract or misrepresentation by the supplier. In plain English, that means if you buy a kettle, for example, and you get home to find that it doesn't work, you are protected if you bought it with your credit card. Normally, you would go to the shop where you bought it and ask for your money back. But if the shop has gone out of business, you can make a claim for compensation or a refund from your credit-card supplier. Some cards also offer insurance as a standard so that, if you lose or damage an item that you have bought within a set period, you can claim the money back.

The key thing about credit cards is not to use them as a loan facility. The interest you pay on cards is horrific compared to what you could get from a loan through a bank. There are 0 per cent cards, which can be very useful as an effective loan for the period that the 0 per cent deal lasts. But once it's finished you need to be disciplined enough no longer to use it as such. You will be back to square one and liable for massive amounts of interest, which really defeats the object. Pay your balance off every month and, if you don't think you're the kind of person with the discipline or funds to do that, don't have a credit card. You could just stick to a debit card, which only lets you spend what is in your account, or get a prepaid one. Credit businesses make their money out of the interest people pay on the cards, and that's why they keep upping the amount you can borrow. Don't be flattered by having an increased borrowing limit. It is a cynical exercise to increase the amount the credit-card supplier can make out of you, not a reflection of your increased status or your Paris Hiltonesque financial resources.

Debt

As a nation, the British are incurring record levels of debt; however, if you're savvy, our credit society can offer great opportunities. But if you don't know how to work it to your advantage, you can end up sucked in and then spat back out again, with huge debts and no way of paying them. In 1996, just under 60,000 people rang the National Debt Line asking for help, and by 2006, the figure had grown to almost 275,000, split almost equally between men and women. Two-thirds of the debt had been run up on credit cards. Now, we're not great ones for statistics, but we found this a truly staggering increase. Make no mistake, getting into debt is serious; it doesn't just go away if you put those letters in the drawer without opening them. Our best advice if you think you're getting in over your head is to stop, open the letters, work out how bad the situation is and get help as soon as possible. And there are plenty of people and places to go to find help. You're not on your own and, although it may be embarrassing at first to explain that you really did absolutely, definitely need twenty-five pairs of shoes and forty-eight handbags, no one will judge you. But you will get practical advice on how best to pay your debt back, for example by reducing it to more manageable monthly repayments. Just making that first move to get help will often take that horrible tension of worry from your shoulders, and the more you talk about it the easier and less embarrassing it will be.

The National Debt Line is a registered charity providing free independent money advice and they have a few golden rules for you to follow to get you back on track.

◈ **Don't borrow money to pay off your debts** without thinking carefully. Get advice first. This kind of borrowing could lead to you losing your home.

◈ **Check you are claiming all the benefits** and tax credits you can.

◈ **With the Debt Line's help, work out your personal budget.** Make sure you show it or send it to your creditors when you tell them about your difficulties.

◈ **Make sure you tackle your priority debts first** – for example, debts which could mean losing your home or having your gas or electricity cut off.

◈ **Contact everyone you owe money to.** If you make arrangements to pay some creditors but not others, you could run into difficulties again.

◈ **If the first person you speak to is unhelpful,** ask to speak to somebody more senior who may be able to agree to what you want.

There are other organizations which can help, such as the Citizens Advice Bureau and the Consumer Credit Counselling Service and, if you're confused by the array of financial products, try the government's website www.moneymadeclear.fsa.gov.uk. But, whatever happens, don't keep the problem to yourself: it will only get worse.

PPI
Many credit cards will offer you payment-protection insurance or PPI. The idea is that if you suddenly find yourself unable to pay, because you have lost your job or fall ill, for example, the company will pay off a percentage of your debt for a set period.

Be very, very careful with these. They can cost you a lot of money and you need to do your sums to see if it's really worth it. If you are offered a credit card on condition of accepting PPI, walk away and get a card elsewhere. If you are tempted, read the small print to see if you really would be eligible: don't rely on the sales-person to spell it out for you; they are under pressure to make a sale. If you are self-employed, have a chronic condition or are in a temp job, you may not be covered. Fiona has made several programmes about people who forked out for PPI for credit cards or loans only to find they had paid for nothing, as they were not eligible from the outset.

Card-Protection Agencies

A card-protection agency (CPA) is a business that provides card holders with a card-number-registration service. If your cards are lost or stolen, you can contact the CPA, who will, on your behalf, advise your credit-card company or companies so that a stop can be placed against the numbers you have. The benefit is you just have to make one call. We would argue that you shouldn't need to pay a CPA because you should have the minimum number of credit and debit cards anyway. We have just one of each. Having five, ten or twenty cards is madness. If you are managing your finances in a reasonably sensible way, you don't need anything like that. The only reason to need more than that is if you want to have a separate credit card for online transactions.

CPAs do have another advantage: some offer services like emergency cash advances, emergency hotel-bill payment or replacement travel tickets to get home. However, some of those benefits may already be covered by your insurance, so make sure you're not paying twice over.

Prepaid Credit or Debit Cards

These are a great idea to stop someone stealing your card (physically, or virtually via the internet) and draining your account. Unlike a normal credit card, where you can run up a massive debt, or a Switch card, where you can spend, spend, spend until your account runs dry, these cards have a fixed sum that is available to spend on them – rather like prepaid credit on your mobile phone. Money is transferred on to them using either cash or by bank transfer, or even from another credit card. You can use them at any shops or online retailers where you would use your usual credit or debit card. Once you've reached your prepaid limit, you will have no money left on the card, so you (or a thief) will no longer be able to use it. They are really useful for shopping on the internet because you can put the exact sum required for a purchase on the card and a fraudster is then unable to use your details to fleece you. You can get them from Visa or MasterCard, and you don't have to have a credit check, because you are adding cash on to the card up front, as opposed to being trusted by the card provider to pay it back. Some twenty-five companies in the UK now offer these cards, from Barclays and the Post Office to smaller companies, and more are sure to follow. Just make sure you check the small print regarding fees to get the best deal.

Fraud on Your Card

I had spent ten days filming a programme about tigers in India for the BBC. It was the experience of a lifetime. I rode elephants at dawn, saw tigers in the wild just feet away and travelled the length of the country from the capital to dense jungle and mountain ranges. Just incredible. But call me shallow, I also wanted to do some shopping. On the day of our departure, time was running out and we still hadn't managed to find time to go into a single shop or market. My producer took pity on me and we stopped for half an hour in a silk shop on the way to the airport. It was an amazing emporium with everything in the most gorgeously vibrant silks you can imagine and all incredibly cheap. I went into total hyperdrive, as it was coming up to Christmas and I needed to get presents – so much to buy but so little time. In the space of thirty minutes I managed to buy five scarves, three tablecloths, a bedspread, four pashminas and some silk pyjamas. By the end of it I had a stress headache, but it was mission accomplished. A few weeks after I got back to England, I noticed a few strange transactions on my credit-card statement. I'd paid for a few hotels in India, as well as the shopping and some meals, so it took me a little while to work out what the different payments were. But there was one I just couldn't place. And I realized it was a bill for something in a city I'd never visited. Then it all came back to me. When I paid for the silks, there had been some kind of problem with my credit card and there was quite a lot of fuss about re-entering it into the machine and getting it to work. I bet that is when the fraud or cloning happened. I've no idea if the shopkeeper was dishonest or whether the fraud was being perpetrated electronically in cyber-space by someone else, but there was certainly something about that whole business that was fishy. If you're travelling abroad, pay special attention when using your cards, don't let them out of your sight and check your statements carefully when you get back.

FIONA

Chip and PIN has made our cards much more secure here. It's not a perfect system, but it's better than a signature that could be copied by an averagely intelligent ten-year-old. Unlike elsewhere in the world, if a fraudster buys something on your card here in the UK you are not financially liable for it, just remember that many other countries don't have the system yet, so be extra careful when going abroad.

If someone uses your card before you inform the credit-card supplier, or before you tell them that someone else knows your PIN, the most you will have to pay is £50. But if you show that you acted without reasonable care (shouting out your PIN number in a crowded pub after several drinks too many – it has happened) you may have to pay the lot.

To protect yourself from fraud on your card:

- ◈ **Keep your PIN safe and secret.**

- ◈ **Never let your card out of your sight** when making a transaction. Beware of shops and restaurants that want to take your card round the back to a machine you can't see. If things start looking dodgy, just say you've changed your mind and don't make the purchase or go and get some cash.

- ◈ **Only shop on secure websites,** or use a dedicated credit card for transactions on the internet.

- ◈ **Carefully discard credit-card offers which come through the post by shredding them** or tearing them up. Otherwise someone else may take up that offer in your name.

- ◈ **The above also goes for receipts or statements.** When you want to get rid of them, tear them up, never just chuck them in the bin.

◈ **Carefully check your monthly statements** and make sure all the purchases listed are ones you remember making. Don't rely on your credit-card company to inform you if they spot fraud. If you find a rogue payment, inform your credit-card company immediately. They will put a stop on the payment and investigate. You will not have to pay if they can't prove it's yours.

I was reading through my bank statements and noticed that over £100 had gone out of our account towards an AA membership. That would have been fine had it not been for the fact that we were not members. I contacted the bank and established that we had been paying someone else's membership for over three years, and because it only slipped out once a year we hadn't noticed. After a few trying phone calls and some threatening letters, the money was eventually returned. It turned out that the real AA member's direct-debit form had been misread by the bank and had been one digit out. That one digit nearly cost us £340.
JACQUI

◈ **Don't use the same PIN number for all your cards.** More than one in four of us do – it makes it easier to remember, but the dangers are obvious. It's still better than writing your PIN number down though. Even if you think you've disguised it in your diary by pretending it's a phone number, thieves will look out for it.

◈ **If you struggle to remember different PINs,** try to think of the shape you're putting into the keypad rather than the actual numbers. For example, 3179 is the shape of a C, and 1793 is the shape of a U.

If you think you are a victim of card fraud, contact the credit-card supplier straight away and if you still have the card, don't use it. The official advice is to contact the police too but in our opinion, that's almost certainly a waste of your time and theirs. Only do so if the credit-card company wants you to or if you have a genuine suspicion or evidence that the police can investigate to find out how the fraud or theft happened.

In December 2007 an entire village fell victim to an elaborate international credit-card scam. Hundreds of people living in Houghton on the Hill in Leicestershire reported cash being withdrawn from their accounts.The withdrawals were made from countries as far-flung as Australia, India and the Philippines. The owner of the village shop and garage became suspicious that fraudsters were targeting his customers as they bought goods and fuel on their credit cards, so he called in the police. It turned out that an international gang of fraudsters had installed a fake card reader and a secret camera in his shop so that when customers entered their payment cards, their details and PIN numbers became known to the gang, who promptly used them to purchase goods all over the world. One customer said the fraudsters only stopped when they reached the £2,000 limit on the card which he used for petrol and other petty-cash expenses. Another customer used to get petrol on her way to work as a teacher at a local school. Cash totalling £300 was withdrawn from her account at a bank in India seven days after she used her Switch card in Houghton. In total, it's suspected that around £80,000 was taken. The garage owner has now made his credit-card facilities more secure. The police are at the time of writing still investigating who set up the fraud, whether it was an ex-employee or someone else with access to the store and garage. JACQUI

YOUR MONEY ON THE NET

More and more of us spend our money on the net with online shopping and sites like eBay, and about 15 million of us in the UK move our money around on the net with online banking. It's a relatively new development but it is rapidly growing every year and, with the right precautions, it is safe and convenient. But wherever there is money, there is usually some villain somewhere trying to think up ways of relieving you of it.

The key thing is to have a good level of basic computer security. You wouldn't leave your home without locking the doors and closing the windows to stop burglars – so get yourself some form of security for your computer: that is the first step to protecting yourself from all sorts of scams, theft and serious inconvenience. Then, arm yourself with some knowhow about the most common scams. See Chapter 7, OK Computer, for more information.

Online Shopping

How we love it. How it has transformed our lives. From bog roll to Bulgari, from a pint of milk to a pair of Manolo's, internet shopping is the biggest thing to hit the high street since the M&S T-shirt bra. Serious amounts of cash can pass through your hands when shopping online, so you need to make sure that you will receive the goods you pay for, that the payment you transfer arrives to the right account and that you are paid for anything you sell. Sign up whenever you are given the option to Verified by Visa (www.visaeurope.com/verified) or MasterCard Securecode (www.mastercard.co.uk/securecode). When you shop online you will increasingly be asked if you want to sign up to these schemes using a password. This is another level of security to prevent a fraudster using your card details on a participating site, as they won't know your password.

Only shop at secure websites. Check that you can see a security icon (the locked padlock or unbroken key symbol) before sending your card details. The beginning of the retailer's internet address will change from 'http' to 'https' when a purchase is made using a secure connection. Unless you are linked via a secure connection do not give any information which you would not want anyone else other than the vendor to see. As simple as that.

If, during a transaction, a window pops up telling you that you are about to view secure and non-secure items, you need to check that the site still says https in the top-left corner and that the padlock logo is still showing. If they are, the window doesn't mean that you are about to go to a totally insecure site. It is simply the supplier covering themselves that, even though they have security in place, the site is not completely immune to all hackers. The same could be said of any site, so you shouldn't necessarily feel deterred from completing the transaction. But if you have any doubts as you progress through the sale, stop. If anything smells fishy to you, your suspicions are probably right.

Other handy hints for shopping safely online:

- **Use a prepaid credit card** or use a specific credit card solely for online shopping.

- **Stick to reputable websites** which have been recommended to you or from a company with which you're familiar.

- **Print out your order** and make copies of the retailer's terms and conditions. If you want to make an allegation of fraud, it'll be a lot easier to prove it to your bank if you have all the details on paper. Consider additional costs like post and packaging, particularly if you're buying from abroad. It's also harder to seek redress if something goes wrong with a purchase from abroad.

◆ **Check your bank statements as soon as you receive them.** They are likely to be your first tip-off if someone has used your online shopping as an opportunity to nick your details to go on a spending spree of their own.

◆ **The retailer should be able to supply you with a certificate of authenticity** on their website. This means that the company has been authenticated by an external company such as Verisign or Comodo to gain certification. It is a global standard, so if the company does not have one of these, do not proceed.

◆ **If you're nervous of buying on the internet, just stick to reputable names** which you already know from the high street and you shouldn't go wrong.

◆ **Be careful when buying from sites outside the UK:** what seems like a bargain can become extortionately expensive by the time Customs have got hold of it.

I was trying to buy my nephew an extra-special present for his birthday and I knew he particularly wanted a Harry Potter Firebolt Quidditch Broom. I managed to locate one in the US which seemed like a bargain at around £30. Unfortunately, I was in a bit of a hurry and didn't check either the delivery charge or the customs rates properly and ended up having to pay a total of £75. It's the most expensive present I've ever given him. It's probably in his room somewhere gathering dust now! KAREN, SURREY

Drugs

With the price of prescriptions these days it's not hard to see why many people are looking for cheaper deals on the internet. E-pharmacies are a growing area of internet shopping, and the reputable ones can offer a good deal if you have to take a particular drug for a long period of time. But remember: anyone, in any country, can set up an e-pharmacy, and you won't be protected by the UK controls as to the quality and quantity of the drug you order. This goes for illegal drugs as well. However tempting, please don't buy any type of drug from an unknown source, particularly without medical advice or supervision.

Online Auctions

The phenomenon of internet auction sites means we can all become shopkeepers from our own homes. It can be a real buzz as you watch the bids rise for something you are buying or selling, especially if you end up with a bargain. Reputable sites, like eBay, are generally very secure, but you still need to have your wits about you.

- When shopping on auction sites such as eBay, **make sure you know who you are dealing with.** Get the seller's phone number (a landline, not a mobile) and a postal address.

- **Read the safety advice on the website before trading.** Never step outside it, no matter how tempting, as that's one way online con artists can try to scam you.

- **Compare prices.** If someone is offering you a deal well below the current bid or reserve price, it's probably too good to be true, especially if the dealer is trying to contact you direct.

- ◆ **Check out the seller's history.** If they have little or no selling history, you should think carefully before entering into a deal with them.

- ◆ **It is never too late to ask questions** to ensure you are completely happy with what you are buying. Don't get carried away in the excitement of the auction. Be on the look-out for fraud at all times.

- ◆ **One area particularly open to abuse is the purchase of second-hand concert or theatre tickets.** There have been many recent complaints about tickets which initially were advertised as 'front row' turning out to be halfway to Timbuktu, or forgeries. Bearing in mind you are generally going to pay way over the odds for the ticket in the first place, check out the seller and the tickets on offer as much as possible before parting with your hard-earned cash.

- ◆ **If you get offered 'second chance' bidding,** check that you are being notified of this opportunity through the official website, not a bogus one. Carefully check the email address or contact the website using its published website address.

- ◆ **Always enter the website through your internet browser,** not via a link in an email. If you've traded once, the auction or shopping site will send you regular emails to entice you to spend money with them again. It's not always easy to tell if these emails are the genuine article, so it's best not to use them as a way of accessing the site. Save the website address in your favourites and always enter it that way.

While internet auction sites offer us, the home shopper, some tremendous advantages, equally, they do so for your average thief. No longer do they have to fence their goods through a backstreet handler – instead, some have become computer literate and use internet auction sites to sell their ill-gotten gains. If you buy something that is stolen and the police find out (and, yes, they do check the internet), then you could lose that much-sought-after purchase and your money into the bargain. If you bought it thinking or believing it could be stolen in the first place, you could face a hefty fine and, in really serious cases, prison. Let's face it, if you end up before a judge, you're going to have some difficulty explaining that, although the brand-new laptop you saw advertised on the net cost just £50, it never occurred to you that it might have fallen off the back of a lorry.

Also have a look at www.checkmend.com. This is a separate company with linked access to the Immobilise stolen property data-base. It will help you to avoid buying stolen second-hand goods or blocked mobile phones on the web by providing an online or text report. It's particularly useful if you're buying a large expensive item from an auction site. They charge £2.99 for the report which includes a seller's report. One word of caution though, just like an MOT it will only be valid up to the date of the report so anything subsequently registered as stolen you still won't know about.

────────── INTERNET SELLING – PAYMENT ──────────

This is where it can all go pear-shaped if you're not careful. You can take all the security precautions under the sun up to this point but then lose everything at the crucial moment when money changes hands. And, infuriatingly, just because money appears to have turned up in your account from the buyer, that doesn't mean it will stay there. There are nasty tricks which mean the money can be reclaimed or stopped.

DOS

Pay or receive money through the online payment options or a reputable escrow account such as Paypal. Escrow is a system where both buyer and seller's financial details are held separately by a legitimate, third-party company which acts as a middleman. This is how it works: the buyer makes a payment into the escrow account; the seller only receives the payment when the goods have arrived and are deemed satisfactory. Never enter an escrow website sent to you by anyone in case it is fake. If you don't know of a reputable escrow site, look for one by using your internet browser, but make sure it's verified by the Financial Services Authority and based in the UK.

Paypal is an online banking system that is generally regarded as very secure. However, it's a favourite target for fraudsters sending emails purporting to be from Paypal. The company is very proactive about combating this and encourages anyone to contact them if they are not happy with the way the service is working.

Protect your online auction details with as much zeal as you would those concerning your bank account. Keep the possibility of identity theft uppermost in your mind and watch out for phishing emails that look as if they come from the auction website but are from fraudsters instead. For example, a genuine eBay email address will read from 'eBay Administration [admin@ebay.com]'. A fake one will look very similar, but look out for rogue letters or numbers, for example [admin@ebayz.com].

The CHAPS system of transferring money is irrevocable and therefore secure. It is an immediate bank transfer, which is made for a fee of £20–30.

DON'T'S

Never deal in cash. The notes could be counterfeit.

Don't accept cheques or banker's drafts as payment. When a cheque or draft is 'cleared' into your account, you could be forgiven for thinking that's it, transaction satisfactorily completed. Think again. All that means is that the money has passed between banks. You remain liable if the cheque turns out to be forged or stolen. The person who paid the cheque just needs to query or put a stop on the payment and the money will be taken back from you.

Don't be drawn into cash-back deals. These are a very common form of fraud and this is how they work: a buyer will ask the seller to accept more money for a particular item than it is on sale for. The reason given may be that it is to cover some kind of shipping charge. The buyer will then transfer the payment (including the extra over the asking price) to the seller's account. Once the money has cleared, the seller will be asked to send the overpayment to some kind of shipping agent. The seller will be offered a percentage of the overpayment as an incentive. It's a way of laundering money, but the seller will find that, far from being up on the deal, the payment that 'cleared' into her account will turn out to be bogus and the money will be stopped. The fraudster is basically taking advantage of the seller's lack of understanding of the bank's clearing system. Remember: just because the money has cleared into your account, it doesn't mean the money is yours to keep. Take a look at these examples from the Metropolitan police where people have been conned by cash-back deals.

♦ **A woman advertised her car for sale in** *Autotrader* **for £3,000.** Within one week she had received three different approaches from 'buyers' abroad offering to purchase it by banker's draft or

UK cheque for a sum significantly above the asking price on the proviso that she transferred the difference via 'money transfer' to a 'shipping agent'.

◆ **A man advertised a church organ for sale for £800** on the Royal College of Music website and was contacted by a 'buyer' via email. Over a series of emails he was informed that a 'client' of this buyer would pay him a UK cheque for £4,800. Upon the cheque clearing he was to send £3,800 by money transfer to a 'shipping agent' and keep £1,000 for himself (£800 for the purchase and £200 for his efforts).

◆ **A woman advertised her daughter's horse for sale** on *Horse and Hound*'s website and was contacted by a 'buyer' via email. Over a series of emails she was informed that she would be paid £5,000 by way of a UK cheque and this would cover the £2,250 purchase of the horse and £2,750 for engaging a 'shipping agent'. She was told to send the higher amount via money transfer to the 'shipping agent' once the cheque had cleared.

The Fraud Squad's advice is not to accept a cheque or banker's draft for an amount above the original asking price. Most buyers would want to view an expensive item (or at least ask to see photos, etc.) before parting with their cash, so beware of prospective buyers who want to rush a sale without asking many questions. If your suspicions are raised, don't go ahead with the sale – it really isn't worth the risk.

THE FUTURE: A NO-CASH SOCIETY

There are all sorts of new technologies in development which will mean that in the future we won't have to carry cash at all. As we write, a trial is starting in London using NFC (near-field communication) technology consisting of a mobile phone combined with a credit and Oyster card (an automatic payment method for the London Underground). It works by holding your mobile close to an electronic reader that operates in much the same way as a barcode scanner and allows you to pay for small things like parking meters, vending machines and travel tickets. The technology has already been used in Japan for some years and has also spread through some parts of Europe. The trial here is just for six months, but if successful could end up a permanent fixture.

So like it or not, this is likely to be the future – some of the larger mobile phone manufacturers like Nokia are already incorporating the technology into their latest phones. Soon your mobile phone will not only play music and videos, surf the net, take photos and video footage (and make phone calls, of course), but will also become a mobile purse which has your credit and loyalty card details. Anything that makes your handbag lighter has to be good news but, as you can imagine, it will certainly throw up a whole new load of challenges for fraudsters and law enforcers alike, and if you lose it you're in real trouble . . .

FURTHER INFORMATION

CREDIT CARDS

www.choosingandusing.com is a free and impartial guide to choosing and using a credit card and Martin Lewis's **www.moneysavingexpert.com** has a good guide to prepaid credit and debit cards.

The UK Payments Association, at **www.apacs.org.uk**, gives details of Card Protection Agencies accredited by APACS.

DEBT

Find advice at **www.citizensadvice bureau.org.uk**, the Consumer Credit Counselling Service, **www. cccsatl.org** and **www.moneymadeclear. fsa.gov.uk**.

CREDIT REFERENCE AGENCIES

Equifax plc, Credit File Advice Centre, PO Box 1140, Bradford BD1 5SU. Tel: 0870 010 0583; web: **www.equifax.co.uk**

Experian Ltd, Consumer Help Services, PO Box 8000, Nottingham NG1 5GX. Tel: 0870 241 6212; web: **www.experian.co.uk**

Call Credit plc, One Park Lane, Leeds, West Yorkshire. LS3 1EP. Tel: 0870 060 1414; web: **www.callcredit.uk**

SHOPPING OR FINANCIAL SERVICES ONLINE

Bank payments advice (CHAPS) at **www.apacs.org.uk**

Financial Services Authority at **www.fsa.gov.uk**

Escrow information at **www.escrow-fraud.com**, or search for 'escrow' at **www.getsafeonline.org**.

For information on using your card safely online visit **www.cifas.org.uk**. CIFAS is the UK's Fraud Prevention Service, a not-for-profit membership association solely dedicated to the prevention of financial crime.

Sign up whenever you are given the option while shopping online to Verified by Visa – **www.visaeurope.com/verified** or MasterCard SecureCode at **www.mastercard.co.uk/securecode**.

See also **www.tradingstandards.gov.uk** or call Consumer Direct on 08454 040506.

And visit the websites **www.cardwatch.org.uk**, **www.banksafe online.org.uk**, **www.getsafeonline.org.uk**, **www.identitytheft.org.uk** for more information about how to shop and bank safely online. For practical consumer advice see **www.consumerdirect.gov.uk**.

CRIME

See **www.met.police.uk/fraudalert**, **www.dcpcu.org.uk** (Dedicated Cheque and Plastic Crime Unit) and **www.banknotewatch.co.uk**.

For information on NFC (near-field communications) see **www.nfc-forum.org** and **www.nokia.com**.

7

OK Computer

B EING A VICTIM OF ONLINE CRIME CAN BE AS DISTRESSING AS being robbed in the real world, and just as intrusive. Don't kid yourself that the risks are tiny and the consequences trivial. You could lose a lot of cash and, even if you don't, the hours you will have to spend on the phone and the letters you will have to write to prove that it wasn't you who spent £500 on a pair of shoes but someone who stole your identity, will convince you that it's in your interests to take a few precautions. Neither of us are tech-heads so you don't have to be versed in mega-gigabyte-URL-VPN-Wi-Fi-talk to be able to make sure that your computer is protected. Believe us: if we can do it, so can you. And be warned – internet crime can lead to:

- Your computer becoming so slow it is unusable
- Criminals using your computer to send viruses or spam without your knowledge
- Paying for goods that never arrive
- Your credit rating being ruined

- Loans or credit cards being taken out in your name
- Criminals gaining access to your bank account or credit cards
- Debt collectors hassling you about loans you never took out
- Sensitive personal information being read and possibly used by strangers
- A deluge of porn
- An enormous bill as your dial-up connection is hijacked
- Children being targeted by paedophiles.

One security software firm we looked at has a database of over 340,000 different fraudulent emails or viruses, and adds over 450 per day. As each one is received, they have to ensure their software can deal with it, which is why all security software is regularly updated online.

We can all come up with 101 excuses not to do anything to protect ourselves . . .

I've got anti-virus software so I don't need anything else. Wrong. That only protects part of your system. It's like closing your car door but forgetting to lock it. It won't keep hackers or fraudsters out.

No one is interested in me. Well, admittedly, you may be very boring. But don't feel down about it – there are plenty of people out in the internet ether who would love to get to know you better. Stealing your identity can be a lot more profitable than breaking into your house. And criminals use programs that can scan tens of thousands of computers an hour over the net.

I back up everything. Good for you. That means you won't lose anything stored on your computer, but it won't stop you losing money or being attacked by viruses. And of course if you back everything up without regularly protecting yourself from a virus, the probability is that you are backing up the virus, so the minute you reinstall the files, bingo, they have got you again.

If I lose money, I'll get it back from the bank or credit-card company. Thanks to the banking code, yes, you will, subject to you not being proved negligent. But it can take a long time to be reimbursed and it is a serious hassle. Ultimately, we all pay the price in increased bank charges.

It takes too long, I'm too busy. Come on, you must be able to find a better excuse than that. It will take an hour or two, but it can take months, even years, to restore a ruined credit rating.

My internet service provider protects me, why should I bother? Some major internet service providers do offer services when you sign up with them. For example, Virgin Broadband offers a package called PCguard which offers the following protection – anti-virus, spyware, a firewall, ID-theft protection, parental control, pop-up blocker and a privacy manager. If you have signed up to their top broadband package it's all free, but if you have a basic package you only get a firewall, anti-virus, pop-up blocker and privacy manager and therefore will need to get additional coverage. Virgin Broadband supplies the additional features for a charge.

But, remember: some ISPs provide nothing at all, so you'll have to install your own. Major stores selling computer hard- and software will stock security software; the major providers are Norton and McAfee, and it will cost anything from £15 to £60 depending on the services, level of cover and number of computers involved. You can also download their packages direct from their websites very easily, and they have good and clear descriptions of what is on offer. If you're worried or confused, print off the instructions before starting the process so you can keep track of what's happening. If you work from home you may find you need greater cover to ensure the security of your work. You can download free basic cover from the internet but be very careful: don't download anything unless you are 100 per cent sure it's from a reputable source.

BASIC SECURITY

Experiments have shown that if you switch on a computer that has no anti-virus protection and log on to the internet, within six minutes it will be infected by a virus. So, the minimum you need for computer protection is a firewall, anti-virus software, regular back-ups and a strong password. The jargon can be confusing if you're not used to hearing it, so here's our guide. If you want to know more, there are some useful books on the subject, but make sure they're up to date, as things change very quickly in the technology world. It's easy to be overwhelmed by the products on offer, but it's like buying any other product. Would you buy a handbag without thinking about the colour, whether it's the right size to fit everything in, does it go with your coat, etc.? You buy what suits you, and it's the same with software. Shop around and buy only what you need.

Firewalls
These act as a barrier between the public internet and your private computer or network. They can make it a lot more difficult for hackers to break into your computer, and stop some viruses called worms, which spread from computer to computer

over the internet. You can also set controls on the type of information which can be accessed by the computer user, such as blocking pornography sites – particularly useful if children or the easily shocked have access to it. Unfortunately, this is not necessarily 100 per cent safe, and the odd thing may sneak through, but it is better than nothing. But on its own, it's not enough. You also need . . .

Anti-virus Software

This is one of the main defences against online crime. It continually scans for viruses, including incoming emails, but it won't protect you against spam or a hacker trying to break into your computer and you need to keep it up to date to make it as effective as possible. When you get a message on your computer offering to update your security, do it straight away. Don't think: I've only got five minutes, I don't have time for that now; I'll do it next time. Do it now.

You can buy either of the above separately or buy a security suite package that includes spam filtering and spyware too (more on them on pp. 279, 283).

Regular Back-ups

Whatever you use your computer for, you need to back up your data, not just in case of fire or someone physically stealing your computer but also to protect yourself from damage caused by an online security breach. The worst scenario is if you have a catastrophic virus or major spyware infection, in which case you will have to erase your hard disk and reinstall everything. It's a good idea to keep all your important data in one place, such as My Documents, to make it easier to back up. Don't keep your back-up disks in the same place as your computer or they may get stolen at the same time.

There are three broad options for backing up information on your computer:

Some broadband suppliers, such as BT, provide automatic back-up capability with their package for an additional charge. This is around £6 per month, which is quite expensive for just personal use but may be worthwhile if you run a business or work from home and keep all your contacts and data electronically.

Back up your system with an external hard drive. This just plugs into your PC or laptop and you can copy everything on to it and then store it in another part of the house or even at a friend's house. This is also good practice in case of fire or total system breakdown.

Back up on to a CD. If you have a CD- or DVD-writer then you have the ability to copy your files on to a disk. You should do this at regular intervals, depending on your amount of usage – say once a week, or once a month if you're a light user. Again, remember to keep the disk in a safe place away from the computer.

Passwords

These are the keys to the castle. It may not have occurred to you before to think about the quality of your password. Most of us just choose something obvious that is easy to remember. But think – if your password is weak, anyone can get in.

─────── WHAT MAKES A WEAK PASSWORD? ───────

1   Plain words that can be guessed by a hacker's program that tries
     every word in the dictionary.

2   The same password for every site. Then the hacker only has to get it right once to gain access to everything.

3   Something that is easy to work out with little or no background knowledge i.e. your birthday, husband's name, favourite footie team, etc.

4   The word 'password' – it's the most commonly used password of all, so steer clear.

5   A password you haven't changed in a couple of months.

6   Your mother's maiden name.

─────── WHAT MAKES A STRONG PASSWORD? ───────

1   First off, it needn't be a word at all. It can be a combo of letters, numbers and keyboard symbols. This will also get round hackers' software which goes through the dictionary looking for matches.

2   Make it at least seven characters long. Shorter words are easier to decipher.

3   Don't use your real name, company name or user name.

4   Use a mix of upper and lower case.

5   Change it regularly.

I have to admit I struggle with the whole password business. At the BBC I have to change mine what feels like every other day, so I never manage to get the new one really fixed into my memory. I have lost count of how many times I have gone into the news-room, ready for a shift on the *Ten O'clock News* and tried to log on, only to find I've forgotten my password. It drives me crazy. Every time, I have to ring up our computer-support people and they come and supply me with a temporary password while I think up a new one. The worst is if I go on holiday. It is a racing certainty that when I come back I will have forgotten my password and have to go through the whole business all over again. Surely I can't be the only one? FIONA

─────── HOW TO KEEP YOUR PASSWORD SAFE ───────

1   Never tell it to anyone. Obviously . . .

2   Don't enter it when others can see what you're typing.

3   Use different passwords for different sites.

4   Have a unique password for banking sites.

5   Don't write it down, even if you hide it in another word.

6   Don't recycle passwords e.g. newsroom1, newsroom2.

7   If you think someone knows it, change it straight away.

If, like many of us, you use the internet more and more for banking and shopping and are therefore suffocating under an ever-increasing list of passwords to remember, then you might want to consider investing in some password-manager software. Not more software, we hear you cry, but software like Roboform can save you time filling in forms as well as keeping your passwords safe. It memorizes your passwords and logs you in automatically. It costs around £16 for the basic licence and package and about £6 for the USB key, but read the extensive website on www.roboform.com if you want to find out more. It's safer than any normal password-protected program as it can remember your passwords (unlike the one written on that handy notebook next to your PC), encrypt them and even generate randomly selected words – all making it more difficult for someone else to access. Of course, it is even more important to secure your Roboform password, but at least you've only got one to worry about. Alternatively, Roboform2go runs from a USB key plugged into a port on your computer which acts as a key to the software and works with all the main software packages. This offers another level of security, so long as you store the key separately from your computer! There are other companies offering this facility so have a look around and see what suits you best.

Spam

If you have your own place, rented or owned, you will already be familiar with the familiar *thunk* through the letterbox every morning as a deluge of junk mail is deposited in the hallway. Spam is simply the electronic version of it, designed to try and part you from your money and, would you believe, it makes up over 70 per cent of all email sent? If that wasn't bad enough, it is also a means by which computer hackers or the maliciously minded can install unwanted viruses or programs on to your computer. It comes in constantly changing forms – inexplicable offers of Viagra (why is it *always* Viagra?), strange emails with random words and lots of capital letters, ads for bizarre health cures and offers for penis extensions. (Do you think they do it with weights or some kind of splint contraption? The mind boggles.) Every time you open up the inbox on your home computer to find 153 new messages, it makes your heart sink, because you know that most of it will be spam – unless you have a lot more friends than we have.

Spammers can find out how to contact you from other spammers – it's possible to buy lists of email addresses by the million online. They can also harvest your address from websites, from insecure online services and by using automated software that generates millions of random fictitious addresses, some of which will turn out to be genuine. Often when we sign up for newsletters or buy goods online, we are inadvertently offering our email addresses up for abuse. Look for a check box on the site to 'opt out' of offers to send you further information about products and services from companies – unless of course you really, really want it.

Spam not only slows down your computer and wastes your time, it also propagates fraud and can contain offensive images and viruses. If you open up a spam email, you are potentially exposing yourself to a con artist. NEVER reply to or click on a link or an attachment within the email. It's the online equivalent of handing a stranger your bank card.

———— HOW TO SPOT SPAM ————

 Is the email from someone you don't know?

 Does it have strange spelling mistakes and random capital letters and numbers? Fraudsters use them because they can often get past your spam filter, which can only be programmed to block emails containing preselected words.

 Is it selling something?

 Do the subject line and the contents not match?

- Avoid spam cancellation services. These offer to stop unwanted emails but may actually be just collecting addresses.

- Avoid spam opt-out lists. These are bogus; there is no such thing.

- Get a spam filter. Not all email accounts offer one. If yours doesn't, switch to one that does. It blocks unwanted messages by searching for keywords which are programmed into the software, such as 'Viagra'. It scans each message and, if it finds the keyword, the message is blocked. You can add new words to the filter if you are receiving unwanted messages from a particular source or unblock certain words if you really want to receive them – perhaps you need the Viagra after all! Set up a separate email address for online transactions and only give your primary email address to people you know.

Trojans

These take their name from the term 'Trojan horse'. Remember those Greek soldiers trying to get at the Trojans barricaded inside a fort? They hatched a cunning plan to construct a massive, hollow wooden horse and leave it outside the fort gates as a gift. It was wheeled in by the grateful but gullible Trojans, who were then killed when the horse turned out to be full of Greek soldiers.

Anyway, nowadays they are a type of virus which can be installed on your computer without you realizing.

Horrifyingly, Trojans can install a 'keystroke logger', which captures all the keystrokes entered into your computer keyboard.

Basically, this means that every time you press a key on your keyboard it appears on someone else's screen in a different location. Some try to capture passwords entered on certain websites or bank account numbers and entry codes by capturing the keystrokes or taking screen shots of sites you visit. Usually, fraudsters send out emails at random and, if you click on a link, you will be transported to a website where vulnerabilities in the web browser are exploited to install the Trojan. If you take the basic precautions outlined above and treat emails with caution, you should be able to avoid falling victim.

Incidentally, keystroke-logger software can also be used in places which offer internet access to the public, such as cafés and libraries. The computers are attached to a central server and this means someone can remotely track whatever sites you are accessing and what keys you are pushing. So it's not a good idea to log on to a financial site in such places using a secure password or code as that can be instantly copied. And better to have a strong password that you never have to reveal in full. A lot of banks are using drop-down lists from which you select random letters from your password, which is a lot more secure than typing the whole thing in.

Cookies

Not the tasty little biscuits that linger for seconds on your lips but forever on your hips but little software programs planted in your computer which instruct it to do certain things, some welcome – some less so. When you connect to an internet site you open up a two-way conversation between computers. To save the computers having the same conversation if you visit or speak regularly, shortcuts can be used to make the conversation more efficient. For example, when you register your details with a shopping website and want them to remember those details for the next time you visit, their software will plant a cookie in your system so that the next time you visit the shop (site) both your computer and their system will remember and you won't have to key in the same details again. If you are on a secure site from a reputable source, this is not a problem and it can be handy not to have to keep re-keying in all your details every time you visit – particularly if you use the site a lot. Think Tesco, Sainsbury's and Ocado online shopping – we'd be lost without them.

But cookies can also be planted by unscrupulous sources without your knowledge when you visit a site or open an email, which is why you need security software to block the ones you don't want. Most security packages will allow you to view a list of the cookies on your system at any one time and the source of them, and if you check the list regularly you can delete the ones you don't like or recognize.

Spyware

Spyware is a software program that stops hackers or other soft-ware programs from instructing your computer to do certain things – generally without your knowledge or permission.

There are different ways the hackers can target you. They can, for example, try to get you to visit commercial websites, typically for gambling and porn, through unwanted pop-ups or by putting new icons on your desktop. Or, at its most sinister, they can scan your hard disk for private data such as credit-card numbers, log your keystrokes, take screen shots of sites you visit to capture personal details and pass on information gleaned from all of the above to cybercrims.

It's a complex form of fraud and it's not easy to get rid of. To sum up: be careful about which sites you visit; be wary of 'free' programs; buy reputable software from reputable companies; and use anti-spyware programs.

Rogue Diallers

These are programs which divert your PC's modem to a premium-rate phone number instead of the usual number it uses to connect to your internet service provider. So when you log on to the internet (if you have a dial-up connection as opposed to broadband), you are in fact making lots of phone calls to the premium-rate number without realizing it. The scammer makes his money by taking a percentage of the fee earned by the premium-phone-number company when the call is made. The first time you'll know it's going on is when you faint at the size of your telephone bill. If it happens to you, contact your service provider and ask them to ban all numbers starting with 09, and report the numbers to Phonepay Plus (www.phonepay plus.org.uk), the regulatory body for premium-rate telephone services.

Too Late

What should you do if you should be unlucky enough to find that your PC has already been infected by a virus, worm, Trojan, etc.? (If you have security software, it should tell you.) Indications that this has happened might include your friends receiving strange emails from you, you seeing unexpected pictures or messages on your computer, the system slowing up or freezing, or just behaving strangely, in a way you haven't seen before. Firstly, disconnect your PC from the internet, then back up your data and use your security software to scan everything. If it does find an intruder it will lead you through a process to get rid of it. If you have any problems removing the infected files, the security-software provider should have a helpline for you to ring.

Wi-Fi

This is supposed to free us from the tyranny of our desks and miles of cables and make us more mobile. We can log on to our computer wherever we are, at the kitchen table, in the airport, in the office canteen, in a bar. It's freedom of a kind, we suppose. But another other way of looking at it is that you can never be unavailable for work. And, technology being what it is, with every development come opportunities for cyber-criminality.

A break-in at a post office showed nothing missing, so police assumed the burglars had been scared off by the alarm before they could take anything. A month later, it became apparent that there had been large withdrawals from newly opened accounts. After an investigation, staff realized that a wi-fi access point had been added to the post office's internal network and was being used to hack into the accounts. It was only because the unauthorized withdrawals had been spotted that the wi-fi scam was uncovered. Otherwise, it could have gone on indefinitely.

But that is nothing compared to a wi-fi scammer in Canada. A man was stopped by the police because he was driving erratically. When they approached his car they saw that he was naked from the waist down and downloading child porn courtesy of open wi-fi systems in the houses in the streets around. That's bad enough, but if someone did that using your wi-fi network, the pornographic downloads could be traced back to your user address and you could find yourself interviewed and arrested for downloading child porn. Ultimately, it's unlikely you would be charged, but the stigma of being investigated for such a horrible offence would be hard to shake off. JACQUI

Whenever you log on to a wi-fi network, anyone in range can intercept the signal or transmit on the same frequency, rather like you can with radio signals. That means a wi-fi network is at risk from eavesdropping, hacking and freeloading – where someone shares your connection without your permission and for free. Every time you log on to a public access point, you are transmitting your log-in name and password over the open airwaves – often a credit-card number too.

You might think that your information is of little interest to a hacker. But by now you have hopefully realized that just your name and address is potentially useful to a fraudster, let alone anything else that might be on your hard drive.

Most wi-fi network equipment doesn't arrive safe and secure. You need to sort that out yourself. Enable the 'encryption' button on the software package options. Encryption is when your normal data is converted into a code before travelling across a connection.

- Each device has an SSID (Service Set Identifier) which announces itself to the web (i.e. the world!) that you are online – you can switch this off.

- Make sure your computer has a firewall (and every other computer on the network if it's in an office).

- Use public access points with care and check what the safeguards are. Some public wi-fi networks are set up by crims to trap unsuspecting users. They sit in on the wi-fi traffic waiting for something interesting to come along, such as a password or credit-card number.

 Use a strong password.

 You will find, if you connect a new wireless network system, there will be an administrator default password already set. Change this, otherwise a hacker may all too easily guess it and get into your system when sitting outside your house.

Phones

Unless you're a member of the Royal family or the likes of Victoria Beckham, you're unlikely to have to worry about people tapping your phone, though, if you have an analogue cordless mobile phone around your flat or house, did you know that someone concealed nearby with an appropriate scanner could listen in? Most people have digital phones with a degree of encryption attached, so it doesn't happen too often, and most of us are not interesting enough to be fodder for the tabloids or the secret services.

But phones are yet another way of carrying out fraud, in particular through the use of Voice Over IP (or VOIP) or internet telephony services, such as Skype. Using the internet for phone-like conversations is convenient and cheap and remarkably secure if done in the right way.

 Running your phone line through your broadband internet connection or PC means that it is even more important that your computer is secure, not only for the reasons we've already mentioned but also to stop hackers running up extortionate phone bills using your connection. So this means that anti-virus, anti-spyware and firewall software plus regular updates are even more important.

 Make sure your wireless connection is encrypted and secure; otherwise, anyone could sit outside your house and use your broadband connection to make free phone calls.

 If you want to avoid cold calling, set up your service to allow connections only from people you know and block everyone else. Be aware that if you use a VOIP phone to replace a landline, it will depend on your broadband internet connection and a router to work. If there is a power cut or other problem with the equipment, you may not be able to call 999.

INTERNET SCAMS

We live in one of the world's richest countries, which makes us a target for thieves from all over the world. From fake lotteries to Nigerian businessmen needing help to transfer sums of money into the country – the variety of internet scams out there is endless. But they all amount to the same thing: they are unsolicited requests for you to part with your cash. The fact that so many otherwise sane, intelligent, worldly-wise, professional people have fallen for these tactics is testament to the elaborate stories and professional ability of the hoaxers but, as a general rule, if you keep the following things in mind, you should avoid being caught out.

 You can only win a lottery if you enter it.

 When you do buy a ticket for a lottery, the lottery operator has no way of knowing who you are or of contacting you. Only you know if you have the winning number, and it's up to you to contact the operator and claim it. That is why there is so much unclaimed lottery money out there.

 There is no such thing as free money. If someone is offering you money, you will inevitably have to pay some kind of processing fee first, and then you will never receive a bean.

 Never hand over money to strangers on the net, no matter how plausible the sob story.

 Never reply to spam or log on to a website connected to it.

There are so many scams out there, it would take more than this book to warn you about all of them, Plus, new ones start up every day. But we've prepared a selection for you, a little *hors d'oeuvre* of scams *du jour*, to give you a flavour of what you could sample in your inbox.

1　Bogus emails (or letters) from what appear to be the Financial Services Authority or the Financial Ombudsman asking for your personal information or money

2　Miracle health cures

3　Career opportunity scams

4　Bogus holiday clubs

5　Bank-charge cold callers – emails (or phone calls) out of the blue offering to help reclaim your charges

6　Share scams – a stranger contacts you and tries to offer you shares in a company you've never heard of

7   Chain letters – emails or letters that contain a list of names and guarantee you a huge return for your small initial investment

8   Fake lottery wins

9   Work-from-home scams

10 Fake Viagra offers

Judging from the content of our inboxes, among the most popular scams are what are known as fund transfer schemes, in which someone asks to use your bank account to place funds; fake websites or 'phishing', which crooks use to get your personal details and your money; and, finally, identity theft.

Fund Transfer Schemes
Or 'please can I place an unfeasibly large sum of money in your bank account?'

We seem to get offers like this on at least a weekly basis, for example, an email from a Nigerian businessman needing to bank a serious amount of dosh into our personal account because he is not allowed to hold a foreign account and then offering us a percentage of the sum. The emails often refer to hundreds of thousands of pounds. Sometimes they are sent to individuals, sometimes they are sent to small- or medium-sized companies, but the scam is always the same. It's known as the 4-1-9 fraud, after the section of the Nigerian penal code which covers this kind of crime. It's a global deception that's been going for several years and often (but not always) involves the unsolicited receipt of an email from someone who claims to work for the Nigerian Central Bank or the Nigerian government.

In the email the scam artist will tell you he is seeking an account into which he can deposit funds overpaid by the government on some procurement contract. The idea is to delude you into thinking that you have been singled out to participate in a very lucrative, though very dodgy, arrangement. The set-up can be very elaborate, with fake letters of credit, letterheads, payment schedules and bank drafts. A meeting may even be arranged between you and the so-called government officials. You may be asked to travel to Nigeria, where you will certainly come under some form of coercion to part with your money. Alternatively, just at the point when you are waiting to receive the massive money transfer into your account, something will go wrong. You will be asked to provide one or more sums of money to save the venture – for example, a bribe to a Nigerian official to permit the money to be transferred. The fraud can be stretched out over many months if you get sucked in.

Here's an example of the kind of email you should delete as soon as it hits your inbox (note the lack of correct grammar, spelling and punctuation, which is often a feature of these letters):

Dear Friend,

   I wish to approach you with a request that would be of immense benefit to both of us. I am an attorney based in Scotland. I want you and I to make some fortune out of a situation that I am obviously left with no other better option. The issue that I am presenting to you is a case of my client that willed a fortune to his only daughter. It is unfortunate that he and his daughter died on the London Bomb attacks on 7 July 2005. The wife died of heart attack on receiving the sad news a week after. I am now faced with a problem of getting a trusted person who I will make the beneficiary that I would pass the fortune to. And according to the law such fortune is supposed to be bequeathed to the government if there is not any relatives or next-of-kin of the decease that would surface for claim of the fortune.

However, I personally don't belong to such school of thought that proposes that such fortune be given to the government because this is cheating and is possible that the top government officials for their own selfish interest could divert the fortune. Because of this I am contacting you to seek your acting as the beneficiary of the will. I am my client attorney and I alone knew about his will. Upon indication of your interests, all I will do is to amend the will by fitting in your name as the supposed next-of-kin and back it up with a sworn affidavit, which automatically became valid. This amendment should be between us and must not leak out to anyone. It is absolutely confidential.

I have complete information of his bank account details with an outstanding balance of $48,550,000.00USD ($48.550 Million USD). To make you be sure of this, I can provide you with details of his bank to enable you to log on to his account to confirm this balance. I know that you would be apprehensive and feel that this is a big sum, but it does not matter because this is a legacy being passed on to a next-of-kin and you are the available next-of-kin.

As I am not very sure of getting your consent yet on the issue, I prefer not to divulge my full identity so as not to risk being disbarred. Until I am sure of your consent and full cooperation then I will not be afraid to give you my full identity. In the meanwhile, I would prefer that we maintain correspondence by email and fax. At this point I want to assure you that your true consent, full cooperation and confidentiality are all that are required to enable us to take full advantage of this golden opportunity.

I shall make representation to the legal courts to facilitate the amendment process within three working days. Since this is a transaction of immense benefit to both of us, I would want that we shared all expenses according to our agreed sharing ratio of the fortune. The sharing ratio shall be 60% for me and 40% for you. This shall also be applicable to all expenditures that would be incurred in the course of the transaction because I wouldn't want either of us to feel cheated. Please note that this is a legal and risk free transaction that does not in anyway hamper the monetary laws of your country. It is an inheritance fund.

If you are interested to work with me, please provide me with your name, address, nationality, age, and date of birth, height, and phone and fax numbers as required for the amendment of the WILL. On completion of this, I will send you a copy of the amended WILL which you will fax to the bank with a back up letter written by your good self requesting for the release of the fund to you. I will also write to the bank as the legal representative of my client before his demise, ordering for the transfer of the fund to you, as the beneficiary of his will.

I will appreciate your urgent response in this regard. Thanks for your anticipated cooperation. You can as well reach me on murdock@walla.com

Yours faithfully,

Kirk Murdock.

Phishing

In case you're not familiar with the term, this is basically a fraudulent attempt through the email system to steal your personal identity and financial information. The best way to protect yourself is to learn to recognize phishing emails. These generally appear to come from reputable, well-known organizations, such as banks, and ask for various personal details to be verified, such as bank details, account numbers, credit-card numbers or other personal details, such as social-security numbers. Basically, in order for them to 'phish' for your personal information they need you to go from the email to a fake website made to look like the real deal, so they will almost always ask you to click on a link where you are then asked to fill in your details.

Apparently, 5 per cent of us respond to spam emails. Don't be one of them or you could find yourself phished out of your funds. Just delete it as soon as you see it.

Most of us have received one or several emails purporting to be from our bank asking us to verify our details. Millions of these emails are sent out every year. Sometimes we are told that our bank details are needed or a stop will be put on our account because the bank needs to combat fraud – in fact, we are being asked to become the victims of a fraud. The con artists only need a small minority of people to respond in order to make large amounts of cash – so don't be one of them. In fact, the way to avoid phishing is very simple. Just remember one thing: banks or other reputable financial institutions never, ever ask for information in this way, so just ignore it. If you really are not sure, ring the company to verify.

This is what phishing emails can look like and how they try it on:

- 'Security update: Our new security system will help you to avoid fraudulent transactions and to keep your investments safe. Due to a technical update we recommend you reactivate your account.'

- 'Your Mastercard account: Your Mastercard debit account has been inactive for more than three months. In order to confirm your membership with us and avoid account cancellation we will transfer a random amount between 0.25 GBP and 0.99 GBP into your debit card.'

'Job in UK: The company deals with many overseas partners, but for the time being we have offices only in Russia and the USA. At the moment we receive a lot of orders from the United Kingdom, so we are looking for agents. Our clients stipulate that they pay for our services only in UK banks such as Barclays and National Westminster.'

If you click on the link in a phishing email and update your personal information what you are in fact doing is logging on to a website run by a criminal gang. They will then recruit people who have accounts at the same bank by advertising by spam email or in chatrooms for 'money processors'. These people are told they will receive a percentage of the money that they handle. Your money is then transferred from your account to that of the processor, who is given instructions to withdraw the money in cash and hand it over to a named individual or send the money to the gang. In one way it's horribly complicated and requires a lot of wasted effort to find an unwitting victim. In another, it's so beautifully simple.

The good news is that, if you can show that you have been duped by this kind of fraud, you will get your money back from the bank. But phishing is so widespread and banks so keen to increase their profits that it is surely only a matter of time before they start requiring customers to demonstrate they have made the proper checks before they hand over personal details.

So what should you do if you receive an email from what you think is your bank? Well, a bank or any other financial organization will never ask you for PIN numbers, passwords or other personal data, no matter how genuine the email looks. If you think you're being phished, forward the email to your bank and let them alert the police or Serious Fraud Office.

Identity Theft

This is perpetrated by someone you never see, no one gets physically hurt, it's inconvenient but not something to get really worried about – if that's what you think, have a look at the ordeal suffered by Derek Bond, a pensioner from Bristol.

Derek Bond, a retired engineer aged seventy-two, was arrested while on a wine-tasting holiday in South Africa with his wife. For nearly three weeks he was held at a police station in Durban, shared a cell with rapists, murderers and slept on a concrete floor. From the outset he protested that he was an innocent man and demanded to know why he was being detained. To his horror he found out that his arrest had been instigated by the FBI, who believed he was one of America's most wanted, a man called Derek Sykes, responsible for defrauding people to the tune of millions of dollars through a telemarketing scheme. Back in 1989 he had assumed the identity of Derek Bond and had taken a British passport in that name. So when the real Mr Bond passed through South African immigration control at the start of his holiday, he was marked as an international criminal. It took weeks for the FBI to realize they had the wrong man and the case was only resolved after they got a tip-off that the man they were really after was living in Las Vegas. They arrested the real criminal, who by now had assumed yet another identity, and a traumatized Derek Bond was released and flew home to Britain to his family. JACQUI

That's extreme, but the reality of ID theft is that someone can pretend to be you and run up massive debts and commit crimes in your name and then it will be up to you to prove that you are innocent. The government estimates ID theft costs us nearly £2 billion a year. Even Jeremy Clarkson was stung for £500 by a fraudster, when he put his financial details in a newspaper. (He was trying to prove that people worry unnecessarily about ID theft, but he ended up losing money out of his account and proving exactly the opposite.)

The UK's Information Commissioner claims a horrifying number of companies and public bodies are in breach of data-protection rules, which means they are playing fast and loose with what should be secure information about you. And then, when you have the Inland Revenue inadvertently releasing details of some 25 million of us into the public domain in 2007, bank account numbers and all, it makes us feel like throwing in the towel. But, while we can do little or nothing about the mind-blowing incompetence of a government department, we can and should take steps to protect ourselves in our daily lives and when conducting our own transactions.

Fraudsters can use our identity to gain access to our bank accounts, run up bills, launder money, create false documents such as passports or birth certificates and carry out benefit fraud. While you will not normally be liable for any stolen money, the onus is on you to prove that ID theft has taken place, and one credit-reference agency reckons it can take up to 300 hours to resolve just one case.

In the mid-nineties my husband investigated an identity fraud. The fraudster advertised for a chauffeur and invited applicants to send in details of their driving licence, national-insurance number and other personal information. Naturally, no one got the job, but the fraudster did get three complete identities. Over about a year he himself got a job using one of the identities and built up debts using the others of over £100,000 before he emigrated. While he eventually got his comeuppance, the three victims' lives were devastated by the bad credit rating that this man had built up in their names. It took almost four years before their financial reputations were restored and their blacklistings removed. Imagine: four years without being able to get credit, a bank account, a mortgage, hire purchase or anything else we take for granted in our everyday life. JACQUI

HOW TO SPOT THAT SOMEONE HAS STOLEN YOUR IDENTITY

Well, if you find yourself arrested like the hapless Derek Bond, that's probably a fair sign that something's amiss. But, otherwise, look out for the following:

- You are turned down for credit even though you have a good payment record

- There are entries on your credit or bank statements you do not recognize

- Large amounts mysteriously disappear from your account

- You are pursued for outstanding debts that are not your own

- Mail you normally expect from banks and building societies does not arrive

- You have lost or had stolen important documents

🖱 **You apply for benefits and are told you are already claiming when you are not.**

I was on a family summer holiday in Italy when I got a call from my bank. They told me there had been some unusual transactions on my account and that they wanted to check them with me. To begin with I assumed they had picked up the bills that we were incurring in Italy and just wanted to check that I was abroad. Imagine my horror when they calmly informed me that virtually the entire contents of my joint savings account with my husband had been drained over the last week – some £30,000. There was only £200 left, and the bank had thought it best to contact me and double-check before it was emptied completely. I was so shocked I began to cry. It had taken us so long to save the money and it was to be used to put down on our next house so that we could get some-where bigger. The bank were sympathetic and seemed to believe that it wasn't me who had spent the money, so that was some relief, but they said they still needed to check that it definitely was fraud before they could talk about reimbursing us. The worry of it ruined the rest of our holiday. It was resolved once we got home and we did get our money back, but it was a horrible fright. And I've no idea how it happened. JAN, STROUD

Identity Theft via the Post

It is important to remember that identity theft happens not only via your computer but also via your letter box. Chucking letters containing personal details in the bin is an easy way to become a victim. It is not just organized criminal gangs that go through rubbish bins for financial records and identity documents, your average burglar or street thief has also found it to be a way of increasing his income. All documents that contain personal information should be shredded or at the very least torn up into tiny pieces. Shredders are not expensive and the best type is a cross shredder, which makes it almost impossible to reassemble the document again afterwards. All junkmail or offers of credit cards should be destroyed too. Anything that contains your name and address is valuable to a fraudster.

A good tip is to limit the amount of junk mail that comes through your letterbox in the first place. The Mailing Preference Service is free; it was set up twenty years ago and is funded by the direct-mail industry. It enables you to have your name and home address removed from 95 per cent of lists used by the industry. It won't stop mail coming from abroad or that is addressed to 'the occupier'. It takes up to four months for the service to have a full effect, though you will notice your mail gradually decreasing from the outset.

When you move house, have your mail redirected using the Royal Mail for at least a year. That will stop anyone nicking your letters from your old address and using them to assume your identity. And while we're on the subject of houses, make sure you lock up valuable documents such as passports and birth certificates so that they don't disappear during a burglary.

Under no circumstances reply to any unsolicited requests for personal information or respond to letters stating you have won anything – once you do that, not only could you end up being the victim of theft, but your details will be sold on to others who think you are a soft touch and you will be inundated with the stuff.

What to Do If Someone Steals Your Identity
Call your bank and credit provider immediately. Official advice is to report it to the police, but unless you have clear reasons to

believe you know where and how the fraud has taken place, the police are unlikely to investigate it. Discuss it with your credit provider. If you have had documents stolen and you are worried you could become a victim, one of the things you can do is contact CIFAS, the industry body that works with the majority of the financial services to prevent fraud. They will supply you with extra protection through their registration service. It costs £11.75 and places a warning on your credit files so that if anyone applies for credit under your name, further identity checks will be made.

Check your personal-credit file to ensure that no one is using and abusing it. You can get a copy for a couple of quid from one of the three main credit agencies – Equifax, Experian or Callcredit. It can be difficult to read so they offer a more expensive but easier to read version too.

Be prepared for hours of answering lots of questions, explaining yourself on the phone and writing letters. Remember: you may end up contacting a bank or companies you have no history with, so they will be suspicious. And once you make an allegation of fraud, you cease to be the victim and the loss is passed on to them, so don't expect them to welcome you with open arms. Every time you speak to someone note their name and the time and date of the call. Photocopy letters you send and keep the ones you receive in a safe place. Don't be put off if a company continues to hold you liable, and keep persevering, because you won't get the debt written off otherwise. If you are really struggling, get a solicitor to represent you.

Make sure your credit file is restored to what it was before the fraud took place when you do get the debt written off. Ask the company to advise the credit-reference agencies accordingly.

DISPOSING OF YOUR COMPUTER

Just sticking your old computer out on the pavement for the council to take away or even taking it to the recycling centre can be as secure as putting all your bank statements in a bin bag and leaving it on your front doorstep. Your computer is full of important personal information that is extremely useful to fraudsters. If you are going to take your computer to the recycling centre for the council to dispose of, check that they wipe the computers thoroughly so that your information isn't left on it. If the council doesn't seem too clued up, do it yourself. Just deleting your files isn't enough to permanently erase your computer. You can buy special data-destruction software, but by far the cheapest, most effective and most secure way is to take out the hard drive and bash it as many times as you can with a big hammer. Very satisfying as well.

When I was presenting a current-affairs series called *Real Story* for the BBC, I made a programme about what can happen to the information on our old computers. We traced a batch of discarded computers that had been exported from the UK to Nigeria. We uncovered several workshops that were in the business of extracting data – details on a hard drive were sold on a disk to criminal gangs for as little as £15. We bought three computers and took them to a special lab in Switzerland that could legally analyse the information on them. What we found was astonishing. In one case, we traced the PC back to the name and address of a man in Surrey. We paid him a visit and told him about the research we had been doing. He was horrified to find that, as well as his name and address, we knew all his bank-account details, where he worked, confidential details about his company, the ages and names of his children, his hobbies and even the name of his daughter's pet rabbit. FIONA

An excellent way of safely disposing of your unwanted computer is to give it to charities that pass on second-hand PCs. Computer Aid, for example, runs data-destruction programs on all computers donated so that they are completely wiped of all information, and then gives them free to schools and colleges in developing countries.

Mobile Phones

Would you believe, 50 per cent of all street crime involves mobile phones? And with twelve- to seventeen-year-olds making up 49 per cent of the victims and 60 per cent of the offenders, clearly young people are the most at risk.

Having your phone stolen these days has more implications than just an inability to make phone calls. Surfing the net has added a whole new dimension, not to mention the loss of pictures, videos, emails, diary dates and personal contacts lists. Keep it as secure as possible.

With so many phones now able to access the internet, there is always the possibility that viruses may become an issue for mobiles as well as computers. At the moment, this is not a major problem, unless you are downloading pirated software, but just be careful – as phones become more and more like computers, the risks will rise.

Bluetooth is a short-range wireless network that allows devices like phones, computers and headsets to communicate with one another. While not inherently unsafe, it needs to be properly used to avoid risks. Only connect with trusted devices like your headset or laptop and do not accept documents transmitted via

Bluetooth from unknown or suspicious sources. If you're not using it, switch it off. If you should lose a Bluetooth-enabled device, delete the pairing from your other devices in case a hacker tries to make a connection.

There is growing evidence that criminals are using SMS text messages in phishing scams. For now, be careful about clicking on embedded internet links in text messages, particularly if the message is unexpected. And remember that an announcement of a lottery win will always be a con trick and the 'free' anti-virus software could well turn out to be an actual virus.

You may feel that, while the phone is in your possession, everything is safe and secure. But did you know that an ex-boyfriend or criminal could easily be listening in on your voicemail messages? Almost every mobile with voicemail has a default password applicable to the service provider. It is amazing how many of us either do not know how to change it or bother to do so. This means that someone could dial into your messaging service, input the default PIN and listen to your private messages. The best and only way to make sure you are not a victim is to change the PIN the minute you receive the phone but, as with the rest of the advice we have given, remember what it is without writing it down somewhere obvious, like inside the phone.

FURTHER INFORMATION

Phonepay Plus, **www.phonepayplus.org.uk**, is the regulatory body for premium rate telephone services

To avoid telephone canvassing register with the Telephone Preference Service at **www.tpsonline.org.uk**.

To register your address as not wishing to receive direct mail (adverts) go to the Mail Preference Service, **www.mpsonline.org.uk**.

Go to **www.jiwire.com** for a complete guide to wi-fi security.

Stamp out scams with the Office of Fair Trading, see **www.oft.gov.uk**.

8
Fearing the Worst

THE CRIME THAT MOST OF US WORRY ABOUT IS ONE WHICH involves some kind of personal attack – mugging, assault or rape. It's featured on *Crimewatch* month in month out, it's the stuff of screaming headlines and it's what makes us look anxiously over our shoulder when we walk down a dark street. But what are the chances of it actually happening to you?

We've already talked in Chapter 2 about the impact of alcohol on your level of risk. A night on the sauce will seriously impair your judgement, cause you to lower your guard and possibly make rash or foolish decisions affecting your personal safety which you would never make in the cold, sober light of day.

But, even then, attacks on women are mercifully rare. Less than 1 per cent of women have reported to the police that they have been a victim of a serious assault. With a conviction rate for rape as low as 6 per cent (more on this later), it may be that many women are not reporting when they've been attacked and the actual number is higher. But, to put your mind at rest, remember these two key facts:

Most victims of attacks are young men.

Most rape victims know their attacker.

The idea of the stranger lurking in a dark alleyway who will pounce as you pass is a reality, but incredibly rare.

Mugging is the most common form of public assault, a nasty type of street theft often involving some form of physical attack. You may be hit or punched as someone tries to take your bag from you. You may be shouted at or intimidated. The mugger may have a weapon and threaten you with it. It's easy to dismiss mugging as a minor crime, a bit of a nuisance, but if you've ever been mugged, you'll know it's frightening and can feel very threatening.

We featured a horrifying mugging on *Crimewatch* a few years back. It wasn't the kind of case we usually show because it can be hard to find enough facts to make an appeal to the viewers with. Most of the time, people would report a mugging but have few details about who had done it and be unable to give a good description. But when this case came into the office, we thought it was too serious to ignore.

A woman was walking along a residential street in Manchester with her baby in a buggy. She was just taking him out to get some air and decided to pop to the shops. She noticed a man cross the road, coming quickly towards her, and as he came up to her he shouted at her to give him her handbag. She hesitated, more out of fear and uncertainty than any desire to fight back. But the mugger clearly thought she wasn't handing over her bag quickly enough, because he pulled a gun out of his pocket and put it to her baby's forehead. He was sweating, and shouting that he would kill her baby if she didn't give him her money. Panic-stricken, she thrust her bag towards him, and he ran off, leaving her rooted to the spot and the baby crying.

It's hard to imagine what kind of person could do something

like that to a tiny baby. There's nothing the mother could have done to stop him but, thankfully, after we featured the story on *Crimewatch*, the mugger was caught and imprisoned. FIONA

So what can you do to prevent yourself becoming a victim of a mugging, or worse? There will be occasions, such as the one above, when you can do nothing to stop someone who may be high on drugs or determined to grab your valuables in any way they can. But that is, thankfully, rare. If you follow the advice in Chapters 2 and 3, you will already have reduced your chances of being a victim to virtually zero. It's all the sensible stuff about looking around you and walking confidently, being aware of your surroundings, not flashing your possessions (such as mobiles) conspicuously, carrying your bag securely, not walking in dark, unpopulated areas. We won't go over it all again here. But those kinds of precautions are your first and best line of defence. But if you fancy getting a little more physical . . .

SELF-DEFENCE

If you Google 'self-defence training' you get over 2 million hits, which shows what big business it is. And if you're physically fit and want to learn a new skill or even a martial art, why not? As you can see from the following comments, whether it's the best thing for you is entirely a personal decision.

'I wouldn't use self-defence on a mugger or advise it. Material things can be replaced, you can't.'

'It should only be used in defence of a physical attack or a sexual attack. Even then it depends on the individual and how they react to the situation and whether it's any use to them or not.'

'Taking up self-defence is a good thing, even if you only learn enough to throw someone off balance so that you can hightail it out of there.'

Ultimately, you have to make your decision based on how at risk you feel. If your life is restricted because you're nervous about going out in the evening, then taking a course may help bolster your confidence, which in turn will lower your chances of becoming a victim of a stranger attack. But it's impossible to know how you're going to act in a situation in which you feel physically threatened until, God forbid, it actually happens.

There are no hard and fast rules when it comes to dealing with an attacker of any kind. People often ask us: is it better to cooperate with your assailant or to scream and shout and try to hit back? There are as many responses as there are individuals, because it depends entirely on the particular attacker and whether or not he is armed. When it comes to protecting your possessions, we are with the first comment: just let them go. It doesn't matter if it's your handbag, your purse, your laptop, your passport, etc. They are all replaceable. You are not. If someone wants to take them from you, let them. You could fight back and you could be lucky and they might be discouraged and run off. But they could also punch you. And you don't know which response you are likely to get. Letting them go doesn't make you a wimp, it makes you sensible. It doesn't do much to discourage crime, of course. Muggers bank on being able to grab a bag off an unresisting victim and leg it – child's play. But our concern in this book is not about reducing the general crime rate; it's about keeping you safe.

In our view, self-defence training can be useful, but in a limited way. It is not something you can ever rely on. Don't be lulled into thinking that just because you've been on a course or two, you will know how to handle yourself if you ever find yourself in difficulty. The problem is that, when you are faced with a threatening situation, basic animal instinct comes to the surface, and you may not be in a position to remember that really smart move you learned in class last week that should have any attacker flat on his back. You may find yourself just paralysed with fear. Or if you do manage to summon up a few moves, you may find that fighting back aggravates your attacker further. You can't know until you find yourself in that situation – we hope you never do and, statistically, it is unlikely.

In Chapter 4, Emma told us how she was attacked while travelling in Venezuela. Here she explains how it affected her when she got home and what she did about it.

I had another trip already planned, to do the Inca Trail in Peru with friends a month later, and although I was very nervous I didn't want to let this incident get the better of me or spoil my friends' plans, so I went. I was very nervous but, as I was with friends, it wasn't too bad, and I was absolutely determined not to let it affect my life. So determined, in fact, I went to Bolivia for a week by myself but, unfortunately, found that I was no longer comfortable on my own, plus, I kept hearing more and more stories about the police in South America. Luckily, I linked up early with a group of travellers and stayed with them throughout the trip.

Subsequently – although I felt I'd dealt with it at the time and was determined not to let it influence my life – it was always in the back of my mind. My confidence had been knocked: I didn't travel abroad any more and, even in this country, I hated getting into cars, particularly taxis. I felt it had been my fault – how stupid I had been to get into the car – and I was too embarrassed to tell people what had happened. I suppressed all these feelings for about a year.

The final straw was when I was walking home after work one day and got jumped by two guys – I think they were after my mobile phone. They knocked me over but ran off without getting anything, thankfully. I reported the incident to the local police, as a result of which I was offered counselling help and also the opportunity to go on a self-defence course. This latest incident really knocked me for six again, making me realize how much I needed help, and I jumped at the opportunity to do both of these things. The self-defence course was brilliant; it was six weeks of theory and practical, and the local council, Tower Hamlets, did it for free.

Afterwards, I felt so much more assertive and confident walking down the street. I even got into taxis again. They taught me things like sitting behind the driver in the back so you can see him at all times, that sort of thing.

I'm also really pleased I did the counselling. In the end, I went through my GP and was offered the counselling on the NHS. I thought the sessions would take months to come through but in fact I only waited about six to eight weeks before it started. After six sessions I felt so much better, more confident and streetwise – not to be too complacent or trusting. Talking about what happened in Venezuela with the counsellor openly and repeatedly, I gradually became less anxious, and I was able to put a positive spin on the whole thing. I recognized that in fact I dealt with the actual attack quite well, getting help and getting away from that horrible situation and that my instincts were right. Suddenly, I wasn't a victim any more. I would recommend counselling to anyone: no matter how long ago the incident happened, still talk about it – it helped me come to terms with and recover from my ordeal.

I've started travelling again, although I would probably think twice before going on my own now, and I certainly haven't regained that carefree, fancy-free feeling that I used to have, but maybe that's a good thing, because I am more cautious, less likely to put myself at risk.

Take some self-defence-training classes; it really does wonders for your confidence. EMMA, LONDON

Accepting its limitations, if learning a bit of self-defence would help you feel more confident, then give it a try – it obviously worked for Emma. The courses tend to vary from learning very basic manoeuvres to in-depth courses that include psychology and martial arts. There are also some which are vocationally based, depending on your profession. We couldn't find any evidence of a regulatory governing body, so it appears that just about anyone can set themselves up in business.

It's best to check out the sporting, martial-arts and training qualifications of the instructors and to speak to other customers, if possible, before parting with your hard-earned cash. Also ask to see their training policy, health and safety guidelines for the course and evidence of their qualifications. The courses can vary from a few pounds a week for a class lasting an hour to hundreds of pounds. If other people in your office are interested, you could investigate the possibility of getting someone to come and run a course in a meeting room during lunchbreaks, particularly if your work involves unsocial hours or lone working.

I remember doing some basic self-defence training at university. It was advertised in the local college bar and seemed like a good idea, so a few of us went along. It took place over the course of an afternoon and could be summed up in the phrase, 'Grab, twist and pull.' You get the general picture. There were a few other tips, too, if the attacker's privates were not readily accessible, things like pressing your fingers into a man's eyes or behind his ears (very tender), how to release your arm from someone's grip and what appeared to be a slightly more technical version of giving someone a Chinese burn. It was good fun and it felt like it would be useful.

Fast-forward to a couple of years later, when I was walking home one evening. It was only about 5 p.m., but it was winter and already dark. As I walked past my local parade of shops, I became aware that someone was behind me. I hadn't spotted him before and he seemed to have crept up on me from nowhere. I began to feel uneasy and quickened my pace a bit. So did he. I looked around to see if anyone else was walking nearby but couldn't see anyone.

Just as I was contemplating breaking into a run, he came right up behind me and put one arm around my body and his other hand between my legs. It can only have lasted a few seconds but I was utterly paralysed. My throat closed so tightly I couldn't make a sound. I couldn't move a muscle and I just stood there. The man then let go and ran off ahead of me. I still stood there, unable to move or shout out.

When he had gone about 20 yards, he stopped, turned round and stared at me. He was wearing a parka jacket with the hood done right up around his face, so I couldn't see what he looked like. But I could see that he was about a foot smaller than me. As

I stood there wondering if he was going to come back and have another go, it dawned on me that I could probably overpower this guy, he looked like a real wimp. I remembered my self-defence training and thought that this would be the time to use it. But I just couldn't. I was too frightened, even of this pathetic character, who can't have been much over five feet. He looked at me for what felt like a minute or two and then turned on his heel and loped off.

I think the reason I remember that incident so clearly is not just because it was frightening – though not particularly serious. It's because I didn't do anything to fight back against what seemed a pretty weedy opponent and I am still furious with myself about that. But it did teach me how utterly paralysing fear can be and why it can be so hard to defend yourself when threatened. FIONA

While in my initial police training at Hendon Police College I attended the regular self-defence-training classes. Initially, I was quite worried about them, as I suspected I too would react like Fiona did and freeze when faced with an attacker. Police training obviously goes further than basic self-defence, as you are responsible for protecting others as well as yourself and, these days, in the era of stab-proof vests, quick cuffs, CS gas and tasers, officers have much more available to them than we did. I was issued with a whistle, fiddly handcuffs and a small lightweight truncheon which was only good for . . . well, nothing really, the only time I hit someone with it, they laughed at me!

When I arrived at my first station posting, Clapham in south London, as one of the very few women in the job at the time, I was met with a barrage of comments like 'She's going to be useless in a fight,' 'I don't want to be stuck with her – what sort of back up can she give me?' – and a lot worse, believe me. I have to admit that I too was worried about letting my colleagues down.

My first experience of a violent situation was going to a fight in a local pub mainly frequented by Irish builders. It was payday and, basically, they liked to have a fight after a good drink – it was traditional. While several of my male colleagues stormed in, fists flying – there were no weapons involved thankfully – my instinct was to stand back for a minute, figure out who was doing what to who, and who the main instigator was. I grabbed another PC and we cleared everyone else out, exposing the main protagonists, who in fact started to lose interest once the audience was gone and the whole thing calmed down. I learned very quickly that, although I wasn't six feet tall and oozing testosterone, I could be just as effective by using different skills and often found that just being a woman acting calmly defused many situations.

The uniform probably helped a bit too! During my career I came face to face with both knives and guns, and on each occasion I survived unhurt because I stayed calm and used my head, not because of any physical techniques I was taught at Hendon. That's not to say I've never been assaulted – I got kicked in the face and stomach by a fleeing villain once – but I'm not convinced a male officer would have come off any better. Thankfully, I've never been attacked by a mugger or stranger in the street, but I like to think that I'd be able to deal with it, if only by turning round and running like hell in the opposite direction. JACQUI

While researching this book we looked through lots of self-defence websites, trawling for useful tips that might come in handy. Some advocated shouting 'Fire!' rather than 'Help!' because they thought it would encourage people to come to your aid more quickly. Others suggested using assertive commands to a would-be attacker (such as 'No!', 'Back off!' or 'Get away!') rather than shouting 'Help!', as that was too passive and might make you appear even more vulnerable. Maybe. You can only trust your instinct if you should ever be unlucky enough to have to put any of the above to the test. And as for the relative merits of fighting back or not, have a look at the two cases below, which we have featured on *Crimewatch*.

Case 1

Every few months we showed reconstructions of cases which had happened several years, sometimes decades ago, but which had never been solved. It was amazing how viewers still remembered important details after such a long time. Or, occasionally, they had harboured a guilty secret or held a key bit of evidence for many years and only felt able to come out with it now. On this occasion, the police wanted to find a rapist who had struck back in the 1970s, attacking at least two women, possibly more. During his first attack, the woman was asleep in her bed, when she was awoken to find a man in a balaclava standing over her. He tied her up and raped her. She didn't at any point try to stop him or protest. She was too terrified, as he threatened her and said he would use a knife on her if she cried out or tried to get away from him.

The same attacker struck in the next county a month or so later. This time, he let himself into a woman's house during the late afternoon. The woman was elderly, in her sixties, and making herself a cup of tea in her kitchen when the man came in. You can imagine how frightening it was to suddenly see him standing there, and the way he was dressed made it clear his intentions were pretty evil. He told her not to say anything and started to touch her. But the woman was made of strong stuff and was as outraged as she was scared. So she told him in no uncertain terms to get off her, to get out, and that he was behaving despicably. And, remarkably, he did as he was told and left. It was only once he'd gone that she realized what a close call it had been and started to shake all over.

Case 2

Another reconstruction we showed was much more recent. A young woman was walking home through a quiet section of woodland near a railway line. It was a sunny day, and it was a route often used by dog walkers. When a man in his twenties walked by her, she thought nothing of it and got out her mobile phone to make a call. But a couple of minutes later, the man doubled back and came up behind her. He dragged her off the path and into the bushes. She said 'No!' several times, as strongly and loudly as she could, but he ignored her and started to rip off her trousers. She struggled and tried to push him off her and shouted for help. He punched her hard several times in the face and told her to shut up or he'd do it again. He sexually assaulted her and left her with a fractured cheekbone.

There's no way of knowing whether any of these women could have made their attacker stop if they had acted in a different way. If the woman in the first case had tried to fight off her attacker, would he have left her alone – as he did the elderly lady a month later? If the young woman in the second case had not resisted her attacker, would she have avoided coming in for such a beating? It's impossible to know. You can only do what you think is right in the situation that you are presented with.

In order to get to school I used to have to get two trains and either take a bus or have a long walk, which I generally did with a group of friends, enjoying the opportunity to have fun and chat about our day. One day, when I was about twelve, I left school a bit later than usual and my friends had already gone. I got on the train and found myself in an empty compartment; I didn't think anything of it and happily sat there thumbing through a magazine.

At the next stop, about six older boys from another local school got into my carriage. I did feel a bit nervous being on my own but just raised my magazine a bit higher and tried to blend into the corner seat. Initially, apart from the odd silly comment, they didn't bother me too much, but as the journey wore on I began to feel more and more uncomfortable being leered at, so much so that when the train was a couple of minutes away from my station I stood up ready to get off as quickly as I could. Big mistake. The next thing I knew I could feel hands up my skirt, pulling at my underwear. Then one of them put his hands up my skirt between my legs and indecently assaulted me. I was frozen with fear and panic, not to mention horror, and didn't know what to do. I kept slapping at the hands, trying to get them off me. They were still shouting and jeering at me, and I think I was crying by then as well. Luckily, we soon arrived at my stop. I got off so quickly I fell on to the platform and twisted my ankle. My last memory of those boys is hearing them laughing from the train as it pulled away.

Anyway, I limped home and hid in my room for a while before putting all my clothes in the wash and washing myself. I felt dirty and humiliated and, sadly for me, couldn't bring myself to tell anyone about it. I had made up my mind that somehow it was my own fault, and the effect on my self-esteem stayed with me for many years. In fact, the first person I told about the incident was a counsellor a couple of years ago, the second was Fiona and the third is you, dear reader.

Having experienced so much as a police officer over the years, I know that, in the general scheme of things, this wasn't a serious incident, but it had an enormous effect on that naïve young girl. The positive side was the effect on my ability to empathize with victims of crime. Just being told that it isn't your fault and realizing that you're not to blame can start you on the road to recovery. For many, it's a lot more complex than that, of course, but I would always urge anyone who's been a victim of such incidents to tell someone as soon as they can, so they can start dealing with it then and there. Internalizing just stores up problems for the future and stops you moving on so that, instead of being a victim for a few minutes, you end up being a victim all your life. JACQUI

RAPE AND SEXUAL ASSAULT

Just to get the terminology clear, rape is when a man intentionally penetrates the vagina, anus or mouth of another person with his penis. Serious sexual assault is penetration of those same parts of the body with a part of the attacker's body (like a finger), or with anything else, without the person's consent. Sexual assault is committed when a person intentionally touches another person in a sexual way and the other person does not consent. There's no research we could find to back this up, but we think most women have probably experienced some kind of unwanted sexual touching at some point in their lives – from that strange school caretaker who used to stroke your leg when you were a kid to the drunken bloke in a pub to the commuter-train groper or some boor in the office who thought reaching for your breasts in the lift was an acceptable way of trying to chat you up. It's a horrifying thought and, overwhelmingly, it's pretty minor, though none the less upsetting for that. But the chances of any of us experiencing a serious sexual assault or rape, as defined by the law, are, mercifully, tiny. Remember: less than 1 per cent of women report that they have been the victim of a serious assault. In the vast majority of cases it is by someone they know. And, in most of the cases, alcohol plays a part. But if the worst should happen, what should you do?

Remember, first and foremost: it's not your fault. Rape and sexual assault is an appalling power game in which a man subjugates a woman to his will. It is his fault – not yours. Not ever.

Get help. Not as obvious as it sounds. Frequently, women who have been raped or sexually assaulted are ashamed of what has happened to them. They feel soiled by it, they feel that they must have done something to invite it upon themselves and they worry that people will shun them if it becomes known. But if you have undergone such a terrible ordeal, you will need help to get over it. Tell a friend and let them help you through.

Report it to the police. This can be very hard. The last thing you may want to do is go over the details of something so traumatic with a complete stranger. And, given the likelihood of a conviction down the line (just 6 per cent of reported cases result in a conviction), you may think there's little point. But, despite the lamentable state of justice for rape victims, we can only recommend that you do go to the police. It's the only hope of catching the person who did it and stopping him from doing it to anyone else. And don't forget that, in order for the right amount of resources to be dedicated to a problem, the police and politicians rely on statistics – if no one reports the crime, then they deduce there isn't a problem and don't dedicate sufficient money to it.

The way that police officers investigate rape and deal with the victims has always been a contentious issue. The first allegation of rape I dealt with as a young officer was a seventeen-year-old woman who arrived at the station during the night saying she'd been grabbed off the street on her way home from a night out. Her legs were covered in cigarette burns and she was generally in a terrible state. I spent several hours with her, trying to establish what had happened and getting a description of her attacker – the earlier you get that circulated, the more chance you have of catching him. I was desperate to get it right. She was examined by a doctor and related the whole story in a lot of detail.

At first she was very reluctant for us to contact her family, but eventually she agreed and her mother arrived pretty quickly. The night-duty detective arrived and took charge of the investigation. He was in his late forties, world-weary and worldly-wise, and I remember thinking that, if I was in her position, I'd feel quite intimidated by him but maybe also reassured, as he was confident and in control.

Imagine my surprise, not to mention horror, when, having listened to the complete story, he walked into the interview room and accused her of making the whole thing up. I was appalled and about to intervene when she stared at him and admitted that she had. Apparently, she'd been seeing a boy her parents disapproved of. They'd got carried away that night and had sex in his car, and she was really, really late home. Rather than suffer the consequences of her parents' anger, she burnt herself with cigarettes, rolled around in the dirt and tore her clothing. Later, when I asked the detective what had convinced him she'd made it up, he said it was a combination of her story not really adding up and instinct.

Making false allegations is not as rare as you may think, but generally they are sussed out pretty quickly. In my service I came across many, but I have dealt with many more genuine incidents with victims of all types, from young girls to older women, secretaries to prostitutes, but have always prided myself on trying my best to be as supportive and understanding, not to mention professional, as I can. Even with false allegations there is often an underlying problem which needs help.

These days the investigation process is much more controlled by specialists, and the interviewing techniques for both victim and suspect scrutinized very carefully. The biggest barrier to securing more successful prosecutions is the general cynicism and lack of understanding by the legal profession, particularly the judiciary, who ultimately steer and advise juries.

A few years ago I investigated an allegation by an Indian cleaner who had been attacked and raped by a young white co-worker as she was cleaning an office block during the night. When I interviewed him, he admitted being a racist and was extremely arrogant. He denied attacking her and said she'd made it up. DNA later proved they'd had sex. During the trial at the Old Bailey he changed his story, saying she'd agreed to have sex with him. Anyone looking at this timid young woman would have realized how ridiculous that was, and during cross-examination he admitted several times that she had in fact said 'No' on several occasions, although he decided she was still willing! Despite this, his counsel submitted that, although he had changed his story, it still differed from her account sufficiently for there to be doubt about how this had happened and indeed what had happened. Although her account hadn't changed from the first report, the judge concurred and, unbelievably (particularly as there were nine women on the jury), he was found not guilty.

I found it difficult for a while afterwards to justify persuading women to go through the legal processes, although I had several successful prosecutions subsequently. Ultimately, things won't get better until courts are able to discriminate between their own prejudices and the basic facts. Women are entitled to say no and receive the support of the law. JACQUI

What to Do if You are Attacked

If the worst does happen there are many places you can turn to. Men who attack women rarely do it just the once. They are usually serial predators. Most police stations have a female police officer who is trained to deal with victims of sexual offences in a sensitive way. If there isn't one on duty, the police should call someone in from another station or even from home. Many stations have special suites where you can be medically examined, where samples may be taken and where the details of the crime will be noted down. If you've waited a few days, weeks or even years before reporting the rape, it's not too late to try to catch the attacker. The police have a duty to take all allegations seriously, although, clearly, the passage of time may make it harder to gather evidence and get a conviction.

It's important not to wash or change your clothes as there may well be vital DNA evidence on them. If you cannot bear to stay in your clothes, keep them in a bag.

Go to what is known as a 'haven' if there is one in your area, if you can't face talking to the police. It is a special service for victims of sexual assault or rape and is a way of getting help while you make your mind up about whether you want to report what has happened to the police. You need to phone before visiting to make an appointment but they are open twenty-four hours a day. You can get medical help, be screened for sexually transmitted infection, talk to a counsellor, have samples or swabs taken (so that you can have the option later if you decide you want to press charges), have a shower and be given new clothes if yours need to be kept for evidence. If you do decide you want to report your crime to the police, the workers at the haven will arrange that for you. They will also inform you about victim organizations which can help, such as Rape Crisis and Victim Support.

Call the Rape Crisis line. You can get information, sources of help and talk to someone anonymously if you choose. We can't stress enough the importance of dealing emotionally with what has happened to you. As with Emma and Jacqui's anecdotes, however strong you think you are, or however much you think you've dealt with what happened, the effects can go much deeper than you realize and store up enormous problems for you in the future. Even if you spend one hour with a counsellor and discover that you really have not been affected by it in any lasting way, it's still worth it.

Some women who are raped or assaulted feel it is something they will never get over. It can take months or years for someone to feel safe once more in their own home or walking down the street or in the company of the opposite sex. But you can survive it. We want to share with you the ultimate story of survival, the story of a woman we both admire enormously who has shown extraordinary courage in the face of not one but two horrific ordeals.

Rachel North's Story

I came home after an evening out with my sister and went to bed. My partner, J, was still at work; he often has to work till the early hours at his law firm. I was woken by the doorbell. I went to the door, thinking J must have forgotten his key. When I saw the shadowy figure was not him I hesitated, but a voice said: 'It's your neighbour – there's been an accident.'

I opened the door a crack, and a stranger pushed me back into the dark hallway of the flat with overwhelming force, punching and kicking me to the floor.

He took off his T-shirt and forced it over my head like a hood before hitting and biting me. I can't tell you in which order the blows came, as I experienced almost immediate and total sensory deprivation in the darkness. But I can remember the warm gush of blood as my tongue split and my lip burst like a tomato. The punch on the nose was especially painful. Choking under the blood-soaked hood, I then realized he was raping me. Telling me not to move, he went off and rummaged through a wardrobe. Hearing me scrabbling about trying to find my mobile, he came back. More kicks. My pleas were useless. He tied my arms behind my back and attempted to assault me sexually again, unsuccessfully. Another huge beating ensued. The only possible survival strategy was to submit, to try to minimize the force before it became lethal. And then to play dead.

I waited for a blow to the head, and when it came I collapsed, gurgled, exhaled and held my breath. (Yoga and scuba training helped here, and I was good at this as a child; it used to be my party trick, playing dead.)

He said 'shit' and kicked me, lit a cigarette and stubbed it out on my face. There was a hiss as the blood extinguished it, causing minimal burning. I did not flinch but continued to pretend to be dead. In fact I was losing consciousness.

Perhaps two hours later I started to come round. I can remember floating in darkness, looking down at my body, thinking: 'Shall I come back? It's very peaceful here. It's going to hurt coming back into my body.'

Then I thought: 'He might still be in the house. He might be about to burn the house down. You have got to escape while you can see he is not in the room! Come on, Rachel, wake up, get up, get up, get up!'

The carpet rushed up to my face and I was back in my body, with my arms tied behind me. My weak wriggling gradually became stronger. I could kneel and then stand.

I shook my matted hair from the one eye that could still see and found I was naked, with something hanging round my neck.

I managed to stagger upstairs to another of the flats in the house. No sound would come out of my mouth so I threw myself repeatedly against their door. No answer.

Blundering downstairs again, barely able to see or walk, I put my back to the front door to the street, raised myself on tiptoes and managed to unlock it. (Yoga flexibility came in handy again.)

In a final blast of adrenalin, I threw myself down the concrete steps, spraining both ankles and tearing ligaments, as a police car screeched to a halt. There had been somebody upstairs, after all, and they had dialled 999.

I suddenly found my voice in an ear-splitting, roaring scream. The police were in total shock. When I was able to speak words I told them to take the bloody noose off my neck. They said they couldn't because it was evidence. I screamed at them and forced them to cut it off. It turned out to be the lead from my electric-toothbrush recharger. How, when or why he had tied it there I don't know.

While dozens of police officers began frantically to search the area for the rapist, an ambulance took me to hospital covered in a blanket, and the forensic examination of the two crime scenes, my flat and my body, began before they could even treat my injuries.

At last, J was brought in, and the first words he said were: 'Oh, honey.' He wanted to take my hand, but they made him wear rubber gloves. This was when I cried, because he was the first person to treat me like a person that night – not a crime scene or prey – and they wouldn't let him touch me.

The police investigation was as painfully slow as my fight to recover.

After five months they arrested an itinerant mugger who had beaten and robbed many other women. His DNA matched that found inside me. He was seventeen. I had been thirty-one at the time of the attack.

In January 2004 I faced him in a courtroom. I had changed and he had changed. This time I was stronger and he was weakened. As he lied and blustered, I drew my outrage and anger to me like armour and faced him down. For violently raping me, and for robbing and beating other women, he was sentenced to fifteen years.

Six months after he was sentenced I felt ready to talk about what had happened. I gave an anonymous interview to a magazine. That piece was published on 7 July 2005. As I boarded the Piccadilly line train, and stood reading my story in print for the first time, I was proud that my life was going so well. I had a wonderful new job; my partner and I were celebrating six years of being in love with each other; we had bought our first flat; we had been enjoying a summer of growing flowers and tomatoes in our garden, catching up with friends, dancing, cooking and drinking wine. My magazine article was a story of hope. I wanted to help other women to come forward and seek justice after being assaulted.

And then a young man detonated his bomb, 7–10 feet away from me.

I was once more on the floor, in darkness, struggling under a heavy, gasping body. Once more the overwhelming blow to the head, the utter darkness, the blindness, the struggling for breath. Once more the wet on my face. Is it sweat? Is it blood? Is it my blood or someone else's? Do I still have a face? Am I still here or am I dead? But this time I was prepared. By the strange chance of my having just read my own near-death story, I was already pounding with adrenalin. This time it would be different. This time I was not alone.

People later asked me what it was like, being caught up in the terrorist bombings in London. They said they couldn't imagine it. For a long time I couldn't say. It was like a dream you can't remember, a puzzle you can't solve. But then I saw a television documentary about the bombings. Immediately, I began to have flashbacks.

Night diving, without a regulator. Breathing in liquid, drowning. The taste of blood. Sharp grit in my mouth. Choking, lung-filling dust.

It was no longer air that I breathed but tiny shards of glass. Have you ever changed a Hoover bag? Imagine pushing your face into the open dust bag, and taking deep breaths. It makes your tongue swell and crack and dry out like leather. I never covered my mouth. I had nothing to cover it with, and there didn't seem any point.

Then imagine a metallic wet taste on your mouth, like vaporizing copper particles. It tastes as if you are sucking a coin. That is the blood. It sprays you, your clothes, your face, your hair. Your lips are wet with it. The walls drip with it. It is black blood, viscous like oil, because it is mixed with smoke.

The temperature rises. Try to imagine the acrid smell of peroxide and burning rubber and burning hair. It fills your nose. It takes over the memory of every smell you have ever remembered and wipes it out. It burns into your mucous membrane.

At first your ears are deaf. The explosion has punched your eardrums so violently that your cheekbones and sinuses ring with it and ache with it. Then you hear the screams. They do not sound human.

You realize that you are on the floor and that there are bodies lying on top of you. The bodies are squirming. You are alive. They are alive. Your hand locks into another woman's hand. You hiss air out, pat your legs, arms, you are still here. You hear a voice, far away. A hubbub of murmurs and an endless scream that does not seem to draw breath, ever. There is a tinkle of glass falling.

You grasp the hand and a voice says, 'Are you all right? Stand up. Stay calm.' It is your own voice. Other voices say the same thing. And you try to stay hopeful; you make yourself stay calm. I have trained for this. My body and mind know what to do.

Time passes. The driver is not dead after all. Ssssssh, listen to his voice. See, here are hands lifting you down the ladder of the driver's cab, a soft Scottish voice warning you not to step on the live tracks.

The screams are fading as we walk away down the narrow tracks. My ears ring. My eyes swim. I start to pant, because this is so hard. And now you are walking through the greenish light of the misted tunnel and you hear yourself and other voices saying that there is hope, there is help, just walk, they are waiting for us all. With water. With blankets. With ambulances and oxygen. Nurses, doctors, helpers, all waiting, they will be there, and all we have to do is keep putting one foot in front of the other. You say it again and again, to drown out the groans of the seriously injured man who is being carried on the man's shoulders, stumbling behind you.

The women walking near you listen; they walk; we all walk. We speak to each other. We try to make jokes. We encourage each other. We babble to drown out the man who is injured. We walk softly, carefully, looking at our bloodied and blackened feet on the uneven tunnel floor. It takes fifteen minutes to walk down the tunnel to Russell Square. Lights will guide us home.

The lights are brighter and I see a small bone poking out of my wrist and I stagger, but here is a woman holding my arm. Here is a man in a fluorescent jacket, pointing the way. Here are hands lifting me out of Russell Square; they are pulling on my split wrist; this is the only time I scream.

In the lift, people are falling sideways, eyes staring with shock. In the ticket hall a white-faced man hands me water. People start to lie on the floor and slump; they stagger. I don't know what to do to help them. I reach down to a woman and ask if she is OK. She stares blankly; I can't reach her.

I need a cigarette. I can't smoke in the ticket hall. I stagger out on to the pavement, opposite Tesco's, by the zebra crossing. I manage to call my boyfriend and leave a message. I am terrified that he is on the train behind me and that he is dead. I say that the train has derailed.

I can't light the cigarette; my hand is wet with blood. I am covered in black film and blood. I don't think the blood is mine. I need to call work, but I can't remember my number.

A Japanese tourist is filming me. People are milling about outside, looking irritated. A commuter shouts: 'I need to get to work!' She sees me, comes up to me. 'What the hell is going on? I need to get the tube to work!' I am black-faced, shuddering, Einstein-haired. I tell her that she won't get to work on the tube today. She mouths a curse at me.

Someone lights my cigarette for me and I take an enormous drag, anything to take the taste of peroxide and blood from my mouth. I find a number on my mobile: Jenna, who passed her first-aid course last week. She works in Covent Garden. I tell her to please come in a taxi; I need A&E. I say I don't need an ambulance. The people I left behind need the ambulance. I don't want to think about who I left behind.

I start to faint. The taxi comes. I tell Jenna to ask if anyone wants a lift to A&E. My mouth is numb; my ears are humming; I can't see properly. I am panting again.

Jenna wraps a bandage around my wrist. The taxi drives past Tavistock Square. It is nearly 9.45 a.m. As we leave the drive there is a dull 'crump'. Later I find out that it was the bus exploding on the other side of the trees. We get to University College Hospital. The taxi driver demands a tenner for a journey of only a few hundred yards. I pass it over. I find my way to A & E, where they X-ray me and stitch me up . . .

Before the first attack on me I had few reasons to fear strangers. I was innocent of the overwhelming and implacable hatred that some young men harboured. My life was ordinary, sometimes stressful, usually busy and generally good.

I look back at that time, and it is like looking back through the wrong end of a telescope. That headstrong, determined, passionate, selfish girl seems a long way away. The teenage stranger-rapist had yet to unleash his fists on me; nineteen-year-old Germaine Lindsay had yet to detonate his suicide bomb. In photos my face seems more than just younger; my eyes are different, my top lip is unscarred.

It is hard living now with the knowledge that these two strangers wanted to violate and kill me yet did not even know my name. They had never spoken to me. They knew nothing about me. How do you go on living your ordinary life with this knowledge and first-hand experience of violence and evil?

At first after the rape, I used my anger to protect me and to fire me up. I fought against sinking into despair; instead I struggled to understand what had happened to me and why. I needed explanations. Why me? I read other people's accounts of rape. I studied criminal law, sentencing patterns, psychology, criminal profiling, arguments about nature and nurture, genetics and social conditioning. I read everything I could about violence, why men attack women, why people attack people.

I would not admit I was afraid; but in truth I was deeply frightened. When I could be attacked in my own flat, where could I feel safe? Whom should I fear? Whom should I trust? Certain sounds, certain smells could cause me to double up, breathless with a panic attack. In my dreams I fought faceless monsters. Psychologically, I was often strangely dissociated and numb. I began to feel incredibly alone. Nothing I read made me feel any better; understanding brought no comfort, no healing. I began to fear for my sanity.

What brought me back was the gentle, protective love of my partner, my family and friends. I realized that what I was suffering from had a name, that it was a psychological injury that would heal, and that I was not going mad.

I started to write, anonymously, about my experiences on an internet discussion board. I was encouraged and supported by strangers. If I still could not make sense of the event, why it had happened, that was because there was no sense, no meaning in it. Wrong place, wrong time, bad luck. The world had always contained danger and it had crossed my path. It was not an attack on me, Rachel; I could have been any woman.

I began to realize that when I was attacked I was faceless and dehumanized: I was the Other, Nothing, No One, Not-Human. The attacker, by unleashing his hate and his rage against me, was seeking some kind of release. If I started hating and fearing other people – young men, let us say – I risked in some ways becoming like him. I saw how fear and anger makes people isolated and alone, how it breeds despair and more anger, more fear, self-obsession, alienation and eventually corrosive hatred.

He had told me not to speak, but I spoke out. He told me not to tell, but I told. He had wanted me to feel helpless and degraded and frightened, but here I was, telling my story to the police, then to other people, then to a judge. He wanted me to be ashamed, but here I was smiling into other people's faces.

The more I listened and talked to other people, the more the numbness thawed. By allowing myself to say I had been afraid, I was winning against the paralysing anger and fear. By making myself vulnerable, I was becoming stronger.

It was not easy, but life became richer, sweeter, more vibrant and joyful than before, because I had the gift of knowing that I was loved and cared for. I felt lucky.

And then I was targeted again. But again, the attack wasn't aimed at me, Rachel North. It was aimed at whoever happened to be on the train at the time. But, unlike July 2002, when the world went black and the blows rained down and I believed I would die, this time I was not alone. I remember how the passengers of the 08.56 Piccadilly line train began to hold hands, to talk to each other, to save each other from the panic that could have erupted at any moment, 100 feet down in the darkness of the suicide-bombed train. Behind me were screaming, groaning, injured and dying people whom we could not reach. But near me were calmer voices. People used lights from their mobile phones. They smashed windows to let in air.

I now know that in every carriage of the train people waited to be rescued. They shared water, passed tissues, held each other, prayed. They breathed in the smoke and they listened to the screams. In some carriages they beat at the glass and forced the doors. They stood there for more than half an hour, believing they would die, trapped in this tunnel, with these strangers. They comforted each other until police officers and Underground staff helped them escape down the tracks.

I know what happened in the other carriages of the train because I have spoken to my fellow passengers many times since. We have met up with each other, and we have talked and talked. We have become friends.

I have contact with more than seventy people who were on my train. We call ourselves KCU – Kings Cross United. We stood shoulder to shoulder at the two-minute silence a week after the bombs. We stood with thousands at the vigil when London stood united in Trafalgar Square. We set up a website; we went for beers. We sat together at the St Paul's memorial service and afterwards we went to the pub, where we found the driver of our train and the police officer who rescued us. We gave them a hero's welcome.

We email each other 'Well done mate!' when one of us manages to get back on the tube; we pass on tips for coping with panic attacks; we make each other laugh; we tell our stories, work out where we stood on the train. We put the pieces of the puzzle together.

There are men and women of all ages from different backgrounds with different beliefs and different political viewpoints in Kings Cross United. We are a random demographic of people – gay, straight, black, white – who travelled on the Piccadilly line on a Thursday morning. We could be anyone. We could be you.

These strangers from the train are why I am filled with hope for the future. The events of July 2002 and July 2005 could have destroyed me, could have broken so many of us, but I do not believe they will.

And today, I am married to my love, J. The man who never lost faith in me, whose arms are my home and whose hands are gentle, who makes me laugh, who is my companion and my beloved. Here is my light at the end of the tunnel; here is my joy and happiness and my heart's home. Here is a sweetness and a peace, at last, come to me out of the darkness, and I walk into the sunshine and I bless it, and hold it, with gladness and gratitude, with all of my thankful heart.

Conclusion

Rachel's story is one of extraordinary strength and hope. She survived not one but two horrific experiences, both of which had been meant to end in her death. She found courage and wisdom she didn't know she had to overcome the terror and trauma that followed both events. We find Rachel's story incredibly uplifting. She has managed to find a way through the darkness and forge a life for herself full of light and warmth and love. We included it in our book in part to pay tribute to her, in part to show how it is possible to survive the very worst of experiences.

Terrible things can happen to women – it would be foolish and reckless to try to downplay that just to make this book an easier read. We all fear it. But if we achieve nothing else in this book, we want to put crime in perspective for you. The odds of Rachel being attacked twice and in two such different ways are infinitesimally small. It doesn't make it any better or easier on the rare occasions when it does happen, but it's important for us to remember just how rare it is. It's worth repeating: less than 1 per cent of women report to the police that they have been seriously sexually assaulted and 90 per cent of them know their attacker. You can't always avoid a man who is determined to assault or attack you – as Rachel couldn't – but if you follow our advice you will reduce the chances of it happening to you from tiny to microscopic. After all, what we want to be doing is living our lives to the full, enjoying our freedom, celebrating our independence, not looking over our shoulders, fearful of who might step out from the shadows. We've listed sensible precautions we should all take, but our aim is not to turn you into timid souls, constantly worrying about all the different things that could go wrong. Follow our advice – as much of it as you can – and then you're free to do what you want, safe in the knowledge that you've minimized any danger to yourself. Be smart, be SAVVY, and then you really can do it all without risking it all.

FURTHER INFORMATION

'Out of the Tunnel' by Rachel North is published by The Friday Project Ltd.

For general personal-safety advice for young people visit the following:
www.thesite.org
www.suzylamplugh.org
www.lucieblackmantrust.org
www.wiredsafety.org

For more specific advice, visit:
www.rapecrisis.org
www.met.police.uk/sapphire
www.thehavens.org.uk
www.victimsupport.org.uk (tel: 0845 3030900)
www.crimestoppers-uk.org (tel: 0800 555111)

Index